Accelerators for Convolutional Neural Networks

Accelerators for Convolutional Neural Networks

Arslan Munir
Kansas State University
USA

Joonho Kong
Kyungpook National University
South Korea

Mahmood Azhar Qureshi
Kansas State University
USA

IEEE PRESS
WILEY

Published by John Wiley & Sons, Inc., Hoboken, New Jersey.
Published simultaneously in Canada.

For general information on our other products and services or for technical support, please contact our Customer Care Department within the United States at (800) 762-2974, outside the United States at (317) 572-3993 or fax (317) 572-4002.

Wiley also publishes its books in a variety of electronic formats. Some content that appears in print may not be available in electronic formats. For more information about Wiley products, visit our web site at www.wiley.com.

Library of Congress Cataloging-in-Publication Data Applied for:

Hardback ISBN: 9781394171880

Cover Design: Wiley
Cover Image: © Gorodenkoff/Shutterstock; Michael Traitov/Shutterstock

Set in 9.5/12.5pt STIXTwoText by Straive, Chennai, India

Arslan Munir dedicates this book to his wife Neda and his parents for their continuous support.

Joonho Kong dedicates this book to his wife Jiyeon, children Eunseo and Eunyu, and his parents for their continuous support.

Mahmood Azhar Qureshi dedicates this book to his parents, siblings, and his wife Kiran, all of whom provided continuous support throughout his academic and professional career.

Contents

About the Authors

Arslan Munir is currently an Associate Professor in the Department of Computer Science at Kansas State University. He was a postdoctoral research associate in the Electrical and Computer Engineering (ECE) Department at Rice University, Houston, Texas, USA, from May 2012 to June 2014. He received his MASc in ECE from the University of British Columbia (UBC), Vancouver, Canada, in 2007 and his PhD in ECE from the University of Florida (UF), Gainesville, Florida, USA, in 2012. From 2007 to 2008, he worked as a software development engineer at Mentor Graphics Corporation in the Embedded Systems Division.

Munir's current research interests include embedded and cyber physical systems, artificial intelligence, deep learning hardware, computer vision, secure and trustworthy systems, parallel computing, and reconfigurable computing. Munir received many academic awards including the doctoral fellowship from Natural Sciences and Engineering Research Council (NSERC) of Canada. He earned gold medals for best performance in electrical engineering, and gold medals, and academic roll of honor for securing rank one in pre-engineering provincial examinations (out of approximately 300,000 candidates). He is a senior member of IEEE.

Joonho Kong is currently an Associate Professor with the School of Electronics Engineering, Kyungpook National University. He received the BS degree in computer science and the MS and PhD degrees in computer science and engineering from Korea University, in 2007, 2009, and 2011, respectively. He worked as postdoctoral research associate with the Department of Electrical and Computer Engineering, Rice University, from 2012 to 2014. Before joining Kyungpook National University, he also worked as a Senior Engineer at Samsung Electronics, from 2014 to 2015. His research interests include computer architecture, heterogeneous computing, embedded systems, hardware/software co-design, AI/ML accelerators, and hardware security. He is a member of IEEE.

Mahmood Azhar Qureshi is currently a Senior Design Engineer at Intel Corporation. He received his PhD in Computer Science from Kansas State University, Manhattan, Kansas, in 2021 where he also worked as a research assistant from 2018 to 2021. He received his MS in electrical engineering from the University of Engineering and Technology (UET), Taxila, Pakistan, in 2018 and BE in electrical engineering from National University of Sciences and Technology (NUST), Pakistan, in 2013. From 2014 to 2018, he worked as a Senior RTL Design Engineer at Center for Advanced Research in Engineering (CARE) Pvt. Ltd, Islamabad, Pakistan. During the summer of 2020, he interned at MathWorks, USA, where he was actively involved in adding new features in Matlab which is a tool used globally in industry as well as academia. During fall 2020, he interned at Tesla, working on the failure analysis of the infotainment hardware for the Tesla Model 3 and Model Y global feet.

Preface

Convolutional neural networks (CNNs) have gained tremendous significance in the domain of artificial intelligence (AI) because of their use in a variety of applications related to visual imagery analysis. There has been a drastic increase in the accuracy of CNNs in recent years, which has helped CNNs make its way in real-world applications. This increase in accuracy, however, translates into a sizable model and high computational requirements, which make the deployment of these CNNs in resource-limited computing platforms a challenging endeavor. Thus, embedding CNN inference into various real-world applications requires the design of high-performance, area, and energy-efficient accelerator architectures. This book targets the design of accelerators for CNNs.

This book is organized into five parts: overview, compressive coding for CNNs, dense CNN accelerators, sparse CNN accelerators, and HW/SW co-design and co-scheduling for CNN acceleration. The first part of the book provides an overview of CNNs along with the composition of different contemporary CNN models. The book then discusses some of the architectural and algorithmic techniques for efficient processing of CNN models. The second part of the book discusses compressive coding for CNNs to compress CNN weights and feature maps. This part of the book then discusses Huffman coding for lossless compression of CNN weights and feature maps. The book then elucidates a two-step lossless input feature maps compression method followed by discussion of an arithmetic coding and decoding-based lossless weights compression method. The third part of the book focuses on the design of dense CNN accelerators. The book provides a discussion on contemporary dense CNN accelerators. The book then presents an iMAC dense CNN accelerator, which combines image-to-column and general matrix multiplication hardware acceleration followed by the discussion of another dense CNN accelerator that utilizes log-based processing elements and 2D data flow to maximize data reuse and hardware utilization. The fourth part of the book targets sparse CNN accelerator. The book discusses contemporary sparse CNNs that consider sparsity in weights and activation maps (i.e., many weights and activations in CNNs are zero and result in ineffectual computations) to deliver high effective throughput. The book then presents a sparse CNN accelerator that performs in situ decompression and convolution of sparse input feature maps. Afterwards, the book discusses a sparse CNN accelerator, which has the capability to actively skip a huge number of ineffective computations (i.e., computations involving zero weights and/or activations), while only favoring effective computations (nonzero weights and nonzero activations) to drastically improve the hardware utilization. The book then presents another sparse CNN accelerator that uses sparse binary mask representation to actively lookahead into sparse computations, and dynamically schedule its computational threads to maximize the thread utilization and throughput. The fifth part of the book targets hardware/software co-design and co-scheduling for CNN acceleration. The book discusses hardware/software co-design and co-scheduling that can lead to better optimization and utilization of the available hardware resources for CNN acceleration. The book summarizes recent works on hardware/software co-design and scheduling. The book then presents a technique that utilizes software, algorithm, and hardware co-design to reduce the response time of CNN inferences. Afterwards, the book discusses a CPU-accelerator co-scheduling technique, which co-utilizes the CPU and CNN accelerators to expedite the CNN inference. The book also provides directions for future research and development for CNN accelerators.

This is the first book on the subject of accelerators for CNNs that introduces readers to advances and state-of-the-art research in design of CNN accelerators. This book can serve as a good reference for students, researchers, and practitioners working in the area of hardware design, computer architecture, and AI acceleration.

January 24, 2023   *Arslan Munir*
Manhattan, KS, USA

Part I

Overview

1

Introduction

Deep neural networks (DNNs) have enabled the deployment of artificial intelligence (AI) in many modern applications including autonomous driving [1], image recognition [2], and speech processing [3]. In many applications, DNNs have achieved close to human-level accuracy and, in some, they have exceeded human accuracy [4]. This high accuracy comes from a DNN's unique ability to automatically extract high-level features from a huge quantity of training data using statistical learning and improvement over time. This learning over time provides a DNN with an effective representation of the input space. This is quite different from the earlier approaches where specific features were hand-crafted by domain experts and were subsequently used for feature extraction.

Convolutional neural networks (CNNs) are a type of DNNs, which are most commonly used for computer vision tasks. Among different types of DNNs, such as multilayer perceptrons (MLP), recurrent neural networks (RNNs), long short-term memory (LSTM) networks, radial basis function networks (RBFNs), generative adversarial networks (GANs), restricted Boltzmann machines (RBMs), deep belief networks (DBNs), and autoencoders, CNNs are the mostly commonly used. Invention of CNNs has revolutionized the field of computer vision and has enabled many applications of computer vision to go mainstream. CNNs have applications in image and video recognition, recommender systems, image classification, image segmentation, medical image analysis, object detection, activity recognition, natural language processing, brain–computer interfaces, and financial time-series prediction.

DNN/CNN processing is usually carried out in two stages, training and inference, with both of them having their own computational needs. Training is the process where a DNN model is trained using a large application-specific data set. The training time is dependent on the model size and the target accuracy requirements. For high accuracy applications like autonomous driving, training a DNN can take weeks and is usually performed on a cloud. Inference, on the other

Accelerators for Convolutional Neural Networks, First Edition.
Arslan Munir, Joonho Kong, and Mahmood Azhar Qureshi.
© 2024 The Institute of Electrical and Electronics Engineers, Inc. Published 2024 by John Wiley & Sons, Inc.

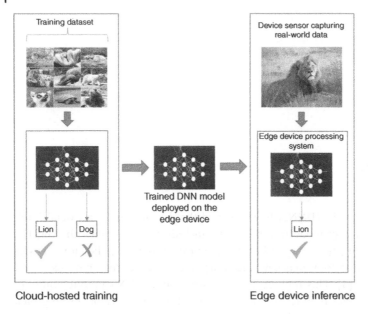

Figure 1.1 DNN/CNN processing methodology. Source: (b) Daughter#3 - Cecil/Wikimedia Commons/CC BY-SA 2.0.

hand, can be performed either on the cloud or the edge device (mobile device, Internet of things (IoT), autonomous vehicle, etc.). Nowadays, in many applications, it is advantageous to perform the inference process on the edge devices, as shown in Figure 1.1. For example, in cellphones, it is desirable to perform image and video processing on the device itself rather than sending the data over to the cloud for processing. This methodology reduces the communication cost and the latency involved with the data transmission and reception. It also eliminates the risk of losing important device features should there be a network disruption or loss of connectivity. Another motivation for doing inference on the device is the ever-increasing security risk involved with sending personalized data, including images and videos, over to the cloud servers for processing. Autonomous driving systems which require visual data need to deploy solutions to perform inference locally to avoid latency and security issues, both of which can result in a catastrophe, should an undesirable event occurs. Performing DNN/CNN inference on the edge presents its own set of challenges. This stems from the fact that the embedded platforms running on the edge devices have stringent cost limitations which limit their compute capabilities. Running compute and memory-intensive DNN/CNN inference in these devices in an efficient manner becomes a matter of prime importance.

1.1 History and Applications

Neural nets have been around since the 1940s; however, the first practically applicable neural network, referred to as the LeNet [5], was proposed in 1989. This neural network was designed to solve the problem of digit recognition in hand-written numeric digits. It paved the way for the development of neural networks responsible for various applications related to digit recognition, such as an automated teller machine (ATM), optical character recognition (OCR), automatic number plate recognition, and traffic signs recognition. The slow growth and a little to no adoption of neural networks in the early days is mainly due to the massive computational requirements involved with their processing which limited their study to theoretical concepts.

Over the past decade, there has been an exponential growth in the research on DNNs with many new high accuracy neural networks being deployed for various applications. This has only been possible because of two factors. The first factor is the advancements in the processing power of semiconductor devices and technological breakthroughs in computer architecture. Nowadays, computers have significantly higher computing capability. This enables the processing of a neural network within a reasonable time frame, something that was not achievable in the early days. The second factor is the availability of a large amount of training datasets. As neural networks learn over time, providing huge amounts of training data enables better accuracy. For example, Meta (parent company of Facebook) receives close to a billion user images per day, whereas YouTube has 300 hours of video uploaded every minute [6]. This enables the service providers to train their neural networks for targeted advertising campaigns bringing in billions of dollars of advertising revenue. Apart from their use in social media platforms, DNNs are impacting many other domains and are making a huge impact. Some of these areas include:

- **Speech Processing**: Speech processing algorithms have improved significantly in the past few years. Nowadays, many applications have been developed that use DNNs to perform real-time speech recognition with unprecedented levels of accuracy [3, 7–9]. Many technology companies are also using DNNs to perform language translation used in a wide variety of applications. Google, for example, uses Google's neural machine translation system (GNMT) [10] which uses LSTM-based seq2seq model for their language translation applications.
- **Autonomous Driving**: Autonomous driving has been one of the biggest technological breakthroughs in the auto industry since the invention of the internal combustion engine. It is not a coincidence that the self-driving boom came at the same time when high accuracy CNNs became increasingly popular. Companies

like Tesla [11] and Waymo [12] are using various types of self-driving technology including visual feeds and Lidar for their self-driving solutions. One thing which is common in all these solutions is the use of CNNs for visual perception of the road conditions which is the main back-end technology used in advanced driver assistance systems (ADAS).

- **Medical AI**: Another crucial area where DNNs/CNNs have become increasingly useful is medicine. Nowadays, doctors can use AI-assisted medical imagery to perform various surgeries. AI systems use DNNs in genomics to gather insights about genetic disorders like autism [13, 14]. DNNs/CNNs are also useful in the detection of various types of cancers like skin and brain cancer [15, 16].

- **Security**: The advent of AI has challenged many traditional security approaches that were previously deemed sufficient. The rollout of 5G technology has caused a massive surge of IoT-based deployments which traditional security approaches are not able to keep up with. Physical unclonability approaches [17–21] were introduced to protect this massive deployment of IoTs against security attacks with minimum cost overheads. These approaches, however, were also unsuccessful in preventing AI-assisted attacks using DNNs [22, 23]. Researchers have now been forced to upgrade the security threat models to incorporate AI-based attacks [24, 25]. Because of a massive increase in AI-assisted cyber-attacks on cloud and datacenters, companies have realized that the best way of defeating offensive AI attacks is by incorporating AI-based counterattacks [26, 27].

Overall, the use of DNNs, in particular CNNs, in various applications has seen exponential growth over the past decade, and this trend has been on the rise for the past many years. The massive increase in CNN deployments on the edge devices requires the development of efficient processing architectures to keep up with the computational requirements for successful CNN inference.

1.2 Pitfalls of High-Accuracy DNNs/CNNs

This section discusses some of the pitfalls of high-accuracy DNN/CNN models focusing on compute and energy bottlenecks, and the effect of sparsity of high-accuracy models on throughput and hardware utilization.

1.2.1 Compute and Energy Bottleneck

CNNs are composed of multiple convolution layers (CONV) which help in extracting low-, mid-, and high-level input features for better accuracy. Although CNNs are primarily used in applications related to image and video processing, they are

Table 1.1 Popular CNN models.

CNN model	Layers	Top-1 accuracy (%)	Top-5 accuracy (%)	Parameters	MACs
AlexNet [30]	8	63.3	84.6	62M	666M
VGG-16 [31]	16	74.3	91.9	138M	15.3B
GoogleNet [35]	22	68.9	88	6.8M	1.5B
MobileNet [35]	28	70.9	89.9	4.2M	569M
ResNet-50 [32]	50	75.3	92.2	25.5M	3.9B

also used in speech processing [3, 7], gameplay [28], and robotics [29] applications. We will further discuss the basics of CNNs in Chapter 2. In this section, we explore some of the bottlenecks when it comes to implementing *high-accuracy* CNN inference engines in embedded mobile devices.

The development of high accuracy CNN models [30–34] in recent years has strengthened the notion of employing DNNs in various AI applications. The classification accuracy of CNNs for the ImageNet challenge [2] has improved considerably from 63.3% in 2012 (AlexNet [30]) to a staggering 87.3% (EfficientNetV2 [4] in 2021). This high jump in accuracy comes with high compute and energy costs for CNN inference. Table 1.1 shows some of the most commonly used CNN models. The models are trained using the ImageNet dataset [2], and the top-1 and top-5 classification accuracy is also given. We note that top-1 accuracy is the conventional accuracy, which means that the model answer (i.e., the one predicted by the model with the highest probability) must be exactly the expected answer. Top-5 accuracy means that any of the five highest probability answers predicted by the model must match the expected answer. It can be seen from Table 1.1 that the addition of more layers results in better accuracy. This addition, however, also corresponds to a greater number of model parameters, requiring more memory and storage. It also results in higher multiply-accumulate (MAC) operations, causing an increase in computational complexity and resource requirements, which in turn, affects the performance of the edge devices.

Even though some efforts have been made to reduce the size of the high accuracy models, they still require massive amounts of computations over a series of network layers to perform a particular inference task (classification, segmentation, etc.). These tremendous number of computations (typically in tens of millions) present a huge challenge for the **neural network accelerators** (NNAs) running the CNN inference. NNAs are specialized hardware blocks inside a computer system (e.g., mobile devices and cloud servers) that speed up the computations of the CNN inference process to maintain the real-time requirements of the system

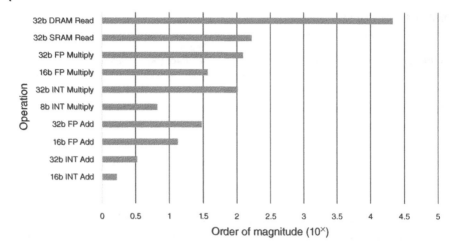

Figure 1.2 Energy cost (relative to 8 bit Add operation) shown on a log 10 scale for a 45 nm process technology. Source: Adapted from [6, 36].

and improve system throughput. Apart from the massive computational require-ments, the addition of more layers for higher accuracy drastically increases the CNN model size. This prevents the CNN model from being stored in the limited on-chip static random access memory (SRAM) of the edge device, and, therefore, requires off-chip dynamic random access memory (DRAM) which presents a high DRAM access energy cost.

To put this in perspective, the energy cost per fetch for 32 bit coefficients in an off-chip low-power double data rate 2 (LPDDR2) DRAM is about 640 pJ, which is about 6400× the energy cost of a 32 bit integer ADD operation [36]. The bigger the model is, the more memory referencing is performed to access the model data which in turn expends more energy. Figure 1.2 shows the energy cost of various compute and memory operations relative to an 8 bit integer add (8 bit INT Add) operation. It can be seen that the DRAM Read operation dominates the energy graph with the 32 bit DRAM Read consuming greater than 4 orders of magnitude higher energy than the 8 bit INT Add. As a consequence, the energy cost from just the DRAM accesses would be well beyond the limitations of an embedded mobile device with limited battery life. Therefore, in addition to accelerating the compute operations, the NNA also needs to minimize the off-chip memory transactions for decreasing the overall energy consumption.

Many algorithm-level techniques have been developed to minimize the compu-tational requirements of a CNN without incurring a loss in accuracy. Since the main compute bottleneck in CNN inference is the CONV operation, *Mobilenets* [33, 34] were developed to reduce the total number of CONV operations. These CNNs drastically reduce the total number of parameters and MAC operations by breaking down the standard 2D convolution into depthwise separable and point-wise convolutions. The depthwise separable and pointwise convolutions result in 8× to 9× reduction in total computations compared to regular CONV operations, with a slight decrease in accuracy. They also eliminate varying filter sizes, and instead, use 3×3 and 1×1 filters for performing convolution operations. This makes them ideal for embedded mobile devices because of their relatively low memory footprint and lower total MAC operations.

A widely used approach for decreasing the memory bottleneck is the reduction in the precision of both weights and activations using various quantization strategies [37–39]. This again does not result in a significant loss in accuracy and reduces the model size by a considerable amount. Hardware implementations like Envision [40], UNPU [41], and Stripes [42] show how reduced bit precision, and quantization, translates into better savings in energy.

1.2.2 Sparsity Considerations

Nonlinear activation functions [6], in addition to deep layers, is one of the key characteristics that improve the accuracy of a CNN model. Typically, nonlinearity is added by incorporating activation functions, the most common being the rectified linear unit (ReLU) [6]. The ReLU converts all negative values in a feature map to zeros. Since the output of one layer is the input to the next layer, many of the computations, within a layer, involve multiplication with zeros. These feature maps containing zeros are referred to as *one-sided* sparse feature maps. The multiplications resulting from this one-sided sparsity waste compute cycles and decrease the *effective* throughput and hardware utilization, thus, reducing the performance of the accelerator. It also results in high energy costs as the transfer of zeros to/from off-chip memory is wasted memory access. In order to reduce the computational and memory access volume, previous works [43–45] have exploited this one-sided sparsity and displayed some performance improvements. To exacerbate the issue of wasted compute cycles and memory accesses, *two-sided* sparsity is introduced in CNNs often by pruning techniques when, in addition to the feature maps, the weight data also consists of zeros. Designing a CNN accelerator that can overcome the wasted compute cycles and memory accesses issues of one-sided and two-sided sparsities is quite challenging.

In recent years, many pruning techniques have been developed for the compression of DNN models [46–49]. Han et al. [46] iteratively pruned the connections based on parameter threshold and performed retraining to retain accuracy. This type of pruning is referred to as unstructured pruning. It arbitrarily removes weight connections in a DNN/CNN but does little to improve acceleration on temporal architectures like central processing units (CPUs) and graphics processing units (GPUs) which rely on accelerating matrix multiplications. Another form of pruning, referred to as structured pruning [50, 51], reduces the size of weight matrices and maintains a full matrix. This makes it possible to simplify the NNA design since the sparsity patterns are predictable, therefore, enabling better hardware support for operation scheduling.

Both unstructured and structured pruning strategies, as described above, result in *two-sided* sparsity, (i.e., sparsity in both weights and activations) which lead to approximately 9× model reduction for AlexNet and 13× reduction for VGG-16. The purning strategies also result in 4–9× *effective* compute reduction (depending on the model). These gains seem very promising; however, designing an accelerator architecture to leverage them is quite challenging because of the following reasons:

- **Data Access Inconsistency**: Computation gating is one of the most common ways by which sparsity is generally exploited. Whenever a zero in the activation or the weight data is read, no operation is performed. This results in energy savings but has no impact on the throughput because of the wastage of compute cycle. Complex read logic needs to be implemented to discard the zeros, and instead, perform effective computations on nonzero data. Some previous works [52, 53] use sparse compression formats like compressed sparse column (CSC) or compressed sparse row (CSR) to represent sparse data. These formats have variable lengths and make *looking ahead* difficult if both the weight and the activation sparsity are being considered. Other than that, developing the complex control and read logic to process these formats can be quite challenging.
- **Low Utilization of the Processing Element (PE) Array**: Convolution operations for CNN inference are usually performed using an array of two-dimensional PEs in a CNN accelerator. Different dataflows (input stationary, output stationary, weight stationary, etc.) have been proposed that efficiently map the weight data and the activation data onto the PE array to maximize the throughput [6, 54]. Sparsity introduces inconsistency in the scheduling of data thereby reducing hardware utilization. The subset of PEs provided with more sparse data have idle times while those provided with less sparse (or denser) data are fully active. This bounds the throughput of the accelerator to the most active PEs, and therefore, leads to the underutilization of the PE array.

Considering the abovementioned issues, many accelerators have been proposed in the past that attempt to strike a balance between hardware resource complexity and performance improvements. The CNN accelerators that exploit sparsity in CNN models are covered in detail in Part IV of this book.

1.3   Chapter Summary

This chapter discussed the history and applications of DNNs, focusing on CNNs. The chapter also highlighted the compute and energy bottlenecks as well as the effect of sparsity in high-accuracy CNN models on the throughput and hardware utilization of edge devices.

2

Overview of Convolutional Neural Networks

This chapter gives an overview of the composition of different deep neural network (DNN) models, specifically the convolutional neural networks (CNNs), and explore the different layers that these neural networks are comprised of. Additionally, this chapter describes some of the most popular high accuracy CNN models and the datasets upon which these CNNs operate. Finally, the chapter reviews some of the architectural and algorithmic techniques for efficient processing of high accuracy CNN models on edge devices.

2.1   Deep Neural Network Architecture

DNNs are a manifestation of the notion of deep learning, which comes under the umbrella of artificial intelligence (AI). The main inspiration behind DNNs is the way different neurons work in a brain to process and communicate information. The raw sensory input is transformed into a high-level abstraction in order to extract meaningful information and make decisions. This transformation, referred to as inference (or forward propagation) in DNNs, results from many stages of nonlinear processing, with each stage called a layer.

Figure 2.1 shows a simple DNN with four hidden layers and one input and output layer. The DNN layers receive a weighted sum of input values ($w_i x_i$, where w_i denotes weights and x_i denotes the inputs) and compute outputs using a nonlinear function, referred to as the *activation function*. Many activation functions have been proposed in the literature, some of which are shown in Figure 2.2. Rectified linear unit (ReLU) is one of the most commonly used activation functions utilized in many modern state-of-the-art DNNs. The weights in each layer are determined through the process of training. Once the training is complete after meeting a desired accuracy, the trained model is deployed on computer servers or often on edge devices where inference is performed.

Accelerators for Convolutional Neural Networks, First Edition.
Arslan Munir, Joonho Kong, and Mahmood Azhar Qureshi.

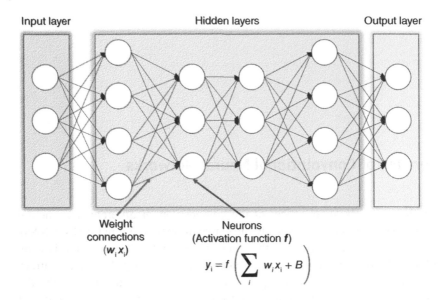

Input layer **Hidden layers** **Output layer**

Weight
connections
$(w_i x_i)$

Neurons
(Activation function **f**)

$$y_i = f\left(\sum_i w_i x_i + B\right)$$

Figure 2.1 A neural network example with one input layer, four hidden layers, and one output layer.

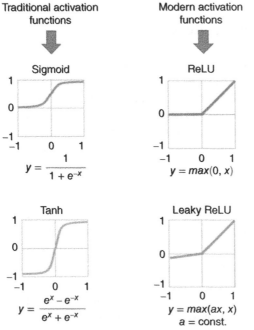

Traditional activation
functions

Modern activation
functions

Sigmoid

$$y = \frac{1}{1 + e^{-x}}$$

ReLU

$$y = max(0, x)$$

Tanh

$$y = \frac{e^x - e^{-x}}{e^x + e^{-x}}$$

Leaky ReLU

$$y = max(ax, x)$$
$$a = const.$$

Figure 2.2 Various nonlinear activation functions. Source: Figure adapted from DNN tutorial survey [6].

DNNs come in various shapes and sizes depending on the target application. Multi-layer perceptrons (MLPs) are DNNs that consist of many fully connected (FC) layers, with each layer followed by a nonlinear activation function. In MLPs, each neuron in layer$_i$ is connected to every neuron in layer$_{i+1}$. In this way, the FC layer computations can be generalized as matrix–vector multiplications followed by the activation function. The FC layer computation can be represented as:

$$y = f(Wi + b) \tag{2.1}$$

where i is the input vector, W is the weight matrix, b is the bias, f is the activation function, and y represents the output activation vector. It can be seen that the DNN in Figure 2.1 is an example of an MLP network.

2.2 Convolutional Neural Network Architecture

CNNs are a specialized type of DNNs that utilize a mathematical operation called convolution instead of general matrix multiplication in at least one of their layers. A CNN is composed of an input layer, hidden layers, and an output layer. In any feed-forward neural network, any middle layers between the input layer and the output layer are known as *hidden layers*. The hidden layers take a set of weighted inputs and produce output through an activation function. In a CNN, the hidden layers include layers that perform convolution operations. In a convolutional layer of the CNN, each neuron receives input from only a confined area (e.g., a square of 3×3 or 5×5 dimension) of the previous layer called the neuron's *receptive field*. In an FC layer of the CNN (further elaborated in the following), the receptive field is the entire previous layer. Each neuron in a neural network applies a specific function to the input values received from the receptive field in the previous layer to compute an output value. The input value received by the function in neuron depends on a vector of weights and biases, which are learned iteratively as the neural network is being trained on the input data. In CNNs, the vectors of weights and biases are called *filters* that capture specific features of the input. A distinctive feature of CNNs as opposed to other DNNs or MLPs is that a filter in CNNs can be shared by many neurons (i.e., weights or filter sharing). As illustrated in Figure 2.3, the same weights are shared between the neurons across receptive fields in the case of CNNs. This sharing of filter in CNNs reduces the memory footprint because a single vector of weights and a single bias can be used across all the receptive fields that share that filter as opposed to having a separate weight vector and bias for each receptive field. The other distinctive feature of the CNN as compared to MLPs is sparse connection between the input and output neurons. It means only a small fraction of the input neurons are connected to a certain output neuron.

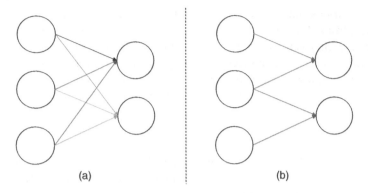

(a)　　　　　　　　　　　(b)

Figure 2.3 The demonstration of (a) MLPs and (b) CNNs.

As shown in Figure 2.3, the neurons are sparsely connected in CNNs, while all the input neurons are connected to all the output neurons (i.e., are densely connected) in MLPs.

An overall architecture of a CNN is depicted in Figure 2.4. The input for CNNs is typically composed of three channels (red, green, and blue [RGB]), each of which comprises two-dimensional pixel arrays. The *convolution layer* performs the convolution operations with filters to extract features from the inputs. The *pooling layer* reduces the size of the feature maps by downsampling the input feature maps. The *flatten layer* flattens the multidimensional tensors to a one-dimensional vector. The *fully connected layer* performs the classification, which is represented by a probability distribution across the classes.

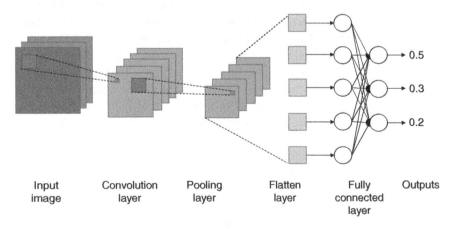

| Input image | Convolution layer | Pooling layer | Flatten layer | Fully connected layer | Outputs |

Figure 2.4 Overview of a typical CNN architecture.

2.2.1 Data Preparation

This first step of using a CNN for any application is to collect data (in most cases images or video frames for CNNs) from different sources. Section 2.4 highlights some of the popular datasets that are often utilized for training and testing CNNs. In case, the publicly available datasets are not suitable for a particular CNN application, a designer needs to collect his/her own dataset. The collected dataset then also needs to be annotated (either manually or with the help of some annotation tool) for training. The data (images or frames) from the dataset often needs to be resized to match the default size for a given CNN. Furthermore, the dataset is also augmented by perturbing the input and/or output of the collected samples to create various altered versions of the same data. *Dataset augmentation* provides additional data to train and provides modified versions of the data. For instance, in case of image data, image augmentation provides a different viewpoint to the CNN model. These different viewpoints can represent changes in the saturation, color, crop, and horizontal and vertical flips [55]. Dataset augmentation also helps to reduce over-fitting of a CNN model to the training data.

2.2.2 Building Blocks of CNNs

A CNN architecture comprises a stack of distinct layers that transform the input to output. In the following, we discuss the distinct layers that are commonly used in CNN architectures.

2.2.2.1 Convolutional Layers

The core layers in CNNs that distinguish CNNs from other DNNs are convolutional (CONV) layers. CNNs contain multiple CONV layers. The parameters in CONV layers are a set of learnable filters (or kernels), which have a small receptive field. During the forward pass, each filter computes the dot product between the filter entries and the input. The filter is then slided across the width and height of the input to produce a two-dimensional activation map of that filter. As the training progresses, the network learns filters that activate when they detect some particular type of feature at some spatial position in the input.

In CNNs, each successive layer extracts features that are at a higher level of abstraction compared to the previous layers. Modern CNNs are capable of achieving superior performance by employing a deep hierarchy of layers. The CONV layers in a CNN are composed of multidimensional convolution operations, as shown in Figure 2.5. The input to the CONV layer is an $H \times W \times C$ matrix, called an input feature map (ifmap or IFM), where H and W are the height and width, respectively, of the IFM and C is the total number of channels[1]. For an input layer

---

1 For a colored image, the value of C at the input layer is 3 which represents the RGB colorspace. For a grayscale image, the value of C at the input layer is 1.

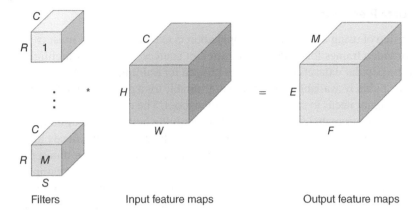

Figure 2.5 Multidimensional convolution operation performed in a CNN CONV layer. There are *M* filters of *R* (filter height) × *S* (filter width) × *C* (the number of input channels) dimension. The dimension of input feature maps is *H* (input feature map height) × *W* (input feature map width) × *C* (the number of input channels). The dimension of output feature maps is *E* (output feature map height) × *F* (output feature map width) × *M* (the number of output channels, which is same as the number of filters).

of a CNN, this IFM is usually a 224 × 224 × 3 image, which is used in the ImageNet dataset. Each channel of the IFM is convolved with a unique 2D filter (weight) from a set of filters, one for each channel. The dimensions of the output feature maps are dependent on the size of the input and the filters. Based on Figure 2.5, the following equation governs the multidimensional convolution operation in a CONV layer of a CNN:

$$O[z][u][x][y] = B[u] + \sum_{k=0}^{C-1}\sum_{i=0}^{S-1}\sum_{j=0}^{R-1} I[z][k][Ux+i][Uy+j] \times W[u][k][i][j],$$

$$0 \leq z < N, \quad 0 \leq u < M, \quad 0 \leq x < F, \quad 0 \leq y < E,$$

$$E = (H - R + U)/U, \quad F = (W - S + U)/U \tag{2.2}$$

where O, B, I, and W denote the output feature map (OFM or ofmap), bias, ifmap, and filter matrices, respectively, U represents the convolution stride, and N denotes the batch size.

A multibatch CONV ($N > 1$) can improve the throughput as compared to a single-batch ($N = 1$) CONV. Figure 2.6 demonstrates the difference between the single-batch and multibatch CONV operations. When executing the CONV operations with N ($N > 1$) batches, N ifmaps (the dimension of a single ifmap is $H \times W \times C$) can be convolved simultaneously. During the multibatch CONV operations, the same filters (M filters with $R \times S \times C$ filter dimension) are shared

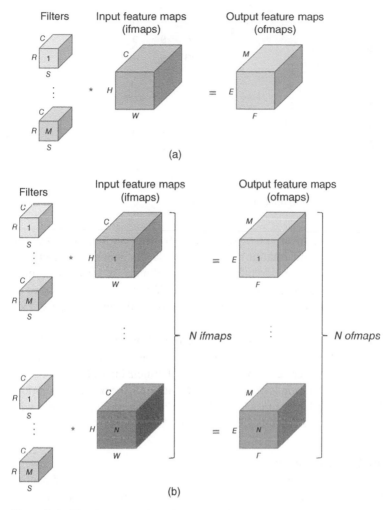

Figure 2.6 The demonstration of (a) single-batch CONV operations and (b) multibatch CONV operations.

across the batches, generating N ofmaps (the dimension of a single ofmap is $E \times F \times M$). Multibatch CONV can also improve the reusability of the filters due to the filter sharing across the batches.

2.2.2.2 Pooling Layers
CNNs contain many pooling layers. *Pooling* is performed mainly for down-sampling the feature maps by aggregating features from local regions to make the CNN less compute-intensive. Pooling also helps CNNs to learn larger-scale

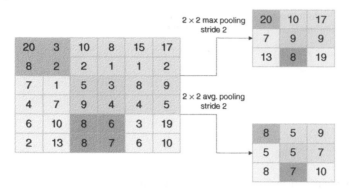

Figure 2.7 Max and averaging pooling on a 6 × 6 ifmap.

image features that are invariant to small local transformations (e.g., translation, scaling, shearing, and rotation) [56]. Pooling layers generally use *max* or *averaging* operations on nonoverlapping blocks of ifmaps. A *stride* of nonunit size is applied to reduce the dimensionality of the ifmaps. Figure 2.7 shows an example of max and average pooling applied on a 6 × 6 ifmap to produce 3 × 3 outputs.

The output of the pooling layer can be determined by the input matrix size ($H \times W$), the spatial extent of pooling (i.e., $K \times K$ pooling filter), and stride S. The pooling layer will generate the output matrix of dimension $((H - K)/S + 1) \times ((W - K)/S + 1)$. For C channels of ifmap (i.e., $H \times W \times C$), the pooling operations can be applied independently to each $H \times W$ matrix, generating the output with $((H - K)/S + 1) \times ((W - K)/S + 1) \times C$ dimension.

2.2.2.3 Fully Connected Layers

A CNN, typically, also comprises a few FC layers after several CONV and pooling layers for classification purposes. Neurons in a layer have connections to all activations in the previous layer, just like MLP networks. The activations of the FC layers can be computed by *affine transformations*, that is, multiplication of the activation values of the previous layer with the weights of their connections with neurons in the FC layer followed by a vector addition of learned or fixed bias terms.

As the FC layer can be calculated by an affine transformation $Wi + b$, where W, i, and b are weights, inputs, and bias, respectively; the output dimension of the FC layer depends on the size of W and i. Assuming that we have I_{FC} input neurons and O_{FC} output neurons, W will be an $O_{FC} \times I_{FC}$ matrix, and i will be an $I_{FC} \times 1$ vector, generating an $O_{FC} \times 1$ vector as an output as shown in Figure 2.8. A bias and a nonlinear activation function can be applied to this $O_{FC} \times 1$ vector to generate the output neurons y.

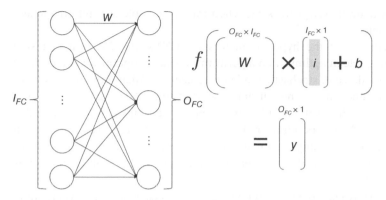

Figure 2.8 Affine transformation in the fully connected layer.

2.2.3 Parameters of CNNs

A machine learning or deep learning model, including a CNN model, is defined or characterized by the model *parameters*. On the other hand, the process of training a model involves selecting the optimal *hyperparameters* that the learning algorithm employs to learn the optimal parameters that befittingly map the input features to the labels or targets to achieve some form of machine intelligence [57].

Parameters of a CNN are internal to the model. The parameters of a CNN model are learned or estimated entirely from the data during training as the algorithm used in the model strives to learn the mapping between the input features and the targets or labels. CNN model training begins with the parameters being initialized to some random values (e.g., using uniform distribution) or zeros. These initial parameter values are continuously updated using an optimization algorithm (e.g., gradient descent) as the training progresses. Although the parameter values are regularly updated as the training progresses, the hyperparameter values set by the model designer remain unchanged. The model parameters constitute the model itself at the end of the training process [57]. For a CNN model, parameters are the *weights* and the *biases* of the model.

2.2.4 Hyperparameters of CNNs

Hyperparameters are variables that determine the neural network structure (e.g., the number of hidden layers and neurons within each layer) and also the variables that control the learning process (e.g., learning rate) [58]. CNNs use more hyperparameters than MLPs. The prefix "hyper" implies that these are "top-level" parameters that control the network structure and the learning process. Essentially, any parameter in machine learning or deep learning that a designer chooses or selects its configuration before training begins and whose value or configuration stays the same when training completes is referred to as a hyperparameter.

Some examples of the hyperparameters for CNNs are [57] train-test split ratio, learning rate in optimization algorithms, choice of optimization algorithm (e.g., gradient descent, stochastic gradient descent, or Adam optimizer), choice of activation function in a neural network layer (e.g., Sigmoid, ReLU, Tanh (Figure 2.2)), the choice of cost or loss function the model uses, number of hidden layers in a neural network, number of activation units in each layer, the drop-out rate (or dropout probability) in a neural network, number of iterations (epochs) in training a neural network, kernel or filter sizes in convolutional layers, pooling size, and batch size.

We can broadly classify hyperparameters into two categories: (i) hyperparameters related to network structure, and (ii) hyperparameters related to training process.

2.2.4.1 Hyperparameters Related to Network Structure

Hyperparameters related to network structure include number of hidden layers and units, drop-out rate (or dropout probability) in a neural network, and the choice of activation function in a neural network layer. We elaborate some of the hyperparameters related to network structure in the following:

Number of Hidden Layers and Units: The layers between the input layer and the output layer are referred to as *hidden layers*. The number of hidden layers in a CNN as well as the number of neurons within each hidden layer are hyperparameters of a CNN. When designing a new CNN, a general rule is to keep adding the hidden layers and the number of hidden units (neurons) in each layer until the test error does not improve anymore. Increasing the number of hidden units within each layer along with some regularization techniques tends to increase the accuracy of a CNN. A smaller number of units in a CNN hidden layer may cause underfitting. A large number of neurons in the hidden layer without appropriate regularization may lead to overfitting the model on the training data, which often result in low accuracy of the model on the validation and test data.

Drop-out Probability: Drop-out is regularization technique aimed to mitigate overfitting of the CNN model to the training data and to help increase the validation and test accuracy of the model. Drop-out, thus, helps to increase the generalizing power of the CNN or the DNN model. Typically, a small dropout value/probability of 20–50% of neurons is chosen with 20% providing a good starting point [58]. A very small value of drop-out probability has a minimal effect and a very high value results in under-learning by the network. Often better performance can be achieved if drop-out is used on a large network, which gives the model a greater opportunity to learn the mapping from input features to target labels.

Activation Function: Activation functions are employed in DNNs, including CNNs, to introduce nonlinearity to models, which enables deep learning models to learn nonlinear prediction boundaries. Generally, the ReLU activation function is the most commonly used activation in DNNs. Sigmoid activation function is typically used in the output layer of a DNN while making binary predictions, whereas Softmax activation function is used in the output layer of a DNN while making multiclass predictions.

2.2.4.2 Hyperparameters Related to Training

Hyperparameters related to training process include learning rate, loss function, optimization algorithm, momentum, number of epochs, and batch size. We elaborate some of the hyperparameters related to training process in the following:

Learning Rate: The learning rate of a training algorithm employed by a machine learning and/or deep learning model determines the step size at each iteration while moving toward a minimum of a loss function. The learning rate influences to what extent or how quickly the newly learned information overrides or updates the older information (model parameters in deep learning context), and thus it metaphorically signifies the speed at which a machine learning model "learns." A low learning rate decelerates the learning process but ensures smooth convergence. A high learning rate accelerates the learning process but may cause the learning process to not converge. Often a decaying learning rate is preferred.

Loss Function: DNNs, including CNNs, learn through a process called *forward propagation* where each training input is loaded into the neural network and given a forward pass. Once the network produces an output, this predicted output is compared with the given target output (label) in a process called *backpropagation*. A *loss function* is a function that compares the target and predicted output values and provides an estimate of how well the neural network models the training data [59]. The average loss J for DNNs can be given as:

$$J(\mathbf{w}, b) = \frac{1}{k} \sum_{i=1}^{k} L(y^{(i)}, \hat{y}^{(i)}) \tag{2.3}$$

where $\hat{y}^{(i)}$ denotes the predicted output value and $y^{(i)}$ denotes the target output value for a sample i, $i \in \{1, 2, 3, \ldots, k\}$ in the training data, and L denotes a *loss function* that measures the "cost" of predicting an output $\hat{y}^{(i)} = f(x_i; \mathbf{w}, b)$ for an input x_i and model parameters $\mathbf{w}$ and b when the corresponding target is $y^{(i)}$ [60]. The goal of training is to find weights $\mathbf{w}$ and bias b to minimize this average loss J between the predicted and target outputs. The parameters of the model (i.e., weights and biases) are then adjusted so that the network outputs a result closer to the target output.

There are two main types of loss functions: (i) regression loss functions, and (ii) classification loss functions. *Regression loss functions* are used in regression neural networks. For a given input value, *regression neural networks* predict a corresponding output value instead of a preselected label. Examples of regression loss functions include mean squared error and mean absolute error. *Classification loss functions* are used in *classification neural networks*. For a given input value, *classification neural networks* predict a vector of probabilities of the input belonging to various preset categories out of which the category with the highest probability can be selected as the predicted category [59]. Examples of classification loss functions include binary cross-entropy and categorical cross-entropy. CNNs often use binary cross-entropy and categorical cross-entropy loss functions. Binary cross-entropy also known as log loss is used in CNNs with binary classification models, that is, the CNN models that have to classify a given input into one of the two preset categories. Categorical cross-entropy loss functions are used in CNN models where the models have to classify a given input into one of the many preset categories where the number of classes/categories is greater than two. One can also define custom loss functions when traditional loss functions may not be sufficient for a given task.

Optimization Algorithm: DNNs, including CNNs, employ an optimization algorithm to update the weights of a neural network through backpropagation. Gradient descent is one of the most popular optimization methods for finding the minimum of a function, and different variants of gradient descent optimization algorithms are employed by DNNs. A vanilla (standard) stochastic gradient descent (SGD) updates weights by subtracting the current weight by a factor (i.e., learning rate α) of its gradient [61].

$$w_{new} = w - \alpha \frac{\partial L}{\partial w} \tag{2.4}$$

where L denotes the loss function. Different variants of SGD algorithms can be obtained by introducing some variations in Eq. (2.4). Three common variations include (i) adapting the gradient component ($\partial L/\partial w$), (ii) adapting the learning rate component (α), and (iii) adapting both the gradient and learning rate components. For the variants that adapt the gradient component, instead of using only a single gradient like in vanilla SGD to update the weights, an aggregate of multiple gradients is used to update the weights. In particular, many of these optimizers use the exponential moving average of gradients. For the variants that adapt the learning rate component, instead of using a constant learning rate, the learning rate component is adapted based on the magnitude of the gradients. The learning rate must be prudently adapted to ensure good progress while thwarting overshooting and exploding gradients [60]. Often, the learning rate is set to a relatively large value at the start of the training process and then it is decreased over time so that the optimization settles into a global minimum.

The modern SGD optimizers aim to enhance the amount of information used to update the weights, primarily through using previous (and future) gradients, instead of only relying on the current gradient. Some of the commonly used SGD optimizers include AdaGrad, RMSprop, Adadelta, NAG, Adam, AdaMax, Nadam, and AMSGrad.

Momentum: Momentum helps to determine the direction of the next step with the knowledge of the previous steps. Momentum speeds up the learning process and also helps the learning process to find a global minimum and not to get stuck in local minima. A momentum value of 0.5–0.9 is typically chosen for DNNs [58].

Number of Epochs: An *epoch* is one single pass of the entire training set through the neural network. Number of epochs is the number of times the complete training data is presented to the network while training [58]. Typically, increasing the number of epochs improves the accuracy of a DNN, including a CNN. As a general rule, a designer can choose to increase the number of epochs until the validation accuracy starts decreasing even when training accuracy could be increasing due to overfitting.

Batch Size: A batch size is the number of samples presented to the network after which the update of model parameters happens. In other words, batch size is the number of samples that are passed through the network at one time. The batch is also commonly referred to as mini-batch.

To better understand the concept of batch size, let us consider an example. Assume our training set comprises 1000 images of cats, and we aim to train our CNN to identify different breeds of cats. Further assume that we select the batch size hyperparameter to be 10. This implies that 10 images of cats will be passed as a batch or group to the network at one time. Considering that a single epoch is one single pass of the entire training data through the network, it will take 100 batches to constitute the full epoch. Number of batches in an epoch N_B can be given as $N_B = S_T/S_B$, where S_T denotes the training set size and S_B denotes the batch size. For the considered example, $N_B = 1000/10 = 100$.

2.2.4.3 Hyperparameter Tuning

A CNN designer selects the hyperparameter values that the learning algorithm will use before even the training begins. Setting the right hyperparameter values is imperative because hyperparameters directly impact the performance of the CNN model as the model parameters learned during the training process depend on the hyperparameters. The process of selecting the best hyperparameters for a CNN model is called *hyperparameter tuning*.

At the completion of the training process, we obtain trained model parameters, which are essentially what we refer to as the model. The hyperparameters that were used during training are not part of this model, that is, it cannot be inferred from the trained model what hyperparameter values were used to train the model from the model itself [57].

2.3 Popular CNN Models

Many CNN models have been developed by researchers in the past. These models have different architectures in terms of layer dimensions, the total number of layers, layer types, and layer connections. This section provides an overview of some of the most popular CNN models.

2.3.1 AlexNet

We start off by discussing the AlexNet [30] model which was proposed in 2012. AlexNet is the first CNN to win the ImageNet challenge [2]. AlexNet has been considered a major breakthrough in the field of computer vision that paved the way for widespread use of CNNs. Figure 2.9 shows the architecture of AlexNet. It comprises five CONV layers and three FC layers. Max pooling is performed after every CONV layer to reduce the layer dimensions. AlexNet has a total of 61 million parameters and achieves a top-1 accuracy of 57.2% and a top-5 accuracy of 80.3% on ImageNet dataset. The CONV layers of AlexNet have three kernel (filter) sizes: 11×11, 5×5, and 3×3.

2.3.2 VGGNet

VGGNet [31] architecture was proposed in 2014. VGGNet has different versions with each version having a different number of layers. The version shown in

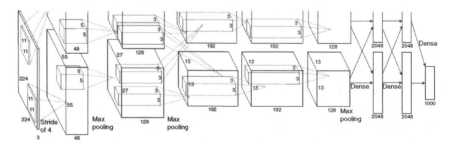

Figure 2.9 AlexNet architecture. Source: [30] Krizhevsky et al., 2012/Curran and Associates.

Figure 2.10 VGG-16 architecture. Source: Adapted from [31].

Figure 2.10 is VGG-16, the 16-layer version of VGGNet, which has a total of 13 CONV layers and 3 FC layers. VGG-16 has a total of 138 million parameters and achieves top-1 and top-5 accuracies of 68.5% and 88.7%, respectively. The accuracy jump in VGG-16 as compared to AlexNet can be attributed to the use of a greater number of CONV layers, which helps to extract more features at different scales as compared to AlexNet. This use of a large number of CONV layers, however, also results in a significant increase in the model parameters which makes VGG-16 much slower than the AlexNet. AlexNet, however, uses variable filter dimensions which make it much more difficult to implement in hardware. VGG-16, on the other hand, only uses filter dimensions of 3×3 making it easier to employ hardware-based acceleration.

2.3.3 GoogleNet

GoogleNet [35], depicted in Figure 2.11, was proposed in 2014 and is a very parameter-efficient CNN architecture. Even though it has a total of 58 layers (57 CONV and 1 FC), it only has 7 million parameters. GoogleNet comprises specialized modules, referred to as the Inception modules, as shown in Figure 2.12. The Inception modules comprise four branches of variable length filters (1×1, 3×3, 5×5). The GoogleNet achieves top-1 and top-5 accuracies of 68.9% and 89.0%, respectively.

2.3.4 SqueezeNet

SqueezeNet (Figure 2.13), proposed in 2016, targets mobile applications by having a relatively smaller number of model parameters (1.2 million), but with accuracy comparable to the AlexNet. It comprises a total of 26 CONV layers and no FC layer. SqueezeNet has eight unique modules, which it refers to as *Fire* modules. The Fire modules are an improvement over GoogleNet's Inception module and use 1×1 convolution and a pair of 1×1 and 3×3 convolutions. It has a top-1 and top-5 accuracy of 57.4% and 80.5%, respectively. SqueezeNet's primary purpose is to provide CNN support for low-cost embedded platforms with accuracy level comparable to the existing models.

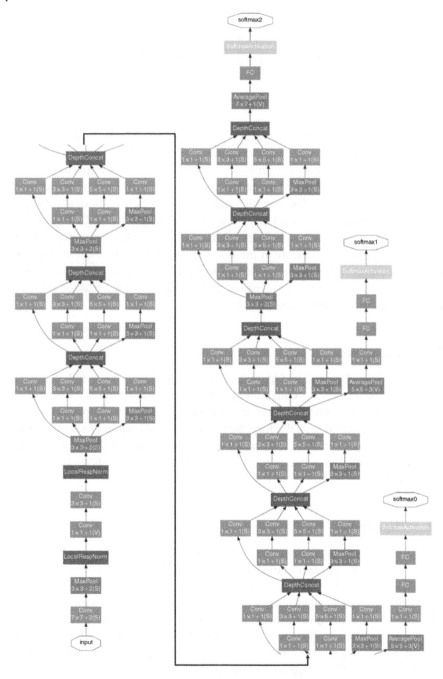

Figure 2.11 GoogleNet architecture. Source: Szegedy et al. [35].

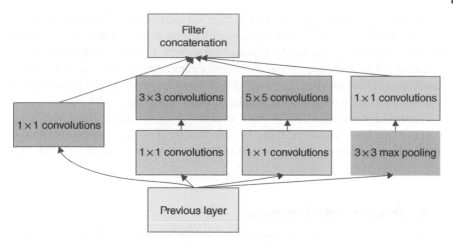

Figure 2.12 Inception module. Source: Szegedy et al. [35].

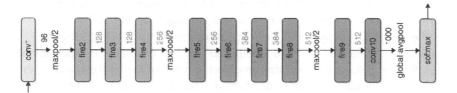

Figure 2.13 SqueezeNet architecture. Source: [62] Iandola et al., 2016/Kurt Keutzer.

2.3.5 Binary Neural Networks

Another class of CNNs that significantly reduce the total number of multiply accumulate (MAC) computations, resulting from CONV operations, are the binary neural networks (BNNs). BinaryConnect [63] modified the weights to only have two possible values (−1 and +1). These modified weights reduced the MAC operations to simple additions and subtractions. BNN [64] further extended the concept to activations as well which reduced the MAC operations to much more hardware-friendly XNORs. This, however, severely impacted the accuracy of the BNN [65].

2.3.6 EfficientNet

Recently, another class of CNNs, referred to as *EfficientNets*, have been proposed [4, 66]. EfficientNet [66], proposed in 2019, uses a dynamic scaling approach to scale all the dimensions of depth, width, and resolution, using a simple yet effective *compound coefficient*. The intuition behind the compound scaling method is that if the input image is bigger in size, then the network requires more layers to increase the receptive field and additional channels to extract more fine-grained patterns on the bigger image. An EfficientNet variant, EfficientNet-B7, has a top-1 accuracy of 84.3% on ImageNet while having a parameter count of 43 million. EfficientNetv2 [4] builds upon EfficientNet and drastically reduces the total number of parameters to 24 million with a slight decrease in accuracy to 83.9%.

There exist many other CNN models, all of which cannot be described within the scope of this book. However, it can be seen that by applying various algorithmic and architectural approaches, the size of CNNs continues to decrease while the accuracy keeps on increasing with time.

2.4 Popular CNN Datasets

A CNN is typically designed taking into account the complexity and difficulty of the task that CNN will be used for. A simple task of digit recognition requires a much simpler CNN than a CNN that is used for classifying an object into one of the 1000 classes of objects. LeNet [5], which is a much smaller CNN, is designed for the task of digit classification, whereas more complex CNNs like AlexNet [30], GoogleNet [35], ResNet [32], and MobileNets [33, 34] are built for complex image classification tasks (e.g., classifying an object into one of the 1000 classes). In the following, we briefly describe some of the datasets that are often used for benchmarking the accuracy/performance of CNNs.

2.4.1 MNIST Dataset

The MNIST dataset [67], introduced in 1998, is used for digit classification. The dataset comprises images of handwritten digits. The images are 28×28 in dimensions and are in grayscale format. There are a total of 10 classes, one for each digit from 0 to 9. The dataset consists of 60,000 training images and 10,000 test images. The LeNet-5 [5] CNN was able to achieve an accuracy of 99.05% on the MNIST dataset. This accuracy has further increased to 99.79% using regularization techniques. The MNIST has become a fairly simple dataset and is, therefore, rarely used as a metric for CNN performance these days.

2.4.2 CIFAR

CIFAR dataset [68] was introduced in 2009 and consists of 32×32 colored images of objects. CIFAR-10 and CIFAR-100 comprise 10 and 100 classes of objects, respectively. In CIFAR-10 and CIFAR-100, each dataset has a total of 50,000 training images and 10,000 test images. Most modern CNNs are able to achieve a high level of accuracy ($\approx 96.5\%$) on the CIFAR dataset.

2.4.3 ImageNet

The ImageNet dataset [2], introduced in 2010, is by far the most widely used dataset for the accuracy benchmarking of modern CNNs. It contains color images of dimensions 256×256 in 1000 classes. There are multiple categories of classes with no overlap between each category. The ImageNet dataset has a total of 1.3 million training images, 100,000 test images, and 50,000 validation images. The ImageNet uses two measures to report a model's accuracy: top-1 and top-5 error rates. The top-1 error rate is the percentage of test images for which the model's most likely label is not the correct label. The top-5 error rate is the percentage of test images for which the correct label is not among the model's top five most likely labels.

Since 2010, an annual software contest, the ImageNet Large Scale Visual Recognition Challenge (ILSVRC), is run by the ImageNet project, where different algorithms/models compete to correctly classify and detect objects and scenes at large scale. The ILSVRC challenge uses a subset of the ImageNet dataset. AlexNet [30] competed in the ILSVRC in 2012 and achieved a top-5 error of 16.4%, which was more than 10% lower than that of the runner up, which didn't use a CNN. The top-1 error achieved by AlexNet in ILSVRC 2012 was 38.1%. These results served as a breakthrough for the use of CNNs for image classification and other computer vision tasks. Since then, the accuracy of CNNs has significantly improved with the latest CNNs having the top-5 accuracy as high as 99.02% [69].

2.5 CNN Processing Hardware

As edge computing is gaining traction in recent years, there is a desire to push CNN inference on edge devices [70]. Furthermore, many of the intelligent edge applications/systems, such as surveillance [71], autonomous vehicles [72, 73], smart grid [74], remote patient monitoring [75], predictive maintenance [76], also require real time response. Since edge devices are often resource-constrained, enabling intelligent real-time applications on the edge necessitates the design of hardware accelerators for CNN inference.

The popularity of CNNs as well as increasing demand of CNN inferences on edge devices has led many researchers and companies to design specialized hardware for accelerating CNN processing. Qualcomm's neural processing engine (NPE) [77], embedded in Snapdragon processors, enables accelerated processing of 8-bit quantized DNN models on mobile devices. Google's tensor processing unit (TPU) [78] is another example of dedicated CNN processing hardware. The TPUv1 is an 8-bit systolic-array architecture comprising matrix multiplication units (MXUs), static random access memory (SRAM) buffers, and activation logic used primarily for CNN inferences. The TPUv2, in addition to inferences, also supports training by employing 16-bit precision. The TPUv3 further improves the computational capability by increasing the number of MXUs, memory bandwidth, clock frequency, etc. Xilinx provides a deep learning processing unit (DPU) [79] for its Zynq Ultrascale+ MPSoC (MultiProcessor System On Chip) devices. The Xilinx DPU specifically targets the acceleration of CNNs in field-programmable gate array (FPGA) devices. Samsung Exynos 2100 mobile processor, powering Samsung Galaxy S21 smartphones, uses triple-core neural processing unit (NPU) [80] and can perform 26 trillion/Tera operations per second (TOPS) for accelerated video processing applications.

If we look closely into the structure of CNNs, we can notice that the basic component in a CNN is a MAC operation. Both the CONV and the FC layers use MAC operation for the generation of OFMs from IFMs. Therefore, the main problem of CNN acceleration boils down to the acceleration of MAC operations. The three most commonly used computation paradigms for CNN processing are temporal architectures, spatial architectures, and near-memory processing.

2.5.1 Temporal Architectures

A temporal architecture is operated by instructions, which eventually provide better flexibility and programmability. Depending on the instruction, the control unit generates appropriate control signals to execute the instruction. The generated control signals control the computation unit and memory in accordance with the required operations to execute the instruction. In the case of the temporal architecture, the data is transferred between the memory (or register) and computation unit when executing each instruction, resulting in high data transfer overhead. Figure 2.14a depicts an overview of temporal architectures.

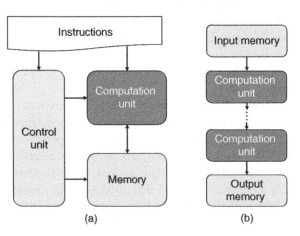

Figure 2.14 A comparison between (a) temporal architecture and (b) spatial architecture.

The temporal architectures are equivalent to central processing unit (CPU) and graphics processing unit (GPU) architectures. These architectures contain a large number of arithmetic logic units (ALUs), all of which can communicate directly with the memory, but cannot communicate with one another. These architectures use single instruction multiple data (SIMD) processing for improving parallelism. Furthermore, computational transforms are applied on the kernel matrices to reduce the total number of computations for increasing the throughput.

Many CPU and GPU architectures are optimized for matrix multiplication operations. These platforms typically implement CONV and FC layers using matrix multiplications. Figure 2.15 shows two of the most widely used convolution transformations for reducing the computational workload. Figure 2.15a uses Toeplitz transformation for converting convolution operations to a general matrix multiplication which can be carried out using efficient specialized hardware of a processor or a GPU. The disadvantage of using such transformation is the additional memory requirement of storing redundant data which can lead to memory inefficiencies.

Figure 2.15b shows conversion of convolution operations into fast Fourier transform (FFT) computations. FFT-based approaches [81, 82] reduce the computational workload of convolution operations from $O(N^2M^2)$ to $O(N^2log_2N)$, where the ofmap size is $N \times N$ and the filter size is $M \times M$ [6]. In FFT-based transformation, the input and the weight matrices are transformed into their frequency domain counterparts and then multiplications are performed in the frequency domain. Inverse fast Fourier transform (IFFT) transformation is applied to the output to bring the result back in the spatial domain, as shown in Figure 2.15b. Even though FFT-based approaches reduce the total number of computations, they require more memory and bandwidth as the size of the FFT is determined

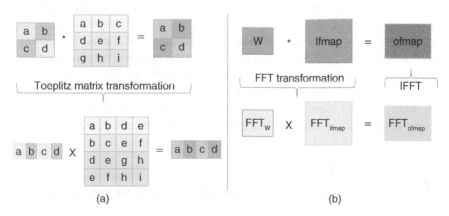

Figure 2.15 Kernel transformation. (a) Convolution to matrix multiplication using Toeplitz matrix and (b) equivalent fast Fourier transform (FFT) computation.

by the size of the output feature map which is typically much larger than the filter size. The FFT also produces complex coefficients which require more storage.

Many other algorithms have been proposed for reducing the total number of MACs required for convolution by applying different transformation techniques. Cong and Xiao [83] use Strassen's algorithm [84] for reducing the total number of multiplications from $O(N^3)$ to $O(N^{2.81})$. Similarly, Lavin [85] use Winograd transformation [86] for accelerating convolution operations involving 3×3 filters.

2.5.2 Spatial Architectures

A spatial architecture has a fixed[2] dataflow for operation, which sacrifices the flexibility and programmability. However, a spatial architecture has a lightweight control unit because of the fixed dataflow and can reduce the amount of the data transfer between the computation unit and the memory. Spatial architectures can lead to better performance and energy efficiency than temporal architectures due to reduction in the data transfer overhead. Figure 2.14b depicts an overview of spatial architectures.

The spatial architectures, used for CNN acceleration in application-specific integrated circuits (ASICs) and FPGAs, use different dataflows for passing data among different ALUs (also called processing elements [PEs]) in an efficient manner to increase the throughput and energy efficiency.

Many previously proposed accelerator architectures have focused on performance improvement; however, one of the major bottlenecks that limit a CNN accelerator's performance is the data movement. CNN inference generates a significant amount of data that needs to be moved to and from the off-chip memory. There are four memory transactions during a MAC operation in a CNN: filter read, ifmap read, partial sum (psum) read, and psum write. Partial sums are intermediate outputs that are generated as a result of a MAC operation. Because of big layer sizes and a limited number of parallel multipliers in hardware, intermediate sums (psums) need to be stored in the memory and then used later to generate the ofmaps. Instead of using the dynamic random access memory (DRAM), which results in higher energy consumption, spatial architectures use local memory hierarchy for storing the intermediate results on the less energy-consuming on-chip SRAM memory. Since the on-chip SRAM memory is very limited, specialized dataflows are designed to maximize the *reuse* of the data brought on-chip from the DRAM.

Many dataflows have been proposed to limit the movement of the data off-chip for minimizing the energy consumption. The *weight stationary dataflow*

---

2 Some spatial architectures can also support the instruction-based execution; however, they support only a small number of instructions for a specific domain.

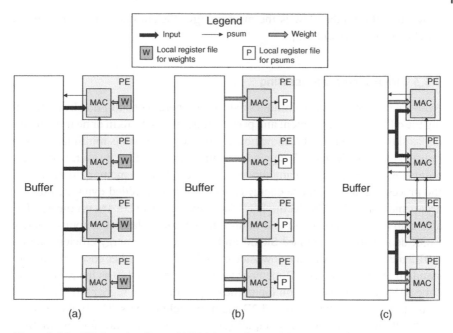

Figure 2.16 Efficient dataflows. (a) Weight stationary, (b) output stationary, and (c) no local reuse. Source: Adapted from [6].

(Figure 2.16a) minimizes the energy consumption of reading weights by storing them in a local register file (RF) of the PE. Since, in a CONV operation, the same weight matrix is convolved with the input feature map, it makes sense to store the weight locally instead of reading it from DRAM for every MAC operation. The global buffer ("Buffer" in Figure 2.16) present on-chip stores the generated psums and accumulates them across the PE array. Accelerator architectures presented in [87] and [88] use weight stationary dataflow for data reuse. *Output stationary dataflow* (Figure 2.16b) stores the psums in the local RF of the PEs. It, therefore, minimizes the energy consumption of psum movement. The psums for a particular ofmap are accumulated locally. *No Local Reuse dataflow* (Figure 2.16c) eliminates the local memory (RF) inside the PEs, and instead, uses a bigger global buffer. This is because, even though the RF memory is energy-efficient, it is not area-efficient. Thus, eliminating RF memory translates into having a larger on-chip global memory for more local data storage. DianNao [89] and DaDianNao [90] use no local reuse dataflow in their accelerator architectures. Another dataflow, referred to as the row stationary (RS) dataflow, was proposed in Eyeriss accelerator [45]. It aims to maximize the reuse of all data types (weights, ifmaps, and psums) for overall better energy efficiency. Comparison of different dataflows shows that the RS dataflow is the most energy-efficient owing to its minimum off-chip data movement [45].

2.5.3 Near-Memory Processing

Near-memory processing techniques reduce the energy consumption by minimizing the off-chip data movement and performing computations in or near the memory as shown in Figure 2.17. show how energy consumption is minimized by the reuse of data locally instead of going off-chip. There have been several enhancements toward bringing data and processing much closer to memory to accelerate the processing and minimize energy consumption. Embedded dynamic random access memory (eDRAM) technology places high-density DRAM on the accelerator chip for faster execution and minimum memory delays. It is approximately 2.85× denser than a standard SRAM and is 321× more energy-efficient than a DDR3 memory [90]. A major downside of eDRAM is its higher cost compared to standard DRAM memory. 3D memory technology, referred to as hybrid memory cube (HMC), stacks DRAM on top of the chip to provide a higher bandwidth for better performance than standard 2D memory architectures. The higher DRAM bandwidth with near-memory computing enables more data transfer per unit time

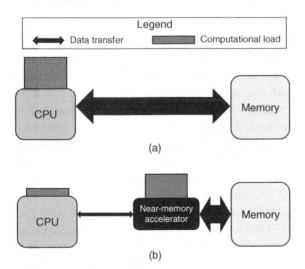

Figure 2.17 Difference between (a) traditional architecture and (b) near-memory processing. In a traditional architecture, all computations are performed in the CPU incurring a huge data transfer overhead between the CPU and memory. When using near-memory processing, the near-memory accelerator can take over a large amount of the computations from the CPU. It leads to much less data transfer between the CPU and memory as compared to the traditional architecture.

due to the reduced transfer latency, which also results in better PE utilization and computation throughput. Works like Neurocube [91] and Tetris [92] use HMC technology for faster and more energy-efficient CNN inference.

Another approach found in the literature for faster and more energy-efficient CNN inference is processing-in-memory. Since CNN inference requires MAC operations, bringing trivial computations involving MAC into the memory itself would eliminate the need for data movement, which in turn, would decrease the energy consumption significantly. Zhang et al. [93] integrated MAC operations directly in the SRAM array by using binary weights (+1 and −1). This gives an energy saving of 12× as compared to a standard 1b read from the SRAM cell. The approach by Zhang et al. [93], however, hampers the CNN accuracy on the account of using binary weights.

2.6 Chapter Summary

This chapter discussed the architecture of CNNs focusing on the main layers comprising CNNs and the parameters and hyperparameters for CNNs. Afterward, this chapter described some of the most popular high accuracy CNN models, such as AlexNet, VGGNet, and GoogleNet. Subsequently, this chapter highlighted popular datasets on which many of the contemporary CNNs operate on. The datasets that were discussed in this chapter included MNIST, CIFAR, and ImageNet. Finally, the chapter elaborated some of the architectural and algorithmic techniques for efficient processing of high accuracy CNN models.

2.7 Chapter Summary

Part II

Compressive Coding for CNNs

3

Contemporary Advances in Compressive Coding for CNNs

This chapter provides a brief overview of compressive coding as well as highlights recent advancements in compressive coding methods for convolutional neural networks (CNNs). This chapter begins with a brief background of compressive coding methods for general applications. The chapter then discusses compressive coding methods particularly used for CNNs, which are broadly classified into lossy and lossless compression. The chapter then reviews recent advancements of compressive coding methods for CNNs.

3.1 Background of Compressive Coding

Compressive coding techniques have been widely adopted in many applications. These techniques can contribute to reducing the data size, eventually leading to less memory and storage requirement. In addition, these techniques can reduce the amount of the computation as they can reduce the amount of the data to be processed.

The compression ratio can be determined as follows:

$$compression\ ratio = \frac{original\ data\ size}{compressed\ data\ size} \tag{3.1}$$

The higher the compression ratio, the lesser the size needed for the data storage or memory to retain the data within the storage or memory. It also means that obtaining a high compression ratio makes the storage or memory usage efficient. Compressive coding is very important for resource-constrained systems (e.g., low-power edge devices) where the available local storage or memory size is extremely small.

The compressive coding can be classified into two broad categories: lossy and lossless compression. The lossy compression is suitable for applications that are tolerant to data loss. The lossy compression cannot be used where even only a

Accelerators for Convolutional Neural Networks, First Edition.
Arslan Munir, Joonho Kong, and Mahmood Azhar Qureshi.
© 2024 The Institute of Electrical and Electronics Engineers, Inc. Published 2024 by John Wiley & Sons, Inc.

small amount of data loss is not tolerable because every bit of data is critical to the functioning and performance of that application. Thus, the lossy compression should be employed for an application by considering how much the quality of the result is affected by data losses. As compared to the lossless compression, lossy compression can generally lead to a better compression ratio as the lossy compression can reduce the metadata size by exploiting the tolerance of an application to data loss.

The lossless compression, contrary to the lossy compression, can fully recover the compressed data to the original data with the help of metadata. Thus, the lossless compression can be broadly applied to a variety of applications regardless of their tolerance to the data loss. However, as compared to the lossy compression, the lossless data compression techniques generate more metadata when compressing the data, and thus likely have a lower compression ratio. In addition, before using the losslessly compressed data for computation, in many cases, we first need to generate uncompressed form of the data, which are entirely same as the original data, from the compressed data. When decompressing the losslessly compressed data, it is likely to typically incur more decompression latency and energy overhead as compared to the case of decompressing the lossy compressed data. This is because the losslessly compressed data typically entails more metadata and computation for decompression than the lossy compressed data to perfectly recover the original data. Thus, when using the losslessly compressed data that need to be decompressed prior to the operation, in situ decompression and operation are desirable for better performance and energy efficiency. Figure 3.1 summarizes the concept and pros/cons of the lossy and lossless compression methods.

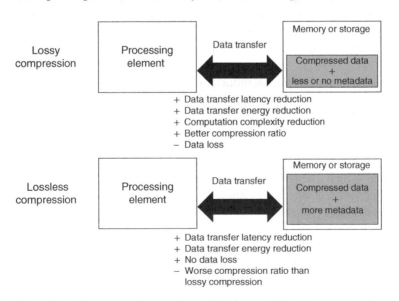

Figure 3.1 Concepts and comparison of the lossy and lossless compression methods.

3.2 Compressive Coding for CNNs

CNNs typically have a lot of data to process at runtime. For inference, the largest amount of data comes from the weights. Specifically, the huge weight (parameter) size of the CNNs is one of the major hurdles for deploying the CNNs in resource-constrained edge devices. For example, ResNet-152 [32] and VGG-16 [31], which are very widely used CNN models, have weight sizes of 235 and 540 MB, respectively (in 32-bit floating-point precision). In addition, for improving the accuracy of the CNN models, CNN models and parameter sizes are expected to be further increased. Though the large weight size causes several important challenges for CNN deployment in resource-constrained devices, one of the most serious problems is limited memory (and/or storage size) of these devices. The large weight data cannot be often fully loaded into the small memory and storage of the resource-constrained devices. In addition, the large weight size inevitably causes latency, power, and energy overhead when transferring the weight data between the storage/memory and the processing units, such as central processing units (CPUs), graphics processing units (GPUs), neural processing units (NPUs), or accelerators, which are not desirable for resource-constrained edge devices. By only storing the encoded (hence, the reduced size of) weight data in device's memory and/or storage, a more cost-efficient deployment of the CNN models in resource-constrained devices can be achieved.

Considering the large size of CNN weights, the data compression is one of the most promising solution to alleviate the storage of CNN weights. The data compression approach for the CNN weights can also be classified into two broad approaches: lossy and lossless compression. Since the CNNs have accuracy-tolerant characteristic, data size and accuracy can be traded off. The lossy compression exploits this characteristic to compress the data, reducing the data transfer size and operation complexity. The lossless compression compresses the data with the metadata, which can fully recover the original data without any loss. In terms of accuracy, the lossless compression can result in a little better accuracy as compared to the lossy compression. However, due to the metadata size and the limit of the information entropy, the lossless compression shows typically a less compression ratio than the lossy compression. In general, the lossy compression does not contain the metadata.

3.3 Lossy Compression for CNNs

For lossy compression, several well-known techniques such as weight pruning [94] and quantization [46] have been introduced. Though the weight pruning does not actually reduce the data size, it increases the sparsity of the weight data by replacing the near-zero weight elements with zero-valued elements, potentially improve the compression ratio when employing the compression methods such as Huffman coding or run-length coding. The pruning can also reduce the number of neurons. If the connected weights to a certain neuron are all zero-values, we can also remove that neuron, resulting in the reduction of the amount of the data size and computations.

The quantization reduces weight elements' size with a negligible loss of the CNN accuracy. For example, while the conventional precision of the elements in CNNs is single-precision floating-point (32-bit), 8-bit integer and 16-bit fixed-point precisions are also widely used for cost-efficient CNN inferences, which can reduce the weight size by 4× and 2×, respectively. Even further, as a more aggressive solution, several works have been proposed to use 5-bit weight elements for deploying the CNN models in resource-constrained systems [37, 95]. The 5-bit quantization represents each weight element with either 5-bit log-based or 5-bit linear-based one. Between the log- and linear-based quantization, the log-based representation is more preferred. This is because (i) log-based approach can achieve a better accuracy as compared to the linear-based approach [37], and (ii) log-based representation is more hardware-friendly as it can replace multiplier with a shifter [96]. It has been reported that the log-based representation shows very small accuracy drops (e.g., 1.7% and 0.5% top-5 accuracy drop in AlexNet and VGG-16, respectively).

3.4 Lossless Compression for CNNs

For lossless compression, entropy-based coding is a widely used approach. It adopts a variable length encoding based on the occurrence probability of a certain symbol in a datastream. Based on the probability, it assigns different code lengths for encoding of the datastream. There are two widely used entropy-based coding schemes: Huffman coding and arithmetic coding. When encoding the data with Huffman coding, one generates Huffman tree (a type of binary tree) which represents how data are encoded for each symbol based on the occurrence probability of each symbol. Figure 3.2 depicts an example of the Huffman tree generated from certain symbol occurrence probabilities. The higher occurrence probability of a certain symbol has, the shorter length of the bits assigned for encoding of the symbol. When decoding the data, one performs a tree traversal from the root node to the leaf node by following the bit sequence. When we find "0" in the bit sequence, we move to the left child, and while we move to the right child when finding "1" in the bit sequence. When we arrive at the leaf node, the corresponding symbol that is defined when generating the Huffman tree is written to the decoded datastream and we perform the tree traversal from the root

Symbol occurrence probability

Symbol	Probability
A	0.375
B	0.2
C	0.15
D	0.15
E	0.125

Generated Huffman tree

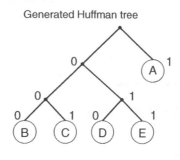

Figure 3.2 An example of the Huffman tree.

node again. The tree traversals are repeatedly performed until we reach the end of the encoded bitstream.

On the other hand, arithmetic coding encodes the data by mapping a stream of the symbols into the real number space [0, 1). Figure 3.3 depicts an example of the arithmetic coding. The example shows an encoding process of the datastream "BDAC.." with the symbol occurrence probability in the datastream as presented in the table of Figure 3.3. The first symbol "B" is mapped to the subrange [0.4, 0.7). The symbol sequence "BD" should be mapped to the subrange within the range [0.4, 0.7), resulting in mapping of the sequence to the subrange [0.67, 0.7). "BDA" is also mapped to [0.67, 0.674), which is a subrange of the range [0.67, 0.7). Similarly, "BDAC" will be mapped to [0.6728, 0.6736) as shown in Figure 3.3. Several weight compression approaches based on Huffman coding have been introduced [46, 97] because of its simplicity whereas little attention is paid to arithmetic coding. However, in general, arithmetic coding is known to result in a better compression ratio as compared to Huffman coding [98]. Moreover, when applying the arithmetic coding to the 5-bit quantized CNN weights, it also results in better compression ratio as compared to Huffman coding [99].

As the CNN weights or feature maps show high sparsity due to pruning and rectified linear unit (ReLU) activation, several lossless coding methods can also be employed for sparse data compression. Since the dense format (i.e., storing the matrix elements in the order of the coordinates in either row-major or column-major order) is not efficient when storing the sparse matrix due to a huge number of zero-valued elements, the compressive coding can also be employed for efficiently storing the sparse data for CNNs.

One of the widely used lossless compression methods is a run-length coding. The run-length coding encodes the datastream with combinations of the symbol

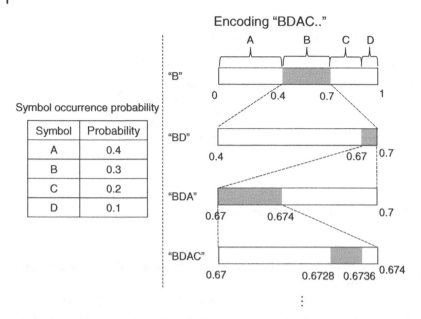

Symbol occurrence probability

Symbol	Probability
A	0.4
B	0.3
C	0.2
D	0.1

Figure 3.3 An example of the arithmetic coding.

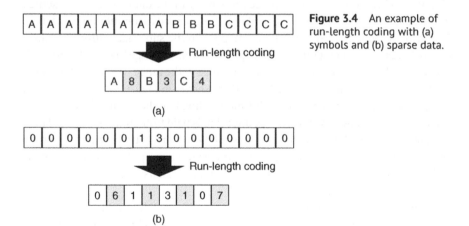

(a)

(b)

Figure 3.4 An example of run-length coding with (a) symbols and (b) sparse data.

and how many times this symbol is presented in a row. Figure 3.4a shows an example of data compression with run-length coding. As shown in the example, symbol "A," "B," and "C" appear eight times, three times, and four times, in a row, respectively. Thus, we encode each symbol with ⟨symbol + unsigned integer number⟩, where the "unsigned integer number" denotes the number of times a symbol appears continuously in a sequence, resulting in the encoded sequence "A8B3C4." Here, run-length coding reduces the number of the elements (numbers or symbols) from 15 to 6.

The run-length coding can be beneficial, in particular, for sparse data compression, where there are many zero-valued elements in a datastream. This is because a long sequence of zero-valued elements can be converted to two elements ⟨"0" + integer number⟩. Figure 3.4b shows an example of runlength coding for sparse data. The encoded datastream by applying run-length coding is also shown in Figure 3.4b. Assuming the size of each element is equal, run-length coding leads to a compression ratio of 1.875 (=15/8). As there are many zero values in a row in the datastream, we can obtain a good compression ratio making the run-length coding attractive to the sparse data compression.

Since the CNN weights are often represented in the form of matrices or tensors, a bitmap-based lossless compression approach is another widely used approach for sparse matrix or tensor compression. An example of bitmap-based lossless compression is shown in Figure 3.5. During the compression, the bitmap-based compression also generates the metadata. The required metadata is a bitmap; each bit in the bitmap corresponds to each weight element. Each bit in the bitmap indicates whether or not the corresponding weight element is zero. For storing the elements, only nonzero elements are stored. When decompressing the compressed data, the nonzero elements are restored in order in the locations where the bits in the bitmap are "1" while the zero value is restored in the locations where the bits in the bitmap are "0." In addition, for sparse weight matrix compression, a coordinate-based (COO) approach [100, 101] can also be used. Similar to the bitmap-based approach, only the nonzero elements are stored, while the coordinate information of the corresponding weight elements are also stored. Majority of the CNN weight compression approaches exploit the characteristics of the data structure in the matrix or tensor to efficiently and losslessly compress the sparse matrix or tensor.

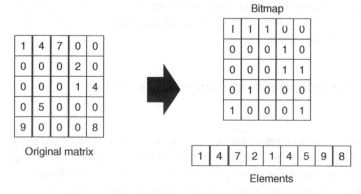

Figure 3.5 An example of bitmap-based coding for sparse matrices.

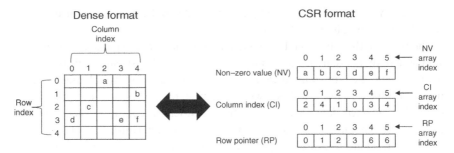

Figure 3.6 A conversion between the dense and compressed sparse row format. The coordinate (x, y) indicates a location of the element in the row index x and column index y with the dense format matrix. In the CSR format, an array index indicates a location in the NV, CI, or RP array. For CSR format, we follow a general C-style representation for indicating a certain array element. For example, NV[2] and CI[2] are equal to "c" and "1," respectively. Source: [102] Lee et al., 2022/arXiv/Public Domain CC BY 4.0.

The most well-known approach for compressing the sparse matrix is compressed sparse row (CSR) format. As shown in Figure 3.6, the CSR format stores three components: values of nonzero elements, column index (CI) of each nonzero element, and row pointers. The CSR format removes the zero-valued elements when storing the matrix while only maintaining the nonzero elements and their location information. The first part, nonzero value (NV), in the CSR format, contains the nonzero value itself. The second part, CI, contains the index of the column location of the corresponding nonzero elements. Since NVs and CIs are maintained in a pairwise manner, the same index value for nonzero element array and CI array can be used for ease of the data structure management. Thus, $NV[i]$ and $CI[i]$ work as a pair (i is a certain index) incorporating the information on a single element in the matrix.

The third part, row pointer (RP), maintains how many nonzero elements exist from the first row to the current row (i.e., cumulative number). For example, $RP[x]$ contains how many nonzero elements exist from the row with index 0 to the row with index $x - 1$ (thus, $RP[0]$ is always 0).

3.5 Recent Advancements in Compressive Coding for CNNs

This section presents recent representative advancements in compressive coding for weight size reduction. In [94], Han et al. have proposed a network pruning technique that removes weak (i.e., a weight value is less than a certain threshold) synapse connections. To improve the accuracy, it re-trains a model with the pruned weights. After pruning, the number of parameters is reduced by 9× and 13× in

AlexNet and VGG-16, respectively, with a negligible accuracy loss. In [46], Han et al. have also proposed a weight compression technique with Huffman coding. They have presented a quantization method which reduces the size of the weight elements with a small accuracy loss. They observed that the accuracy of deep neural networks (DNNs) does not significantly decreases until 4-bit precision (2.0% and 2.6% accuracy drop in top-1 and top-5 accuracies, respectively). When combining the quantization with weight pruning and data compression by Huffman coding, storage reduction of 35× to 49× has been reported. Similarly, in [97], Choi et al. have proposed a weight size reduction technique that exploits quantization and Huffman coding. They proposed an entropy-constrained quantization method which minimizes accuracy losses under a given compression ratio. In addition, with Huffman coding, it achieves over 40× compression ratio with less than 1% accuracy losses.

In [103], Ko et al. have proposed a JPEG-based weight compression technique. In order to minimize accuracy losses from the JPEG encoding, the proposed technique adaptively controls a quality factor according to error sensitivity. The proposed technique achieves a 42× compression ratio for multilayer perceptron (MLP)-based network with an accuracy loss of 1%. In [104], Ge et al. have proposed a framework that reduces weight data size by using approximation, quantization, pruning, and coding. For the coding method, the framework encodes only non-zero weights with their positional information. It is reported that the framework proposed in [104] shows a compression ratio of 21.9× and 22.4× for AlexNet and VGG-16, respectively. In [105], Reagan et al. have proposed a lossy weight compression technique that exploits Bloomier filter and arithmetic coding. Due to the probabilistic nature of Bloomier filter, it also re-trains weights based on lossy compressed weights. The technique by Reagan et al. shows a compression ratio of 496× in the first fully connected layer of LeNet5. However, the technique also shows an accuracy loss of 4.4% in VGG-16 top-1 accuracy. In [106], Choi et al. have proposed a universal DNN weight compression framework with lattice quantization and lossless coding such as bzip2. By leveraging the dithering which adds a randomness to the sources (i.e., weights), the framework proposed in [106] can be universally employed without the knowledge on the probability distribution of the source values. This implies that the compression ratio is not likely to severely vary depending on the source distribution. This also means that the compression method proposed in [106] does not require preprocessing to examine the statistical distribution of DNN weights. In practice, it would result in an easy deployment of the weight compression technique under frequently fluctuating source distribution (e.g., frequent weight updates through model training). In [107], Young et al. have proposed a transformation-based quantization method. By applying the transformation before the quantization, the proposed method achieves a significantly low bit rate around 1–2 bits per weight element.

3.6 Chapter Summary

This chapter provided an overview of the compressive coding methods and classified them into two categories: lossy and lossless compression. For lossy compression, the chapter introduced quantization and pruning, which is widely used techniques for CNNs. For lossless compression, the chapter discussed entropy-based coding and some other coding methods that can be employed for sparse matrices or tensors. The chapter also reviewed recent compressive coding methods for CNNs. In Chapters 4 and 5, this book discusses several compressive coding techniques recently proposed for CNNs. In Chapter 4, this book presents a lossless compression technique for CNN input feature maps [108]. In Chapter 5, this book discusses an arithmetic coding method for compression of 5-bit CNN weights [99].

4

Lossless Input Feature Map Compression

Although convolutional neural network (CNN) model parameter sizes are continuously being reduced via model compression and quantization, the CNN hardware acceleration still entails huge data transfer between the hardware accelerator and memory via direct memory access (DMA). This data transfer overhead aggrandizes latency, memory bandwidth pressure, and energy consumption, which limits the feasibility of many contemporary CNN accelerators for resource-constrained systems such as embedded and Internet of things (IoT) devices. Even though many hardware accelerators attempt to reuse data to minimize off-chip data transfer, the limited on-chip memory of CNN hardware accelerators results in large amounts of data transfer between hardware accelerators and main memory.

The data transfer overhead in CNNs can be classified into two types: latency overhead and energy overhead. The latency overhead could be hidden by double buffering. However, double buffering requires twice more on-chip memory capacity to support the same processing element (PE) utilizations, thus inhibiting its suitability for resource-constrained systems. Furthermore, in case of huge amounts of data transfer between the accelerator and main memory, data transfer latency cannot be hidden completely by overlapping computations with data transfer. Moreover, overlapping computations with data transfer do not hide the energy overhead of data transfer. The only way to minimize data transfer energy is to reuse on-chip data as much as possible. However, a limited size of on-chip memory in CNN hardware accelerators restricts the amount of the data reuse thus resulting in nonnegligible energy overhead. Though processing-in-memory (PIM) has been emerged to minimize data transfer, PIM would be hard to be adopted in resource-constrained systems. Hence, it is imperative to consider both computational performance and data transfer between main memory and the CNN accelerator when designing CNN hardware accelerator for resource-constrained systems.

Accelerators for Convolutional Neural Networks, First Edition.
Arslan Munir, Joonho Kong, and Mahmood Azhar Qureshi.
© 2024 The Institute of Electrical and Electronics Engineers, Inc. Published 2024 by John Wiley & Sons, Inc.

To this end, this chapter introduces a novel input feature map (IFM) compression method [108]. To reduce data transfer overhead between the hardware accelerator and main memory, it is proposed to use an efficient compression method for IFM data. The introduced scheme exploits the activation sparsity in CNN models, which are attributed to rectified linear unit (ReLU) activation function. The presented IFM data compression method, which is performed on the software side, removes the transfer of zero-valued elements in IFMs. In the following sections, this chapter introduces the IFM compression method in detail.

4.1 Two-Step Input Feature Map Compression Technique

Since there is a huge sparsity in CNN feature maps, the presented technique only maintains nonzero values (elements) with metadata for a location, while zero values are omitted in the IFM. In order to record the location of nonzero elements (NZEs) in IFMs, the presented technique also maintains indices of the NZEs in IFMs. Figure 4.1 shows a format of compressed IFM data. The presented compression algorithm maintains three entities: *nonzero elements* (32-bit floating-point for each element[1]), *indices* (8-bit for each element), and *count_table* (one element for each chunk[2]). The first part, that is *NZE* part, stores all NZEs in the IFMs. The second part, *indices*, indicates the location of NZEs in a chunk of IFM. The third part, *count_table*, indicates the accumulated number of NZEs from the first chunk to the current one.

The presented compression algorithm works as follows: Firstly, the 3D tensor IFM is converted into the 1D vector format which is also divided into a granularity of the chunk (256-elements per chunk in this work). It then linearly searches for the NZE from the first chunk. If it finds the NZE in the chunk, it updates the *indices* by storing the location of the NZE in the chunk (i.e., IFM 1D vector index % 256). It also increases the number of the NZEs of the current chunk in the *count_table*. Also, it stores the element itself to *NZE*. After it finishes the NZE search in a chunk, it starts to search for the NZEs in the next chunk and updates the cumulative number of the NZE in the next *count_table* entry. For example, as shown in Figure 4.1, since there are three NZEs in the first chunk (IFM[0]–IFM[255]), it records 3 in the *count_table*[0]. In the next chunk, it found another three NZEs, and thus records 6 (cumulative number) in the *count_table*[1]. Similarly, it records 8 in the *count_table*[2] corresponding to the third chunk as it found two NZEs in

---

1 For explanation of the presented technique, 32-bit floating-point precision for IFM elements is used. However, the presented technique can also be applied to the cases of using 16-bit fixed-point and 8-bit integer elements by applying quantization.
2 Although in this work, it is assumed that 256 elements correspond to one chunk, the chunk size depends on the design and can be extended.

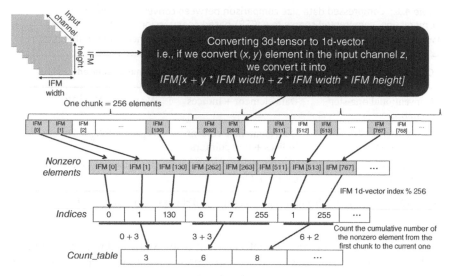

Figure 4.1 The two-step data compression technique.

the third chunk. Following the same procedure, it searches for the NZEs in all the chunks till it encounters the last element in IFM.

Table 4.1 illustrates a comparison among the presented two-step compression, conventional one-step compression which maintains NZEs and the corresponding indices (locations), and well-known compressed sparse row (CSR) compression. In Table 4.1, $N_{\bar{\phi}}$ denotes the number of NZEs and N_c denotes the number of chunks. Table 4.1 indicates that for the presented two-step compression scheme, 4B (i.e., 32-bits) are required for storing an NZE, 1B is required for storing the index of an NZE in a chunk (since it performs index % 256), and 2B are required to store the cumulative number of NZEs in a chunk. Table 4.1 also indicates that for the conventional one-step compression schemes, 4B are required for storing an NZE and 2B are required for storing the index of NZEs. The presented two-step compression scheme leads to a better compression ratio than the conventional one under the condition of $N_{\bar{\phi}} > 2 \times N_c$. Since the maximum allowable number of chunks (N_c) is 256 assuming that the maximum number of elements in the IFM is 2^{16}, the presented two-step compression scheme leads to a better compression ratio as long as the sparsity of the IFMs is lower than 99.2% (($65,536 - 512)/65,536 = 99.2\%$), which is a common case.[3]

The comparison between the introduced compression scheme and the CSR compression scheme is also presented. Please note that we also assume the 256×256 matrix format where 2^{16} elements (at maximum) can exist since the CSR scheme

---

3 Since the presented technique is geared toward resource-constrained systems, it is assumed that the maximum number of elements in the IFM is 2^{16} (256 KB when using 4B floating-point format for an element).

Table 4.1 Compressed data size comparison between conventional one-step compression, compressed sparse row (CSR)-based compression, and the presented two-step compression assuming the maximum number of elements in the IFM is 2^{16}.

Compression scheme	Data stored	Memory required
Conventional one-step compression	Data element + indices	$N_{\overline{\phi}} \times 4\text{B} + N_{\overline{\phi}} \times 2\text{B}$
Conventional CSR compression	Data element + column indices + row pointers	$N_{\overline{\phi}} \times 4\text{B} + N_{\overline{\phi}} \times 1\text{B} + 256 \times 2\text{B}$
Presented two-step compression	Data element + indices + Count_table	$N_{\overline{\phi}} \times 4\text{B} + N_{\overline{\phi}} \times 1\text{B} + N_c \times 2\text{B}$

$N_{\overline{\phi}}$ and N_c denote the number of nonzero elements and chunks, respectively.

can only be used to compress 2D matrix format. The CSR format requires a column index for each NZE and row pointers to maintain (in a cumulative manner) how many NZEs exist in each row. Thus, $N_{\overline{\phi}} \times 1\text{B}$ (8-bits) for column indices is required because of representing 0-255 column indices. For the row pointers, the worst-case requirements are considered because the data size for row pointers depends on the sparsity and data distribution pattern in the matrix. Since the row pointer should record the cumulative number of NZEs until the corresponding row (i.e., from the first row to the corresponding row), the maximum value of the row pointer is 2^{16}, meaning that 16-bits (2B) are required for each row pointer value (technically, though 17-bits are needed for the case where all the elements in the matrix are nonzero value, this case is excluded because it is a very rare case and not desirable to apply CSR compression). In addition, the number of required row pointer elements is the same as the number of rows in the matrix. Thus, 256 (2^8) row pointer values are required. Hence, for the CSR format, $N_{\overline{\phi}} \times 4\text{B} + N_{\overline{\phi}} \times 1\text{B} + 2^8 \times 2\text{B}$ are required. As explained, since the maximum allowable number of chunks (N_c) of our presented compression technique is 256 assuming that the maximum number of elements in the IFM is 2^{16}, the two-step compression technique shows a compression ratio comparable to the CSR format.

On the other hand, the CSR format can only be applied to a 2D sparse matrix because it can only contain the column indices and row pointers which are two-dimensional positional metadata. On the contrary, the presented two-step compression technique can also be employed to compress the 3D tensors because of flattening the sparse tensor to 1D vector before data compression. If one would like to use the CSR compression for a tensor (i.e., input feature maps) compression, one can separately compress each 2D IFM and combine the compressed data of each IFM. However, when performing the compression with a large number of input channels, it may seriously increase the metadata (column indices and row pointers) size because the metadata size will be proportional to the number of input channels. In addition, depending on the IFM size (height and width) and the number of input channels, the metadata size will vary. It may hugely increase accelerator hardware complexity due to variable input dimensions. On the contrary, since our compression technique converts the 3D IFM tensor into 1D vector format, our hardware accelerator (will be explained in Chapter 10) operations are not affected by the tensor dimension, relieving the hardware design complexity. Even though some other compression techniques may be a little better in terms of the compression ratio, they can increase hardware complexity for decompression and convolution, deteriorating the overall performance.

In the presented compression technique, the zero values are removed to reduce the required storage size. At the same time, the nonzero values still remain in the compressed data with their location information within the tensor. Although the zero values are removed in the compressed data, it is not actually removed from the tensor. In other words, if one restores (i.e., decompress) the compressed data to the original data, one can completely restore the tensor same as before compression (i.e., without any data loss). This is because the compressed data only contains the information on nonzero values (i.e., values and locations), whereas all the remaining spots of the tensor can be filled with zero values, meaning that the presented compression technique is lossless compression.

4.2 Evaluation

By applying the presented compression technique, one can obtain a huge amount of transferred data and transfer latency. Figure 4.2 shows the comparison of compressed IFM size normalized to the noncompressed IFM size. The presented technique reduces the IFM data size by 34.0–85.2% across the degree of the IFM sparsity from 50% to 90%. As illustrated in Figure 4.2, there are remarkable differences in compressed data size depending on the degree of sparsity in IFM. The reduced IFM data size can also contribute to the reduction of latency, memory bandwidth pressure, and energy. As shown in Figure 4.3, the presented technique reduces the DMA transfer latency by 41.6%, on average as compared to the case of transferring noncompressed IFMs. These results imply that one can significantly reduce the data transfer latency caused by the large batch of the inputs depending on the input data sparsity. In case of the input sparsity of 50%, one can only obtain the data transfer latency reduction by 4.4% with the presented technique. This is because additional latency for compression is required when applying the presented technique. Although the presented compression technique provides only a small data transfer latency benefit for 50% input sparsity, the data transfer latency improvements imparted by the presented compression technique increase

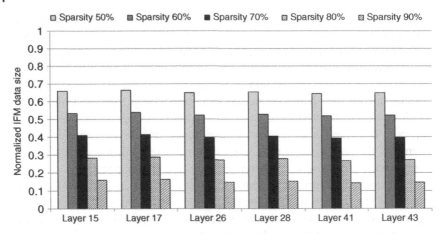

Figure 4.2 Normalized compressed data size (including metadata) comparison of the presented acceleration technique across various CONV layers.

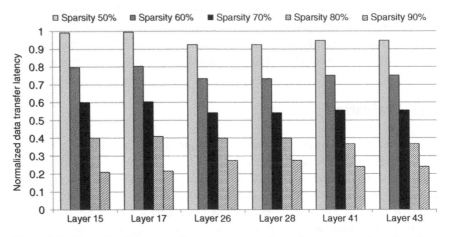

Figure 4.3 Normalized data transfer latency comparison of the presented acceleration technique across various CONV layers.

as the degree of IFM sparsity increases. For input sparsity of 90%, results indicate that one can obtain data transfer latency reductions by 75.7%, on average, with the presented technique.

Though the DMA transfer time may be hidden by double buffering, the reduced data transfer latency can also reduce the required memory bandwidth which is very crucial for low-power resource-constrained edge systems. Moreover, as observed in [109], since power and energy consumption from the dynamic random access memory (DRAM) interface is significant in embedded platforms, the data transfer reduction by the presented technique can hugely contribute to energy efficiency of the system. Apart from the data transfer latency, since the presented technique compresses the IFMs, the decoding latency should also be taken into account when performing convolution (CONV) layer operations. However, the hardware accelerator, which is introduced in Chapter 10 performs the decoding of the compressed IFMs in an in-situ manner. Thus, the decoding latency is inherently included in the latency of the hardware accelerator and therefore the decoding latency in CONV operations is not separately reported.

4.3 Chapter Summary

Sparsity in CNNs provide a huge opportunity for optimizing CNN accelerators and reducing data size. This chapter discussed a lossless compression scheme for compressing IFM data resulting in data transfer reduction between the memory and the accelerator. The compression technique presented in this chapter reduced the data size and latency for IFM data transfer by 34.0–85.2% and 4.4–75.7%, respectively, as compared to the case without the data compression.

5

Arithmetic Coding and Decoding for 5-Bit CNN Weights

To mitigate a large parameter size in convolutional neural networks (CNNs), several well-known techniques such as weight pruning and quantization have been introduced. The weight pruning increases the sparsity of the weight data by replacing the near-zero weight elements with zero-valued elements. The quantization reduces weight elements' size with a negligible loss of the CNN accuracy. For example, while the conventional precision of the elements in CNNs is single-precision floating-point (32-bit), 8-bit integer and 16-bit fixed-point precisions are also widely used for cost-efficient CNN inferences, which can reduce the weight size by 4× and 2×, respectively. Even further, as a more aggressive solution, several works have proposed to use 5-bit weight elements for deploying the CNN models in resource-constrained systems [37, 95]. Though, these works have shown successful results on reducing the weight data size, one could further reduce the weight size by applying the data encoding schemes such as Huffman coding or arithmetic coding. By only storing the encoded (hence, the reduced size of) weight data in device's memory and/or storage, one could enable more cost-efficient deployment of the CNN models in resource-constrained devices.

This chapter introduces an arithmetic coding-based 5-bit quantized weight compression technique for on device CNN inferences in resource-constrained edge devices. Once the weight elements are quantized to a 5-bit format (quantization can be done by other methods such as [95]), it leverages arithmetic coding for weight compression, which has been generally employed for entropy-based data compression (e.g., for image compression in [110] and [111]). In addition, a range scaling for lossless compression is employed, meaning that there is no accuracy loss in CNN inferences as compared to the case of using uncompressed 5-bit weight element. Compared to Huffman coding-based compression, which is commonly used, the arithmetic coding-based technique leads to a better compression ratio (CR), resulting in less memory and storage requirements for weights. In addition, when applying this technique to the pruned weights, one can obtain much higher compression ratio as compared to Huffman coding-based

Accelerators for Convolutional Neural Networks, First Edition.
Arslan Munir, Joonho Kong, and Mahmood Azhar Qureshi.
© 2024 The Institute of Electrical and Electronics Engineers, Inc. Published 2024 by John Wiley & Sons, Inc.

weight compression. For an in situ weight decompression for edge devices which contain a CNN accelerator or NPU, a hardware decoder which can decompress the compressed weight with a small latency overhead will also be introduced.

The contributions of the introduced compression technique are summarized as follows:

- A lossless arithmetic coding-based 5-bit quantized weight compression technique is introduced;
- A hardware-based decoder for in situ decompression of the compressed weights in the NPU or CNN accelerator is introduced, and the hardware-based decoder is implemented in field-programmable gate array (FPGA) as a proof-of-concept;
- The introduced technique for 5-bit quantized weights reduces the weight size by 9.6× (by up to 112.2× in the case of pruned weights) as compared to the case of using the uncompressed 32-bit floating-point (FP32) weights;
- The introduced technique for 5-bit quantized weights also reduces memory energy consumption by 89.2% (by up to 99.1% for pruned weights) as compared to the case of using the uncompressed FP32 weight;
- When combining the compression technique and hardware decoder (16 decoding units) with various state-of-the-art CNN accelerators [112–114], the introduced technique incurs a small latency overhead by 0.16–5.48% (0.16–0.91% for pruned weights) as compared to the case without the introduced technique and hardware decoder.
- When combining the introduced technique with various state-of-the-art CNN accelerators [112, 113], the introduced technique with 4 decoding unit (DU) decoder hardware reduces system-level energy consumption by 1.1–9.3% as compared to the case without using the introduced technique.

5.1 Architecture and Design Overview

For a real-world deployment of the weight compression technique, we introduce a system overview and execution flow to support fast and cost-efficient weight encoding/decoding. The overall architecture and execution flow of the introduced technique are illustrated in Figure 5.1. First, the weight quantization and encoding (upper part of Figure 5.1) are performed offline. In the cloud (or datacenter), the trained 32-bit FP weight elements[1] can be quantized to 5-bit format (and can also be pruned), and compressed by using the presented arithmetic coding-based compression technique, and sent to resource-constrained edge devices for CNN inference. The compressed weight data are stored in the memory or storage of the

---

1 Instead of FP32, the presented compression technique can also be applied to fixed-point (e.g., 16-bit) weight values as long as they can be quantized to 5-bit weight format.

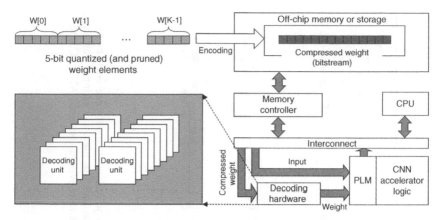

Figure 5.1 Architecture and execution flow of the presented technique.

edge devices and will be accessed when running the CNN inference. We assume there is a CNN accelerator (or NPU) in the edge device because recent edge devices are widely adopting CNN accelerators (e.g., edge tensor processing unit in Google Coral platform [115]). Please note that the 5-bit quantization can be performed with any already proposed technique (e.g., [46], [116], and [38]), and thus the proposal of a 5-bit quantization method is outside the scope of this chapter. A clear description of the contributions and execution flow is depicted in Figure 5.2.

In case of CNN inference in the baseline system (i.e., without the presented technique), the weight data will be directly loaded into CNN accelerator's private local memory (PLM). In this case, non compressed 5-bit weight data are fully

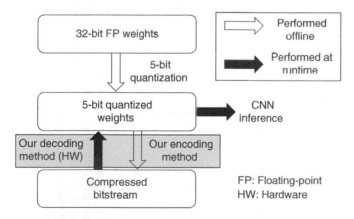

Figure 5.2 A quantization, encoding, and decoding flow for CNN inference in the presented technique. The gray-shaded part denotes the main contributions of the presented technique.

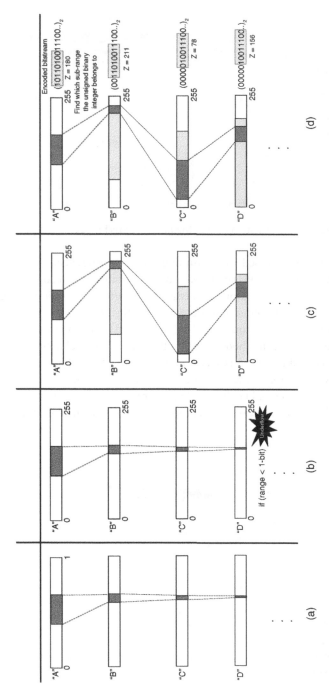

Figure 5.3 An overview of theoretical arithmetic coding (a), binary arithmetic coding with range scaling (b), and decoding algorithm (d). For illustrative purpose, we assume that the unsigned integer binary is 8-bit size (thus, mapping space is 0–255). In this example, we encode or decode a sequence of symbols (weight elements) "A", "B", "C", and "D". In (d), the numbers specified for the bitstream and Z values are merely exemplary values.

or partially loaded into CNN accelerator's PLM. However, with the presented technique, before we send the weight data to the CNN accelerator, we need a fast in situ decompression (i.e., decoding) of the compressed weight data, which necessitate a hardware decoder. The hardware decoder receives the bitstream (BS) of the compressed weight and generates the original 5-bit quantized weight data. In the hardware decoder, there are multiple DUs to expedite the runtime decoding process. Please note that the presented decoding hardware does not have any dependency to the CNN accelerator that can perform convolution operations with 5-bit quantized weight.

5.2 Algorithm Overview

In this section, we describe an overview of the algorithm. Figure 5.3 summarizes the comparison between the theoretical arithmetic coding-based encoding (a), binary arithmetic coding-based encoding without range scaling (b), and the presented binary arithmetic coding-based encoding with range scaling (c), and decoding (d). As shown in Figure 5.3a, arithmetic coding encodes the original data into a certain real number between 0 and 1 ([0, 1)). Theoretically, the arithmetic coding can compress any raw data (i.e., a sequence of the symbols) to one real number since we can have an infinite number of real numbers between 0 and 1. In general, however, when we encode certain data to a bitstream, the encoded data should be mapped to a finite binary number space, which can cause underflow. In this case, the encoded data may be lossy because different binary data can be mapped to the same encoded binary due to the limited space for data encoding. As shown in Figure 5.3b, if we have a long sequence of the weight elements and we do not have a sufficiently large binary mapping space, the underflow can occur. This is because the feasible mapping space will become smaller and smaller as more weight elements are encoded.

In the presented technique, we also map the weight elements into the unsigned integer-based binary mapping space. Since the presented compression (i.e., encoding) technique aims to generate losslessly encoded data, we also employ a range scaling method that can adaptively scale the range of the binary mapping space. In the case of encoding (Figure 5.3c), depending on the mapped subrange for a certain element, we adaptively scale this subrange according to the range scaling condition (we explain the details on the scaling condition in the next Section 5.2.1, Section 5.3, and Section 5.4). In this case, we record the scaling information as well as the information on the mapped and scaled subrange to the compressed bitstream. In the case of decoding (Figure 5.3d), by referring to a sliding window (gray shaded area in Figure 5.3d) within a bitstream, we find which subrange the unsigned integer (the number Z converted from the binary in the sliding window) belongs to. By referring to the found subrange, we decode a weight element to which the subrange corresponds. By shifting the sliding window,[2] we decode the next weight element in the similar way we describe above.

5.2.1 Weight Encoding Algorithm

In this section, we explain how we compress (i.e., encode) the 5-bit quantized weight data in details. Figure 5.4 shows a pseudocode of the presented arithmetic coding-based weight encoding with range scaling. For input, 5-bit quantized weight data (W), the occurrence probabilities for each weight value ($PROB$), and the number of weight elements (K) (i.e., the number of parameters) are required. To obtain $PROB$, we can calculate the probability based on how many times each weight appears in the weight data. The output is an encoded weight bitstream (BS). Prior to encoding, we need to set variables: N means the number of bits for mapping the weight data to an unsigned binary with arithmetic coding. RS contains range scaling information, which is initially set to 0. The MAX, $HALF$, and QTR are calculated according to the N. For initialization, low and $high$ are first set to 0 and MAX, respectively. We also need to collect the cumulative probabilities for each weight value[3] ($F[X] = PROB[x < X]$ where $0 \leq X \leq 32$).

The encoding procedure is performed by per weight element basis. For each weight element (from 0 to $K - 1$), we set the $high$ and low values to a range for mapping a certain weight element to an unsigned integer binary number space (lines 2–4 in Figure 5.4). We call this range ([low, $high$]) as *subrange*. When mapping the elements in the subrange with range scaling, there can be three cases of the range scaling: (a) upper scaling, (b) lower scaling, and (c) middle scaling. These three cases of the range scaling are also shown in Figure 5.5. Lines 5–7 and 11 in Figure 5.4 correspond to the case (a) in Figure 5.5: upper scaling. In this case, we write 1_2 followed by RS-bits of 0_2s in the bitstream (for example, if $RS = 3$, we write $(1000)_2$ to BS), reset RS to 0, and update low and $high$ values by following the upper scaling rule for further range scaling. The reason why we write 1_2 in the upper scaling case is that the subrange is in the upper half of the binary mapping space, meaning that the most-significant bit (MSB) of the mapped unsigned integer binary value will be 1_2. RS-bits of 0_2s incorporate the information on how many middle scaling has been done before. Performing more middle scalings implies that the original subrange (i.e., before performing the upper and middle scalings) was closer to the center point of the range (Figure 5.6a). This is why we write more number of 0_2s as we perform more middle scalings in the previous loop iteration.

---

2 To decode one weight element, the sliding window can be shifted by more than 1-bit depending on the range scaling condition.
3 Though the actual weights are interpreted by 5-bit log-based or linear-based values, here we represent 5-bit binary as an unsigned integer (0–31) for an ease of explanation.

Pseudocode for Encoding (Compression)

INPUT: W – 5-bit quantized weight elements

                PROB – Probability of each weight value occurrence in W

                K – # of weight elements

OUTPUT: BS – Encoded weight bitstream

N = # of bits for mapping the weight data to an unsigned integer number

RS = 0

MAX = 2^{N-1}, HALF = *round*(MAX/2), QTR = *round*(MAX/4)

low = 0, high = MAX

F[X] = PROB[x < X] (X=0 to 32, F[0]=0, F[1]=PROB[0], ... F[32]=1)

```
 1  for i=0 to K – 1
 2     range = high – low
 3     high = low + floor(range * F[W[i]+1])
 4     low = low + floor(range * F[W[i]])
 5     while high < HALF or low >= HALF
 6       if low >= HALF
 7         write 1₂ and RS-bits of 0₂s to BS, RS=0, low=low-HALF, high=high HALF
 8       else
 9         write 0₂ and RS-bits of 1₂s to BS, RS=0
10       end if
11       low=low << 1, high=high << 1
12     end while
13     while low >= QTR and high < 3*QTR
14       RS++, low = (low–QTR) << 1, high – (high–QTR) << 1
15     end while
16  end for
17  RS++
18  if low <= QTR
19     write 0₂ and RS-bits of 1₂s to BS
20  else
21     write 1₂ and RS-bits of 0₂s to BS
22  end if
```

Figure 5.4 Pseudocode of the weight encoding technique.

In case (b) in Figure 5.5 (lower scaling: lines 5 and 8–11 in Figure 5.4), we write 0_2 (MSB of the mapped unsigned integer binary value will be 0_2) followed by *RS*-bits of 1_2s in the bitstream, reset *RS* to 0, and update *low* and *high* values by following the lower scaling rule for further range scaling. As depicted in Figure 5.6b, the reason why we write 0_2 and *RS*-bits of 1_2s can be explained in a similar way of

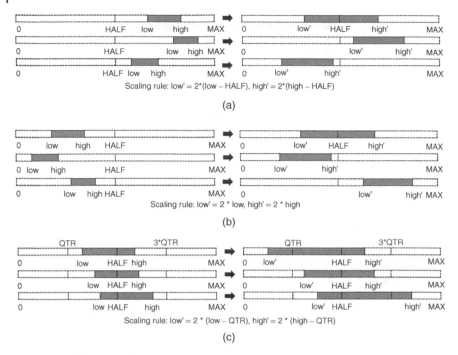

Figure 5.5 Three possible cases and scaling rules for range scaling. (a) Upper scaling, (b) lower scaling, and (c) middle scaling.

the upper scaling case. In the case (c) in Figure 5.5 (middle scaling: lines 13–15 in Figure 5.4), we do not encode the element data and only scale the subrange by following the middle scaling rule as long as the condition of the middle scaling case (line 13 in Figure 5.4) is met while we also keep incrementing RS to track how many times of middle scaling has been done. There can be a case where the subrange does not belong to any of the three scaling cases. In this case, we do not scale the subrange and we move onto the next iteration (i.e., next iterations of the **for** loop or terminate the **for** loop in the case of the last loop iteration). This procedure (lines 1–16 in Figure 5.4) is repeatedly performed until the entire W elements are encoded to BS. After that, lines 17–22 in Figure 5.4 perform a bitstream writing that corresponds to the last part of the weight data which have not been encoded yet. In this part, we do not have a middle scaling case and only record the bits by following either upper or lower scaling rule. Although the presented technique maps weight elements to an N-bit unsigned integer binary number space with arithmetic coding, the encoded bitstream also contains range scaling information (RS) along with iteratively appended binary bits depending on the scaling condition (i.e., lower and upper scaling: Lines 6–9 in Figure 5.4). Thus, the encoded bitstream is typically much longer than N-bits.

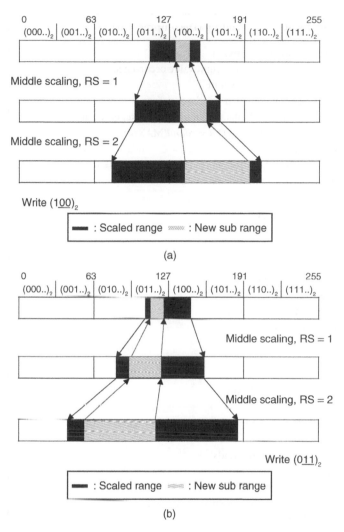

Figure 5.6 Range scalings in the case of middle scaling. (a) Middle scaling before upper scaling and (b) middle scaling before lower scaling.

5.3 Weight Decoding Algorithm

An overall structure of the decoding (i.e., decompression) procedure is very similar to that of the encoding procedure. The decoding procedure exactly follows the range calculation and scaling while we perform the weight element mapping with a part of the bitstream, which is an inverse operation of the encoding procedure. Figure 5.7 presents a pseudocode for the decoding. We need the encoded weight

---

Pseudocode for Decoding (Decompression)

INPUT: BS – Encoded weight bitstream
                    PROB – Probability of each weight value occurrence in W
                    K – # of original weight element

OUTPUT: W – Original 5-bit quantized weight elements

N = # of bits for mapping the weight data to an unsigned integer number

$MAX = 2^{N-1}$, $HALF = round(MAX/2)$, $QTR = round(MAX/4)$

low = 0, high = MAX, idx=0

F[X] = PROB[x < X] (X=0 to 32, F[0]=0, F[1]=PROB[0], ... F[32]=1)

Z(idx) = N–bits starting from bit index 'idx' in BS

 1 Append N−1 '0's at the end of BS
 2 **for** i=0 to K−1
 3   range=high−low
 4   **for** j=0 to 31
 5   high = low + *floor*(range * F[j+1])
 6   low = low + *floor*(range * F[j])
 7   **if** low <= Z(idx) **and** Z(idx) < high
 8   store weight value j to W[i]
 9   **break**
10   **end if**
11   **end for**
12   **while** high < HALF or low >= HALF
13   **if** low >= HALF
14   low = low − HALF, high = high − HALF, Z(idx) = Z(idx) − HALF
15   **end if**
16   low = low << 1, high = high << 1, idx++
17   **end while**
18   **while** low >= QTR **and** high < 3 * QTR
19   low = (low − QTR) << 1, high = (high − QTR) << 1
20   Z(idx) = Z(idx) − QTR, idx++
21   **end while**
22 **end for**

Figure 5.7 Pseudocode of the weight decoding technique.

bitstream (*BS*), the occurrence probabilities for each weight value (*PROB*), and the number of original weight elements (*K*) as inputs while the output of the decoding procedure is original 5-bit weight elements (*W*). We omit the explanation for variable initialization because the variable setting is same as the encoding except for *Z(idx)* which corresponds to the *N*-bits starting from the bit index *idx* in the *BS* where N is the number of bits used for mapping the encoded data to an unsigned binary number space, which is same as in the encoding. For example, if $N = 8$, the $Z(idx)$ will be the 8-bits starting from the bit index "idx," which can also be represented by an unsigned integer number ranging from 0 to 255 ($= 2^8 - 1$). Please note that $Z(idx)$ shifts from the starting point of the encoded bitstream in a sliding window manner as we explained in Section 15.2.1.

The decoding procedure is performed until the encoded bitstream (BS) is fully decoded into original 5-bit weight elements (W). We decode the bitstream by a unit of N-bits ($Z(idx)$). Here, the bit index of the bitstream begins with 0 ($idx = 0$). Thus, the initial N-bit window will be $Z(0)$. Before we perform the iterations, we need to append the $N - 1$ bits of 0_2s at the end of BS in order to enable the decoding of the last $N - 1$ bits in the BS (line 1 in Figure 5.7). As in the encoding procedure, decoding is also performed by per weight element basis (from 0 to $K - 1$: line 2 in Figure 5.7). In lines 3–11, we calculate the subrange ($[low, high]$) for each weight value (i.e., from 0 to 31) and find which weight value's subrange contains $Z(idx)$. If the subrange of weight value j contains $Z(idx)$, we write j to the decoded weight $W[i]$. Similar to the case of the encoding, we then consider the three different range scaling cases: upper, lower, and middle scaling. In the cases of upper and lower scaling (lines 13–16 in Figure 5.7), we also scale the subrange ($[low, high]$) by following the corresponding scaling rule as in Figure 5.5a,b, respectively, while also updating $Z(idx)$. Please note that the $Z(idx)$ can be regarded as a pointer that indicates the N-bits in the BS with a starting index of idx. Thus, updating the $Z(idx)$ also means updating N-bits in the BS starting at the bit index idx, also affecting the following $Z(idx + 1)$ value which will be referenced next (i.e., referenced by shifting the sliding window). In the middle scaling case (lines 18–21 in Figure 5.7), we scale the subrange as in Figure 5.5c while also updating $Z(idx)$. As in the encoding procedure, for three scaling cases, the scaling procedure is repeatedly performed (in a *while* loop) as long as the scaling condition is satisfied. Once K weight elements are all decoded, the **for** loop (lines 2–22 in Figure 5.7) terminates, and the decoding process is completed.

5.4 Encoding and Decoding Examples

Figure 5.8 shows an illustrative example of the presented arithmetic coding-based weight encoding. For brevity, we limit the types of weight values (i.e., possible weight element values) as "0," "1," and "2" (originally, possible weight element values are 0–31: 32 different weight values) and assume that we encode the sequence of the weight elements {0, 1, 0, 1, 2} (weight elements flattened to a

i	Starting range	$W[i]$	Subrange	Scaling case	BS	Updated RS
0	[0, 255]	0	[0, 102]	Lower scaling	0_2	0
1	[0, 204]	1	[81, 163]	Middle scaling	0_2	1
2	[34, 198]	0	[34, 99]	Lower scaling	$(001)_2$	0
3	[68, 198]	1	[120, 172]	Middle scaling	$(001)_2$	1
4	[112, 216]	2	[195, 216]	Upper scaling	$(00110)_2$	0
4	[134, 176]	—	—	Upper scaling	$(001101)_2$	0
4	[12, 96]	—	—	Lower scaling	$(0011010)_2$	0
Out of the loop	[24, 192]	—	—	—	$(001101001)_2$	1

Figure 5.8 An example for encoding by using the presented technique.

form of a 1d-vector.[4]) From the sequence, we can recognize that the $F[x]$ values for a range [0, 3] ($\{F[0], F[1], F[2], F[3]\}$) will be $\{0.0, 0.4, 0.8, 1.0\}$. In this example, we assume that $N = 8$, meaning that *MAX*, *HALF*, and *QTR* are 255, 128, and 64, respectively.

At first, we encode the first weight element "0." By calculating the sub-range ([*low*, *high*]) of the weight element "0," a new subrange will be [0, 102] ($=[0 + \lfloor 255*0.0 \rfloor, 0 + \lfloor 255*0.4 \rfloor]$) which corresponds to the case of lower scaling (*high* < *HALF*). In this case, we write a bit 0_2 in the output bitstream (*RS* is currently 0, thus we do not write 1_2). We then scale the lower bound and upper bound of the subrange by 2× by following the lower scaling rule. A new scaled range will be [0, 204] which does not account for any of the three scaling cases. Thus, we move to the next iteration for encoding the second weight element "1." The next subrange will be [81, 163] ($=[0 + \lfloor 204*0.4 \rfloor, 0 + \lfloor 204*0.8 \rfloor]$), which corresponds to the case of the middle scaling. In this case, we increment *RS* by 1 and scale the range by following the middle scaling rule, which makes the current range [34, 198] ($=[(81 - 64)*2, (163 - 64)*2]$). This range does not correspond to the middle scaling case, which means that we need to encode the following element. When we encode the third element "0," a new subrange will be [34 + $\lfloor 164*0.0 \rfloor$, 34 + $\lfloor 164*0.4 \rfloor]$] = [34, 99], which is the lower scaling case. Thus, we write $(01)_2$ (because of *RS* = 1) to the bitstream and reset *RS* to 0 while we also

---

4 For a sequence of weight elements, we flatten the weight elements starting from the first convolutional (CONV) layer to the last CONV layer of the CNNs.

scale the lower and upper bounds of the subrange by 2×, resulting in the range of [68, 198] which does not correspond to any of the three cases. For the fourth weight element "1," a new subrange will be $[68+\lfloor130^{*}0.4\rfloor, 68+\lfloor130^{*}0.8\rfloor] =$ [120, 172], which corresponds to the middle scaling case. Thus, we increment the *RS* by 1 and scale the subrange by following the middle scaling rule ([(120 − 64)*2, (172 − 64)*2] = [112, 216]). The scaled range [112, 216] does not correspond to any of the three cases, we perform the next iteration. For the next weight element "2," a new subrange will be $[112+\lfloor104^{*}0.8\rfloor, 112+\lfloor104^{*}1.0\rfloor] =$ [195, 216], which corresponds to the upper scaling case. Since the current *RS* value is 1, we write $(10)_2$ to the bitstream and reset *RS* to 0. After the upper scaling, we obtain [(195 − 128)*2, (216 − 128)*2]=[134, 176] as a new scaled range, which is still upper scaling case. Thus, we write 1_2 to the bitstream and scale the range by following the upper scaling rule, which results in [(134 − 128)*2, (176 − 128)*2] = [12, 96]. It accounts for the lower scaling case, resulting in writing 0_2 to the *BS*. By following the lower scaling rule, we obtain a new scaled range of [12*2, 96*2]=[24, 192], which does not correspond to any of the three cases, terminating the main loop (lines 1–16 in Figure 5.4). Since we have already encoded all the weight elements, we need to process the last part of the encoding (lines 17–22 in Figure 5.4). After we increment *RS* by 1, we write $(01)_2$ to the *BS* because the lower bound of the current range (*low*) is 24 which is less than *QTR* (64). Finally, we obtain the encoded bitstream of $(001101001)_2$.

Figure 5.9 demonstrates an example of the weight decoding. Please note that the *N*, *MAX*, *HALF*, and *QTR* values are equal to the encoding example. Before starting the first iteration, we append 7-bits of 0_2s at the end of *BS*. In this example, we will perform five iterations because *K*, the number of weight elements encoded in the *BS*, is 5. We first start with the 8-bit part $Z(0)$, $(00110100)_2$ (=52) in the first iteration. When we calculate the subranges for each weight element, $Z(0)$ is within the subrange of "0" ($[0+\lfloor255^{*}0.0\rfloor, 0+\lfloor255^{*}0.4\rfloor] =$ [0, 102]). Thus, we write element "0" to the weight data *W*[0]. Since the subrange [0, 102] corresponds to the lower scaling case, we scale the lower and upper bounds of the subrange by 2× (thus, a new scaled range will be [0, 204]) while increasing the *idx* by 1. Since the scaled range [0, 204] does not correspond to any of the three scaling cases, we move to the next iteration. In the second iteration, $Z(1)$ is equal to $(01101001)_2$ (=105), meaning that it corresponds to the subrange of the element "1" $(([0+\lfloor204^{*}0.4\rfloor, 0+\lfloor204^{*}0.8\rfloor] = [81, 163]))$ which will be written to the *W*[1]. A new subrange will be [81, 163] (subrange of $j = 1$), which corresponds to the middle scaling case. After scaling the range ([(81 − 64)*2, (163 − 64)*2] = [34, 198]) and updating $Z(1)$ $(105 − 64(QTR)=41((00101001)_2))$, the new scaled range does not correspond to any of the three cases. Thus, we perform the next iteration with $Z(2)$ $((01010010)_2 = 82)$. Similarly, after calculating the new subrange for each weight element, $Z(2)$ is within the subrange

i	Starting range	Sub-range			$Z(idx)$-gray-shaded part	Output w	Scaling case	Updated idx
		$j=0$	$j=1$	$j=2$				
0	[0, 255]	[0, 102]	—	—	(00110100 10000000)$_2$	{0}	Lower scaling	1
					52			
1	[0, 204]	[0, 81]	[81, 163]	—	(0 01101001 0000000)$_2$	{0,1}	Middle scaling	2
					105			
2	[34, 198]	[34, 99]	—	—	(00 01010010 000000)$_2$	{0,1,0}	Lower scaling	3
					82			
3	[68, 198]	[68, 120]	[120, 172]	—	(000 10100100 00000)$_2$	{0,1,0,1}	Middle scaling	4
					164			
4	[112, 216]	[112, 153]	[153, 195]	[195, 216]	(0000 11001000 0000)$_2$	{0,1,0,1,2}	—	—
					200			

Figure 5.9 An example for decoding by using the presented technique.

([34 + ⌊164*0.0⌋, 34 + ⌊164*0.4⌋]=[34, 99]) of the element "0," which will be written to the $W[2]$, and we need to scale the subrange with the lower scaling rule, resulting in the new scaled range [68, 198] (=[34*2, 99*2]). In the next iteration, we have a starting range of [68, 198], while $Z(3)$ is (10100100)$_2$ (=164), which exists within the subrange of the element "1" (164 is within the sub-range [68 + ⌊130*0.4⌋, 68 + ⌊130*0.8⌋]=[120, 172]). Thus, we write element "1" to the $W[3]$, and perform the middle scaling with the subrange [120, 172] while updating $Z(3)$ to 100 (=164 − 64(QTR)). After that, we have a new scaled range [112, 216] (=[(120 − 64)*2, (172 − 64)*2]), which does not correspond to the middle scaling case. Thus, we move to the next iteration to seek for a subrange of $Z(4)$, (11001000)$_2$ (=200). After calculating the subranges for each weight element, $Z(4)$ is within the subrange of "2" ([112 + ⌊104*0.8⌋, 112 + ⌊104*1.0⌋]=[195, 216]) which will be stored to the $W[4]$. Since we have already decoded five weight elements, we finish the decoding procedure with the decoded weight output $W = \{0, 1, 0, 1, 2\}$.

5.4.1 Decoding Hardware

Figure 5.10 shows a block diagram of the decoder hardware with a single DU. There are two buffers, bitstream buffer (for BS) and decoded weight buffer (for W), and one table (probability table for $PROB$). The bitstream buffer contains

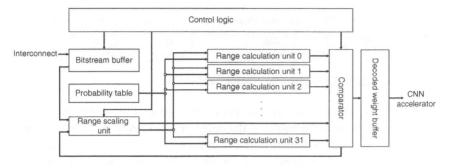

Figure 5.10 Decoding unit (DU) architecture.

the encoded weight bitstream which is delivered from the main memory (or storage). The probability table maintains $F[x]$ for each weight value ($F[0]$ and $F[32]$ are always 0 and 1, respectively, meaning that they do not need to be stored in the table). The decoded weight buffer will store the decoded weight elements. From the bitstream buffer, we send the $Z(idx)$ (where idx is the starting bit index of the N-bits) to the range scaling unit which performs the range scaling according to the three cases (upper, lower, and middle scaling). After that, the scaled ranges from the range scaling unit and probability values ($F[0] - F[32]$ in Figure 5.7) are sent to the range calculation unit, which performs calculations of a new sub-range for each weight value. In the presented design, we perform 32 subrange calculation (corresponds to the lines 4–6 in Figure 5.7) in parallel, improving the performance of the decoder. In the comparator, the $Z(idx)$ value and each subrange are also compared in parallel in order to figure out which weight value should be written to the output in the current iteration. Once the comparison is done, we store the corresponding element to the decoded weight buffer (lines 7–9 in Figure 5.7). This process is iteratively performed according to the orchestration of the control logic.

For proof-of-concept of the decoding hardware,[5] we have implemented the hardware in a FPGA board (Xilinx ZCU106). We have used Xilinx Vivado design suite to implement the decoder design. We have synthesized our design for 150 MHz with 16 DUs (the maximum number of DUs which the FPGA chip can accommodate), which results in 16× higher throughput than the 1-DU decoder implementation. To utilize 16 DUs, we divide the weight elements into 16 chunks as evenly as possible and encode each chunk into a separate bitstream. When decoding the bitstreams, we send each bitstream to each of the 16 DUs. Although the prototype

---

5 Hardware resources for the 16-DU decoder in FPGA are as follows: 141,568 LUTs; 49,379 flip-flops; 1152 DSP48E blocks; and 512 BRAM blocks. If we share the decoded weight buffer with the CNN accelerator, we could further reduce the resource usage though we design a separate decoded weight buffer in the implementation.

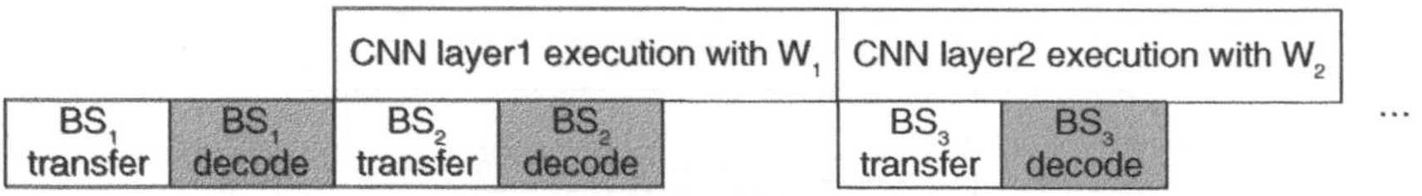

CNN layer1 execution with W_1				CNN layer2 execution with W_2		
BS_1 transfer	BS_1 decode	BS_2 transfer	BS_2 decode		BS_3 transfer	BS_3 decode

...

Figure 5.11 Latency hiding for the decoding hardware.

is implemented with 16 DUs, the number of DUs is one of the design parameters which can be flexibly determined by the designer considering the available hardware resources (we will demonstrate the latency vs. resource usage trade-off in Section 5.6.3). If we implement the decoding hardware with application-specific integrated circuits (ASICs), we could implement more number of DUs, resulting in a better decoding throughput. According to the implementation results, the single DU hardware takes 6.45 clock cycles per one weight element decoding, on average, though the total number of decoding cycles depends on the pattern and sequence of the weight elements in the bitstream.

When executing the CNN inference, the weight decoding must be performed prior to the convolution operations. Without hiding the decoding latency, the latency overhead would be nonnegligible, which is not desirable. To minimize the decoding latency, we can overlap the transfer and decoding latency for weights in the ith CNN layer with the $(i-1)$th CNN layer execution latency in the CNN accelerator (illustrated in Figure 5.11). In this case, the latency overhead will be only decoding latency of the weights for the first CNN layer (where the weight decoding latency cannot be overlapped) as long as the following two conditions are satisfied. First, the input and output feature maps are reused across the CNN layers in the CNN accelerator (hence, the input and output feature maps do not need to be transferred between the memory and the PLM of the accelerator). Second, data transfer and decoding latency of CNN layer i are fully hidden by the execution time of CNN layer $i-1$, where integer $i > 1$. To satisfy the second condition, more DUs in the decoding hardware can be desirable. This is because the decoding latency can be further reduced as we have more DUs in the decoder.

5.5 Evaluation Methodology

We show the evaluation results in terms of three metrics: compression ratio, energy consumption in the main memory, and latency overhead. For benchmarks, we use five CNN models: Network-in-Network (NiN) [117], SqueezeNet [62], GoogleNet [35], AlexNet [30], and CaffeNet [118]. We use 32 for N in the evaluations.

We have used the trained FP32 weights provided by Caffe framework [118]. For 5-bit quantization, we have employed an incremental network quantization (INQ) [95] method to generate 5-bit power-of-two (i.e., utilizing binary logarithm or logarithm to the base 2) quantized weights from the 32-bit full-precision weights. The main reason we choose INQ for the baseline is that it shows comparable or even better accuracy with 5-bit quantized weights as compared to 32-bit full-precision weights when running CNN inferences. Though we use a specific method (INQ) for 5-bit power-of-two quantization, the presented technique can be deployed with any 5-bit quantization method. For AlexNet and CaffeNet, we have additionally employed weight pruning (we used [119] and [120] for weight pruning of AlexNet and CaffeNet, respectively) to figure out how weight pruning affects the compression ratio. Although the top-1/top-5 accuracies show a little fluctuation by applying the weight pruning,[6] the presented compression technique itself does not adversely affect the inference accuracy as the technique is based on lossless compression. In other words, accuracy losses are not attributed to the compression technique, but attributed to the quantization and/or weight pruning. For AlexNet and CaffeNet, we demonstrate the results for two separate cases: (i) only 5-bit quantization (denoted as Q) and (ii) pruning and 5-bit quantization (denoted as P + Q).

Firstly, we present compression ratio (Section 5.6.1), memory energy consumption (Section 5.6.1), and latency overheads for CNN inference (Section 5.6.2). We only compare the compression ratio and memory energy consumption for CNN convolutional (CONV) layers while excluding the fully connected (FC) layers. For latency overheads, we assume that we only compress CONV layers' weights, while the weights of the other layers such as FC layers are not compressed. In this case, we do not have the latency overheads of the layers other than the CONV layers because it does not need to be decompressed. Although early CNN models have a large number of weights in FC layers (e.g., AlexNet [30]), recent CNN models have FC layers only in the last layer of the CNN model (e.g., ResNet [32]), meaning that the CNN layer architecture is mostly composed of CONV layers. For deployment of the presented technique to highly resource-constrained systems, we also demonstrate a trade-off between the CNN inference latency and hardware resource usage (Section 5.6.3). In addition, we further show a system-level energy consumption for a CNN inference in highly resource-constrained systems (Section 5.6.4).

5.6 Evaluation Results

5.6.1 Compression Ratio and Memory Energy Consumption

The *compression ratio* (CR) is defined as the ratio of uncompressed data size S_u to the compressed data size S_c, that is, $CR = S_u/S_c$. Table 5.1 summarizes the compression ratio across five CNN models. In Table 5.1, 32-bit, 16-bit, 8-bit, and 5-bit

---

6 Weight pruning results in top-1/top-5=−0.0%/+0.4% and top-1/top-5=−1.5%/−1.4% for AlexNet and CaffeNet, respectively. The accuracy results are obtained by using Caffe framework [118] with ImageNet dataset [121].

Table 5.1 Compression ratio (for only CONV layers) comparison across five CNN models.

CNN models	32-bit	16-bit	8-bit	5-bit	HC-5bit	AC-5bit	IE-5bit
NiN (Q)					9.335	**9.744**	9.747
SqueezeNet (Q)					8.817	**9.118**	9.157
GoogleNet (Q)					8.801	**9.434**	9.454
AlexNet (Q)					9.652	**9.829**	9.835
CaffeNet (Q)	1.000	2.000	4.000	6.400	9.524	**9.672**	9.678
Average (Q)					9.226	**9.560**	9.574
AlexNet (P + Q)					26.675	**57.498**	57.536
CaffeNet (P + Q)					28.806	**112.154**	112.333
Average (P + Q)					27.744	**84.826**	84.934

Bold values denote the values corresponding to our proposed/presented arithmetic coding technique.

correspond to the cases of uncompressed 32-bit FP, 16-bit quantized, 8-bit quantized, and 5-bit quantized weights, respectively. HC-5bit and AC-5bit (the presented technique) denote the cases of 5-bit quantized weight compressed with Huffman coding and arithmetic coding, respectively. IE-5bit denotes the theoretical bound of compression ratio (information entropy) when losslessly compressing the 5-bit quantized weight data.

In the case of only quantization (Q), the AC-5bit reduces the weight data size by 9.6× as compared to the uncompressed 32-bit weight data. In addition, the presented technique reduces the weight data size by 29.8–34.9% as compared to the uncompressed 5-bit quantized weight data size. It means the presented technique can significantly reduce the required storage and memory. In addition, the arithmetic coding-based compression technique shows better compression ratio as compared to the Huffman coding-based compression technique. On average, when compressing the 5-bit quantized weight data, the presented technique results in 3.7% (up to 7.2%) better compression ratio compared to the Huffman coding-based technique (HC-5bit). Moreover, the arithmetic coding-based compression technique shows near-optimal compression ratios. As compared to IE-5bit, the AC-5bit shows only 0.1% less compression ratio, on average.

In the case of pruning and quantization (P + Q), the AC-5-bit obtains 57.5× and 112.2× higher compression ratio over 32-bit FP for AlexNet and CaffeNet, respectively. The pruning significantly increases the number of zero-valued elements in the weights, which also significantly contributes to the compression ratio. On the other hand, HC-5-bit obtains 26.7× and 28.8× (as compared to the 32-bit FP) better compression ratios for AlexNet and CaffeNet, respectively. However, the AC-5bit results in 2.2× and 3.9× better compression ratios for AlexNet and CaffeNet, respectively, as compared to HC-5bit. As shown in the results (Table 5.1), the presented technique shows more promising results when applying the weight pruning which is a widely used technique for CNN inferences.

We also compare the presented technique with other state-of-the-art techniques in terms of the compression ratio when using AlexNet [30]. Though the comparison in Table 5.1 is based on the compression of the weight in the CONV layers, for a fair comparison, we have compared the presented technique to other techniques based on the compression of the weights in the entire layers including the FC layers. Before applying the presented compression technique, the entire CONV and FC layers are pruned by [119] and quantized to 5-bit format by [95]. As shown in Table 5.2, the presented technique shows better compression ratio as compared to the techniques or methods presented in [46], [97], and [104]. As compared to the method presented in [106]; however, the presented technique shows a little lower compression ratio by 24.7%. In [106], the bzip2 compression is additionally applied to pruned and quantized weights. In this case, there would be a nonnegligible latency overhead for decompressing the compressed weights during the runtime CNN inference. Please note that without bzip2 compression in [106], the compression ratio of the presented technique is better than that of [106] by 14.2%. Since this chapter has also introduced hardware decoder and pipelining which minimizes latency overhead of runtime weight decompression, the presented technique would be more practical and suitable for real-world deployment.

Higher weight compression ratio translates into less memory energy consumption when transferring the weight data to the PLM of the CNN accelerator or the NPU. Table 5.3 presents memory data transfer energy comparison results when the device uses LPDDR4 (5 pJ per bit [122] and 0.43 W static power [123]) dynamic

Table 5.2 AlexNet (full layers including CONV and FC layers) compression ratio comparison of the presented technique with the state-of-the-art methods.

Method	Compression ratio
[46]	34.8
[97]	40.7
[104]	21.9
[106] (w/o bzip2)	57.5 (37.9)
Presented technique (AC-5 bit)	**43.3**

Table 5.3 Memory energy consumption (μJ) when transferring the weight data to the CNN accelerator or NPU on-chip memory.

CNN model	32-bit	16-bit	8-bit	5-bit	HC-5bit	AC-5bit	IE-5bit
NiN (Q)	17532.72	8766.36	4383.18	2924.72	1907.95	**1814.19**	1798.76
SqueezeNet (Q)	2874.67	1437.34	718.67	503.87	353.31	**341.66**	313.94
GoogleNet (Q)	14089.60	7044.80	3522.40	2398.83	1626.18	**1536.88**	1490.30
AlexNet (Q)	5388.55	2694.27	1347.14	902.44	567.10	**556.90**	547.88
CaffeNet (Q)					574.74	**565.21**	556.77
AlexNet (P + Q)					201.99	**93.71**	93.65
CaffeNet (P + Q)					187.06	**48.05**	47.97

random access memory. We have estimated the dynamic energy by multiplying the accessed data size (in bits) by the per-bit access energy and static energy by multiplying the static power by the memory transfer time. The total estimated energy consumption is a summation of the dynamic and static energy. When only employing the 5-bit quantization (Q), the AC-5bit reduces the memory data transfer energy by 89.2% as compared to the case of using uncompressed 32-bit FP weight data. The AC-5bit also leads to 36.4% and 3.4% less memory energy consumption for weight transfer as compared to the cases of uncompressed 5-bit weight and HC-5bit, respectively. When employing both 5-bit quantization and pruning (P + Q), the AC-5bit results in 98.3% and 99.1% less memory energy consumption for AlexNet and CaffeNet, respectively, as compared to the case of 32-bit FP weights. Even compared to HC-5bit, the AC-5bit reduces memory energy consumption by 53.6% and 74.3% for AlexNet and CaffeNet, respectively. Considering that the energy consumption in memory-related parts accounts for a large portion in resource-constrained edge systems [109], the presented technique will enable more energy-efficient resource-constrained edge devices.

5.6.2 Latency Overhead

The presented technique incurs decoding latency before the weight data are loaded to the accelerator on-chip memory. As explained in Section 5.4.1, the decoding latency can be hidden by overlapping bitstream decoding in the decoding hardware with the CNN layer execution in the accelerator or the NPU. Even with the latency hiding, the weight decoding latency for the first layer in the CNN model cannot be hidden, thus incurring the latency overhead. Table 5.4 summarizes the latency overhead results when using the presented decoding hardware combined with various state-of-the-art CNN accelerators [112, 113, 114] ("Combined CNN

Table 5.4 Inference latency (in milliseconds) and overhead comparison across the baseline (w/o the presented technique) and the presented technique (16-DU decoder) w/ latency hiding (LH) and w/o LH when employing various state-of-the-art CNN accelerators.

Combined CNN accelerator	[112]	[113]	[114]	
CNN model	AlexNet	AlexNet	AlexNet	GoogleNet
Platform	Stratix-V GXA7	ZC 706	Xilinx ZU9 MPSoC	
Clock (MHz)	155	156.25	100	
Precision (bits)	5-bits	5-bits	8-bits	
Peak throughput (GOP/s)	206.87	155.10	14.97	15.63
Decode + Transfer latency	3.79	6.70	16.06	42.62
Decode + Transfer latency (pruned)	3.45	3.42	10.94	N/A
Baseline inference latency	8.83	52.80	90.01	202.02
Inference latency of the presented technique w/ LH (overhead)	**9.31 (5.48%)**	**52.886 (0.16%)**	**91.16 (1.27%)**	**204.85 (1.40%)**
Inference latency of the presented technique w/ LH (overhead) w/ pruned weights	**8.91 (0.91%)**	**52.884 (0.16%)**	**90.15 (0.16%)**	N/A
Inference latency of the presented technique w/o LH (overhead)	12.62 (42.94%)	59.50 (13.26%)	106.07 (17.84%)	244.64 (21.10%)
Inference latency of the presented technique w/o LH (overhead) w/ pruned weights	12.28 (39.07%)	56.24 (6.48%)	100.95 (12.15%)	N/A

When estimating the decoding latency, we assume that the presented decoder operates at the same clock frequency as the CNN accelerator.
Source: Adapted from [112–114].

Accelerator" in Table 5.4). We present the latency overhead results when the introduced decoding hardware (Figure 5.10) is combined with the FPGA-based CNN accelerators because the decoding hardware prototype is implemented and verified in an FPGA.

There is also a CNN accelerator [114] with 8-bit precision in Table 5.4, while the main target for weight compression is 5-bit quantized weights. Though we have suggested the presented technique for 5-bit weights, the presented arithmetic coding-based encoding and decoding technique can also be used along with 8-bit precision-based CNN accelerators. In this case, we only compress 5-bits within each 8-bit weight element by using the arithmetic coding, while the remaining bits (i.e., 3-bits) of the weights remain uncompressed (the remaining 3-bits can be transferred directly from the memory to the CNN accelerator without passing through the hardware decoder). In this case, we will have a lower compression ratio, and a higher weight decoding and transfer latency as compared to the case of 5-bit weight compression due to the uncompressed part in each weight element. Nonetheless, to present the versatility of the presented technique, we also present the latency overhead results when adopting the presented technique with the 8-bit precision accelerator [114] in Table 5.4.

When using the presented decoding hardware and various CNN accelerators without the latency hiding, the latency overhead is 13.26–42.94%. On the other hand, with the latency hiding,[7] the presented technique without pruning shows 0.16–5.48% latency overheads when performing the CNN inferences, implying that the latency overhead from the decoding hardware is small. In the case of the presented technique with pruning and latency hiding, the latency overheads are almost negligible (0.16–0.91%). When focusing on the case with 8-bit precision accelerator [114] in Table 5.4, the latency overhead is only up to 1.40%, implying that the presented technique can also be deployed with 8-bit precision accelerator with a negligible latency overhead.

The huge latency overhead reduction when applying the pruning is attributed to the reduced weight data size with arithmetic coding (due to the increase in the number of zero-valued weight elements), resulting in quicker decoding and shorter weight transfer latency. Considering that the main focus of the presented technique is resource-constrained edge devices, this small latency overhead is sufficiently acceptable as the benefits from the reduced memory and storage requirement and reduced memory energy consumption are much greater than the latency overhead.

---

7 The latency hiding does not affect the compression ratio, but reduces latency overhead incurred by the runtime decoding.

5.6.3 Latency vs. Resource Usage Trade-Off

For systems or devices under tight resource constraints, we also present the latency vs. resource usage trade-off when employing 2-DU, 4-DU, 8-DU, and 16-DU decoders.[8] The 2-DU, 4-DU, and 8-DU designs require much less hardware resources than the 16-DU design. Thus, the 2-DU, 4-DU, and 8-DU designs can be suitable for small or tiny embedded edge devices. However, the smaller number of DUs will lead to a higher decoding latency overhead, which also results in increased CNN inference latency. As shown in Figure 5.12, in the case of the 4-DU and 8-DU decoders, performance overheads without pruning can be up to 34.2% and 8.73%, respectively, whereas the performance overheads with pruning can be up to 31.4% and 2.77%, respectively, even with the latency hiding. With the 2-DU decoder, which can be deployed for the systems with extremely stringent resource constraints, the latency overhead can be up to 126.1% without pruning and 108.0% with pruning. The reason why the decoding time overhead seems to be large when used with the CNN accelerator in [112] is that the baseline CNN inference latency in [112] is very small, which makes the latency overhead from the decoder relatively large. For the decoding overhead with the CNN accelerator in [114], even though the baseline inference latency of [114] is higher than that

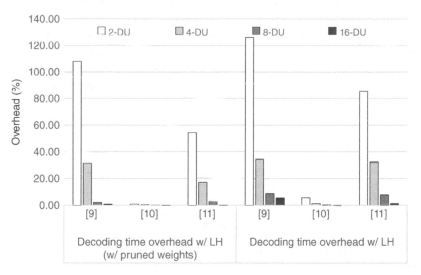

Figure 5.12 A comparison of decoding time overheads across the number of DUs in the decoder (2-DU, 4-DU, 8-DU, and 16-DU) when running AlexNet. Please note that LH stands for latency hiding

---

8 We have additionally implemented and verified 8-DU decoder design in ZCU106. We have also implemented and verified 2-DU and 4-DU decoder designs in Ultra96 platform, which is used in highly resource-constrained edge devices and/or embedded systems.

of [113], the latency overhead is larger as compared to the case of [113]. This is because the CNN accelerator in [114] uses the 8-bit precision accelerator, which implies that the compression ratio will be worse in [114] as compared to 5-bit precision accelerators as the presented arithmetic coding technique is optimized for 5-bit weight encoding (i.e., 5-bits within 8-bits element are compressed while the remaining 3-bits remain uncompressed). This results in relatively high transfer latency when using the CNN accelerator in [114] with the decoder. In the cases of 8-DU and 16-DU with the CNN accelerator in [114], the transfer latency and decoding latency can be mostly hidden by the CNN layer processing time. However, in the cases of 2-DU and 4-DU with the CNN accelerator in [114], the transfer latency and decoding latency cannot be hidden by the CNN layer processing time, leading to the large latency overhead. For [112], though relative decoding time overhead can be large, the absolute inference latency is negligibly affected (+9.54 ms and +2.77 ms with 2-DU and 4-DU decoders, respectively) as shown in Table 5.5. For [114], the decoding time overheads with 2-DU and 4-DU decoders can be decreased if we use 5-bit precision CNN accelerators.

In typical edge devices, the baseline CNN inference latency will not be very small. This is because the CNN accelerator performance will be limited due to the tight hardware resource constraints. In addition, satisfying the deadline of the response time (i.e., latency) is more important in edge or embedded systems, which imply that the increased latency overhead is acceptable as long as it does not violate the response time deadline. Thus, the edge system designers can choose the appropriate number of DUs by considering the performance requirements and resource constraints of the system under design.

Table 5.5 Inference latencies (in ms) across the state-of-the-art CNN accelerators without the presented technique (baseline) and with the presented technique (2-DU, 4-DU, 8-DU, and 16-DU).

| | Combined CNN accelerator | | |
	[112]	[113]	[114]
Baseline	8.83	52.80	90.01
2-DU	18.37	53.23	138.96
4-DU	11.60	53.02	105.46
8-DU	9.02	52.91	92.50
16-DU	8.91	52.88	90.15

5.6.4 System-Level Energy Estimation

We compare the system-level energy when using the presented arithmetic coding-based compression for the 5-bit quantized and pruned weights with 4-DU decoder and baseline (i.e., without the presented compression and decoder while only 5-bit quantization is employed since the combined CNN accelerators supports 5-bit precision arithmetic operations). The system-level energy includes the CNN accelerator (with the 4-DU decoder in the case with the presented technique) energy, DRAM-based main memory energy, and NVMe (Non-Volatile Memory Express) flash-based storage energy. Since the nonvolatile flash storage will be accessed to load the weights into the main memory before CNN inferences, we have included the flash-based storage energy to the system-level energy estimation. Please note that we use the flash energy parameter reported in [124] (1 J/28 MB = 4.26 nJ per bit). Since CNN accelerator power is reported in [112] and [113], while it is not reported in [114], we only include the results with [112] and [113] for the system-level energy estimation. The reason why we choose the 4-DU decoder among the various configurations is that the 4-DU decoder can be accommodated in an edge/embedded platform (such as Ultra96) and shows a good tradeoff between the inference latency and resource usage.

As shown in Table 5.6, for the combined accelerators with the presented technique, power consumption and inference latency are increased, which results in an increased energy consumption in the FPGA by 40.2% and 5.7% with the

Table 5.6 System-level energy comparison between the baseline (Q) and the presented technique (P + Q) with 4-DU decoder.

Combined CNN accelerator		[112]	[113]
FPGA platform		Stratix-GXA7	ZC706
Baseline (Q)	Latency (ms)	8.83	52.80
	FPGA power (W)	8.69	12.02
	FPGA energy (mJ)	76.73	634.66
	Total energy (mJ)	130.27	707.10
Our technique (P + Q) with 4-DU decoder	Latency (ms)	11.60	53.23
	FPGA power (W)	9.28	12.61
	FPGA energy (mJ)	107.59	670.96
	Total energy (mJ)	118.11	699.39

CNN accelerators in [112] and [113], respectively. However, when considering the system-level energy consumption which includes the DRAM memory and flash-based storage energy consumption, the presented technique with 4-DU configuration results in the system-level energy reduction by 9.3% and 1.1% with the CNN accelerators in [112] and [113], respectively. This is attributed to the reduced weight data size from the presented arithmetic coding-based weight compression.

5.7 Chapter Summary

In resource-constrained edge devices, one of the most serious challenges for deploying on-device CNN inferences is huge weight data size which can hardly be fully stored in an edge device. This chapter introduced an arithmetic coding-based 5-bit quantized weight compression technique with range scaling for lossless 5-bit weight compression. The chapter also presented a decoding hardware for fast, yet efficient runtime weight decoding (decompression). Evaluation results revealed that employing the presented weight compression technique to 5-bit quantized weights (not pruned) achieved 9.6× better compression ratio as compared to the uncompressed 32-bit FP weights. When employing the presented technique to the pruned 5-bit quantized weights, the technique resulted in 57.5×–112.2× better compression ratio as compared to the uncompressed 32-bit FP weights. Due to the reduced weight data size, the technique also led to memory data transfer energy reduction by 89.2% (by up to 99.1% for pruned weights), on average, as compared to the uncompressed 32-bit FP weight data. When combining the presented decoding hardware with various state-of-the-art CNN accelerators, the latency overheads of the presented technique with 16-DU decoder along with the latency hiding were only 0.16–5.48% and 0.16–0.91% for nonpruned and pruned weights, respectively. In addition, the presented technique with 4-DU decoder hardware reduced system-level energy consumption by 1.1–9.3% as compared to the case without the presented technique.

Part III

Dense CNN Accelerators

6

Contemporary Dense CNN Accelerators

This chapter provides background on dense convolutional neural network (CNN) accelerators, including the exact definition of the dense CNN accelerators. The chapter then discusses popular architectures of the contemporary dense CNN accelerator. Toward the end, the chapter highlights recent advancements in dense CNN accelerators.

6.1 Background on Dense CNN Accelerators

The CNN accelerators generally perform matrix multiplication (MM) with hardware logic. Since the CNN weights and feature maps contain lots of zeros, many researches have explored the efficient representation of the sparse matrix. However, in the early stages of the CNN hardware development, the dense format representation has been widely used as it is more intuitive and efficient for storing the dense (i.e., low sparsity) matrix.

As shown in Figure 6.1, *we define a dense CNN accelerator as a CNN accelerator that accepts the weights or activation maps (feature maps) in dense format matrices.* Please note that a dense format can also contain a sparse matrix even if the sparsity of the matrix is sufficiently high. Thus, it does not necessarily mean that the dense format always contains dense matrices for representing weights or activation maps. We cover the CNN accelerators that accept sparse format matrices in Part IV of this book (Chapters 9–12).

6.2 Representation of the CNN Weights and Feature Maps in Dense Format

Dense CNN accelerators generally perform matrix multiplications. Thus, it is natural to represent CNN weights (filters) and input feature maps (IFMs) in

Accelerators for Convolutional Neural Networks, First Edition.
Arslan Munir, Joonho Kong, and Mahmood Azhar Qureshi.

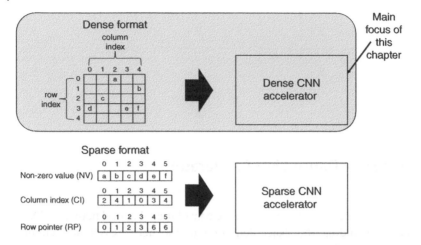

Figure 6.1 The comparison between the dense and sparse CNN accelerators. We have shown the compressed sparse row (CSR) format as an example of the sparse format although other sparse formats, such as bitmap-based compression, can also be used.

a matrix format for dense CNN accelerators. Since the convolution operations are performed like a sliding window (i.e., CNN filters slide onto the IFMs), the IFMs should be unrolled for dense format matrix conversion. The unrolled dense matrix of the IFMs is often referred to as Toeplitz matrix.

Figure 6.2 shows how the IFMs and filters are transformed into a matrix–vector multiplication. For convolution operations, the overlapped area in the IFMs (gray-shaded part in the IFM in Figure 6.2) is flattened into a row vector format with the dimension of 1×4. As we need to perform convolution with four overlapped areas in the example in Figure 6.2, we generate four rows, generating a 4×4 matrix. Similarly, the filter is flattened into a column vector with the dimension of 4×1. Finally, the generated 4×4 matrix and 4×1 vector are multiplied, generating the 4×1 vector as a result.

Most of the contemporary CNN models are employing multiple input and output channels for better feature extraction. Figure 6.3 depicts another example of converting the CNN IFMs and filters into dense matrix–matrix multiplication when performing a 3×3 convolution with two input channels and two output channels. Assuming the filter weights slide onto the IFMs with a row major order, the IFM elements for convolution are unrolled in a form of row vectors to generate one output feature map (OFM) element. Since we generate a 3×3 OFM for a single output channel, we have 9 rows generating the 9×18 matrix. A weight filter also forms a column vector with 18 elements (=9 elements $\times$ 2 input

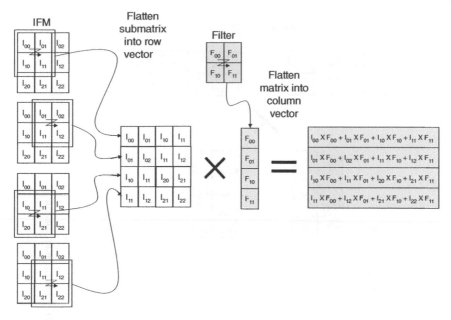

Figure 6.2 The conversion of convolution operations into matrix–vector multiplication.

channels). As we have two sets of filters to generate the two output channels, we append the two column vectors to make a matrix format with the dimension of 18×2. As a result of the convolution of the example presented in Figure 6.3, we obtain the matrix of OFMs with the dimension of 9×2.

6.3 Popular Architectures for Dense CNN Accelerators

The widely used dense CNN accelerators are based on systolic arrays as shown in Figure 6.4a. The systolic arrays employ a dataflow-driven architecture as the data are moved between the processing elements (PEs) and transferred via the fixed routes while minimizing the role of the control logic (i.e., minimizing the impact of the control flow). The systolic arrays are widely used for matrix multiplication (MM) engine.

In systolic arrays, there are multiple PEs which are organized in a grid. In a single PE, multiply-and-accumulate (MAC) is a key operation. Thus, a PE has a multiplier and an adder which perform the multiplication and accumulation, respectively. There are also registers in systolic arrays to temporarily store the

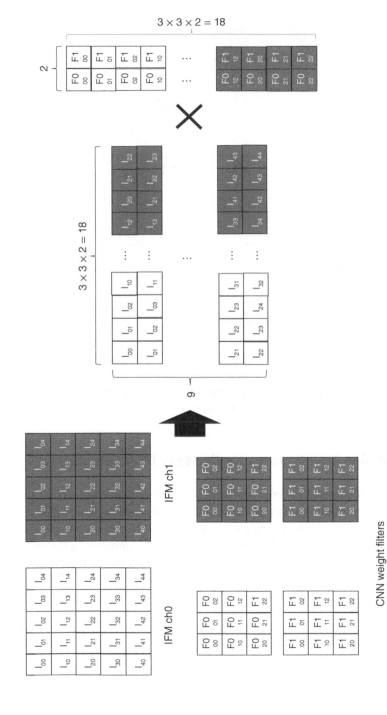

Figure 6.3 The conversion of multichannel convolution operations into matrix–matrix multiplication.

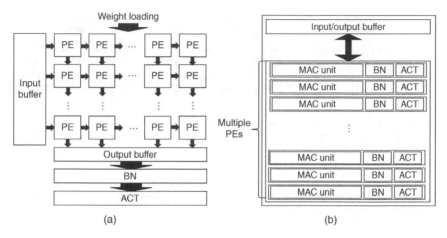

Figure 6.4 Hardware architecture of systolic array- and MAC array-based CNN accelerator. BN and ACT stand for batch normalization and activation, respectively. (a) Systolic array-based CNN accelerator architecture (weight stationary). (b) An array of MAC PE-based CNN accelerator architecture.

weights, inputs, and partial sums (outputs). In systolic arrays, there are two routing paths between the PEs: one in the X-axis direction and the other in the Y-axis direction. These paths can be differently used depending on different dataflows.

In typical systolic arrays, there are three representative dataflows [54]: weight stationary, output stationary, and input stationary. In case of the *weight stationary dataflow*, the weights are pinned into the PEs, and the inputs are streamed across the PEs (in the direction of X-axis). The accumulated outputs are delivered through the PEs in the direction of Y-axis. In the case of *output stationary dataflow*, the outputs are pinned into the PEs while the inputs and the weights are streamed in the direction of X-axis and Y-axis, respectively. In the case of *input stationary dataflow*, the inputs are pinned to the PEs while the weights are streamed in the direction of X-axis, and the outputs are accumulated in the direction of Y-axis. Figure 6.5 summarizes the three dataflows used in systolic arrays.

Instead of systolic arrays where PEs are organized in a grid, one can also utilize a MAC array-based structure for CNN accelerators. As shown in Figure 6.4b, this architecture is similar to the single instruction multiple data (SIMD) architecture where a single instruction triggers multiple PEs in the array. The MAC array-based structure exploits the parallelism of the MACs within the matrix multiplications. For example, when performing the inner products, the MAC operations can be executed in parallel with different rows and columns of the input matrices. In addition, as in [125] and also described in Chapter 15, the multiple MAC PEs in the array can be used in parallel to generate multiple OFMs in parallel.

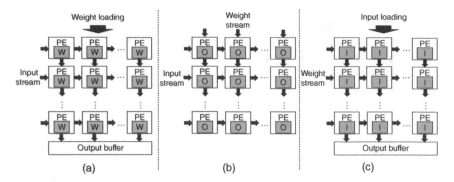

Figure 6.5 Three widely used systolic array dataflows in CNN accelerators. (a) Weight stationary, (b) output stationary, and (c) input stationary.

6.4 Recent Advancements in Dense CNN Accelerators

Many dense architectures have been introduced in the past for the acceleration of CNN inference. The proposed accelerators either optimize the compute [39, 126–130] or the memory bandwidth [131, 132]. Accelerators proposed in [133, 134] use Booth encoding to avoid the use of zeros and reduce the total computations. They, however, still transfer zeros to and from memory which incurs static random access memory (SRAM) area and energy overhead. Block circulant matrices for weights were introduced in CirCNN [135]. CirCNN, however, requires complex fast Fourier transform (FFT) operations in its PE design which significantly increases the area overhead.

In-memory accelerators have also been presented in literature [136, 137] that use analog logic design to perform matrix multiplications within memory. Analog circuits, however, are impacted by noise and variations during the manufacturing process which can significantly impact the CNN model accuracy during inference.

Chen et al. have proposed Eyeriss [45], a nonsystolic array, reconfigurable spatial architecture along with a new dataflow scheme called *row stationary* to maximize the data reuse. This design, however, incurs high PE costs owing to local storage and control in PE. It also has low hardware utilization which results in low throughput per PE. Liu et al. [138] have proposed an field-programmable gate array (FPGA)-based CNN accelerator with an integrated depthwise separable mode of operation. This accelerator, however, has low throughput because of the usage of a 32-bit floating point format. Bai et al. [139] have proposed an FPGA-based CNN accelerator having a dedicated matrix multiplication engine (MME) on Arria 10 SoC. It achieves a frame rate of 266 fps; however, its MME engine has a huge digital signal processing (DSP) cost of 1200+ DSP blocks. Miyashita et al. [37] have introduced the concept of logarithmic data representation for neural network accelerator designs. It also gives accuracy comparison between linear and log quantization. Vogel et al. [38] have proposed an accelerator design using an arbitrary log base. It, however, does not utilize the low hardware overhead of the log-based PE and instead rely on linear PE arrangements. Huan et al. [140] propose a reconfigurable design for various convolution kernels. It uses a propagated input data-flow scheme but incurs high latency and low hardware utilization. Jo et al. [141] have proposed a rescheduled dataflow for convolution to optimize the energy efficiency. Chang and Chang [142] have proposed VWA, a vectorwise accelerator architecture, with the goal of maximizing hardware utilization. It supports various kernel sizes from 1×1 to 5×5. Although some of the recent designs achieve high hardware utilization, they are not able to increase the peak throughput per PE count beyond unity owing to the use of single-core, linear PEs with high area cost.

One of the most well-known dense CNN accelerators from industries is Google tensor processing unit (TPU). The TPUs have been deployed in Google data centers since 2015 [78]. According to [127], TPUv1 is based on 256×256 PE-based systolic array with 8 bit integer precision support. However, for the fast deployment of TPUv1, architectural support for sparse matrix multiplication has not been included, meaning that the TPUv1 only accepts dense format inputs. The TPU has been currently updated to TPUv4i, which shows 1.5× better peak tera floating-point operations per second (TFLOPS) per chip with bf16 (brain floating point) precision support.

6.5 Chapter Summary

This chapter defined dense CNN accelerators and provided background of dense CNN accelerators. The chapter discussed the representation of CNN weights and feature maps in dense format that is required for dense CNN accelerators. The chapter elaborated systolic array- and MAC array-based architectures for dense CNN accelerators. Finally, the chapter highlighted recent advancements in dense CNN accelerators. In the following chapters, this book presents modern dense CNN accelerators that overcome the limitations of contemporary dense CNN accelerators. In Chapter 7, iMAC CNN accelerator is introduced, which is based on the MAC array architecture and is suitable for resource-constrained systems [188]. In Chapter 8, NeuroMAX accelerator is introduced, which supports multithreaded execution and log-based MAC operation [96].

7

iMAC: Image-to-Column and General Matrix Multiplication-Based Dense CNN Accelerator

In resource-constrained systems, cost-efficiency (i.e., performance per unit cost) is one of the key metrics. For cost-efficient design, the approach introduced in this chapter performs finer-grained offloading of the operations required for convolution layers instead of offloading the entire convolution layer operations. We choose im2col (image-to-column) and MAC (general matrix-multiply [GEMM] and accumulation), which we refer to as iMAC (im2col + MAC), for offloading to the hardware (HW) accelerator. Though only offloading GEMM could be a cost-efficient approach, we have determined that im2col significantly increases the amount of data transfer (e.g., 9× in the case of 3 × 3 convolution), and thus necessitates in situ execution of im2col and MAC within the accelerator. This chapter presents implementation results of a prototype of the introduced design in ZED platform (which equips ZYNQ7020) with full-stack software (SW) including operating system (petaLinux).

7.1 Background and Motivation

Inference tasks of convolutional neural networks (CNNs) are often required to be executed on-device (e.g., IoT edge) because of limited communication bandwidth to cloud and security/privacy concerns. However, since IoT devices have a tight resource budget, it is very hard to meet the response time requirement of the CNNs. A major challenge of CNN inferences in resource-constrained IoT devices is to find an optimal point of trade-off between resource cost and response time. A tight budget for hardware resources makes it hard to offload the computational tasks such as convolution operations. In such systems, CNN inferences are typically performed by CPUs. However, CPUs are known to be inefficient for CNN execution because of their meagre performance on data-parallel workloads such as matrix multiplications. Even with the single instruction multiple data (SIMD)

Accelerators for Convolutional Neural Networks, First Edition.
Arslan Munir, Joonho Kong, and Mahmood Azhar Qureshi.
© 2024 The Institute of Electrical and Electronics Engineers, Inc. Published 2024 by John Wiley & Sons, Inc.

instructions, general CPU provides only a few SIMD execution lanes that limit the exploitation of parallelism in matrix or vector operations. In addition, CPUs rely on caches for data transfer between the CPU and main memory, which can be inefficient when running CNNs with large number of weights (i.e., weight size > cache capacity) because of cache misses. These cache misses can result in slower response time and relatively high energy consumption.

To improve response time and energy efficiency, one can employ the GEMM (GEneral Matrix Multiplication) hardware accelerator such as systolic arrays to offload convolution operations of CNNs. In fact, GEMM accelerators can be used not only for CNNs but also for many other embedded/IoT applications, making this design decision very attractive for resource-constrained IoT and embedded systems. As shown in Figure 7.1, when running CNNs with a GEMM accelerator, the GEMM can be executed in a dedicated GEMM accelerator while the other CNN tasks can be executed in the CPU. However, before performing GEMM, we need to unroll the input feature maps (IFMs) to fit the data into matrix or vectors that can be applied to the GEMM hardware. This is often called as "im2col" which is already employed in many CNN frameworks such as [143]. However, decoupled im2col and GEMM execution causes nonnegligible data storage and transfer overhead. The main reason for this overhead is that im2col actually explodes the amount of storage requirements and the amount of data transfer depending on the weight kernel size (e.g., 3×3 or 5×5). For example, to execute 3×3 convolution operations with GEMM on the accelerator, we need to transform the IFM to multiple vectors that have redundant IFM elements resulting in 9× more data storage and transfer requirements for IFMs. To utilize a GEMM accelerator, we need to offload the unrolled vectors, which has 9× larger size as compared to the original data size, which is not desirable for meeting response time and energy constraints due to high data transfer overheads.

The other problem using the hardware accelerators for CNNs is that the CPU remains idle during the direct memory access (DMA) transfer and accelerator execution. If we could find the parallelism among the convolution layer operations, we would efficiently utilize the hardware resources in the resource-constrained systems. To exploit the parallelism, the approach that uses both accelerators and CPUs such as [109] would be beneficial. The presented work also exploits the parallelism in convolution layer operations to utilize both the accelerator and the CPU simultaneously. The exploitation of parallelism and

Figure 7.1 A general flow of the convolution layer execution.

HW/SW co-design eventually leads to better response time and energy efficiency of CNN inference in the presented design.

7.2 Architecture

The iMAC hardware accelerator functions a combined operation of im2col and MAC (we refer to it as im2col+MAC or iMAC). Figure 7.2 shows the conventional software-based im2col with 5×5 input feature map, 3×3 weights, one zero-padding, and stride as one. Since the GEMM or MAC operations can be executed after the SW-based im2col is entirely finished, it just unrolls the IFM into multiple vectors for matrix multiplication and accumulation in a rowwise fashion as shown in Figure 7.2. However, as we discussed in Section 7.1, the im2col actually generates 9× more data (25*9 elements) in the case of 3×3 convolutions, which causes inefficiency in terms of data storage and transfer.

Since im2col, which must be performed before GEMM, replicates IFM data for GEMM execution, only offloading the GEMM to the accelerator increases the required data storage and transfer, which is not desirable for cognitive IoT systems. Hence, we combine the im2col, GEMM, and accumulation operation within a unified hardware accelerator referred to as "iMAC." Figure 7.3 shows

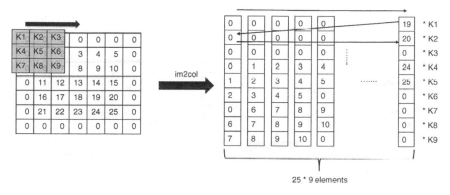

Figure 7.2 Conventional im2col execution in software.

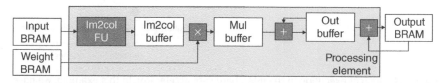

Figure 7.3 Hardware architecture of the iMAC (im2col + MAC) accelerator with one processing element (PE). We can also use multiple PEs to increase throughput.

an overall architecture of the iMAC accelerator. From the input block random access memory (BRAM), IFM data are delivered to the im2col functional units (FUs) that perform im2col operations for a certain area of the IFM. Data that are unrolled from the im2col FU is delivered to Im2colBuffer, which is multiplied by the weights from the weight BRAM. Since we immediately calculate the MAC operation with data from im2col FU, we do not need to maintain replicated data in the memory, implying that we can reduce the amount of the data transfer and required size of the data storage compared to the case of only offloading the GEMM. The multiplied results are temporarily stored in multiplication buffer (MulBuffer) and then accumulated to output buffer (OutBuffer). Finally, the results in OutBuffer are also added to the Output BRAMs for accumulation across the results from the multiple input channels.

To further improve performance, we can employ multiple processing elements (PEs) for parallel executions of the multiple im2col and MAC operations. Figure 7.4 shows an example execution sequence of the iMAC accelerator with two PEs. In this case, we can simultaneously perform im2col operations for two columns which will be temporarily stored into Im2colBuffer in each PE. We also carry out multiplications with weights (K1–K9) and accumulations to OutBuffer and output BRAM for two columns (one column is processed with one PE) at the same time, increasing the computation throughput compared to the case of using a single PE.

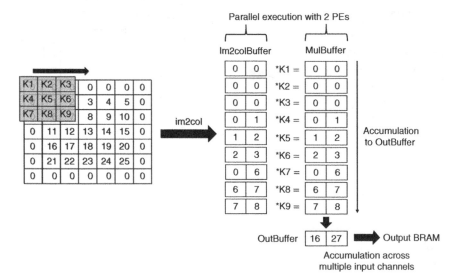

Figure 7.4 Im2col execution in the iMAC hardware accelerator. In this example, we have 5 × 5 input feature map with 3 × 3 filter with 1 zero-padding and 1 stride. Filter weights are assumed to be all 1.0 in this example.

The presented hardware design focuses on cost efficiency. Through fine-grained offloading (we only offload the portions that take a huge latency, e.g., GEMM), we use minimal hardware resources. Thus, the presented hardware is suitable for accelerating CNNs in resource-constrained IoT systems. Due to the limited on-chip memory (BRAMs), the weight data could not be reused in the presented design. We may trade the input BRAMs for weight BRAMs in order to increase the weight reusability. However, decreasing the size of input BRAMs has two important disadvantages: (i) it may also reduce the PE utilization due to the reduced input data supply, and (ii) we need more frequent input data transfer, which results in worse performance and more power consumption.

7.3 Implementation

We implement the presented design in ZED platform [144], which has a Xilinx Zynq 7020 field-programmable gate array (FPGA)-system-on-chip (SoC) that integrates programmable logic and ARM Cortex-A9 CPU. For iMAC implementation, we use Vivado HLS (High Level Synthesis) that translates high-level programming language to Zynq-compatible hardware design. In order to actually implement CNN, we use Darknet [143] framework with PetaLinux. For the CNN model, we use Tiny Darknet [145][1]. The presented implementation is based on 32-bit floating-point CNN model which can be more flexibly applied to many types of different CNN models and frameworks. The FPGA clock frequency is set to 90 MHz. Table 7.1 shows the hardware utilization of the presented implementation for iMAC accelerator with 8 PEs compared to the existing designs [146–148] that use Xilinx FPGA-based platforms. Since the presented design is geared toward resource-constrained system, we use much less logic and memory elements in Zynq FPGA-SoCs. In terms of BRAM, we only use around 600 KB, which is also less than the other implementations shown in Table 7.1. Though the presented design additionally uses 728 lookup table random access memories (LUTRAMs) (not shown in Table 7.1), the hardware cost of an LUTRAM is comparable to an 64-bit storage, meaning that overhead of the additional LUTRAMs is negligible (~5.8 KB). Compared to the existing designs, the presented design is more suitable for resource-constrained cognitive IoT where we have much lower budget for power and hardware resource.

---

1 Please note that the implementation is not limited to Tiny-Darknet and other CNN models can also be implemented with only configuring the network architecture description files in Darknet.

Table 7.1 Logic element and BRAM usage of the design presented in [146–148], and ours.

	[148] (Virtex7)	[147] (Zynq-7045)	[146] (Zynq-7045)	Our design (Zynq-7020)
Register	205 K	127 K	61 K	18 K
LUT	185 K	182 K	100 K	16 K
DSP	2240	780	864	50
36 Kb BRAM	512	486	320	133.5

The numbers of registers and LUTs are approximate values.
LUT, lookup table; DSP, digital signal processor.
Source: Adapted from [147–149].

7.4 Chapter Summary

This chapter presented a cost-efficient design for dense CNN accelerators. For a cost-efficient design, the presented approach only offloaded the most critical parts in convolution layers (i.e., im2col and GEMM) to the FPGA-based iMAC accelerator. The results demonstrated the hardware resource efficiency of the FPGA-based implementation of the presented iMAC hardware accelerator. Please note that the performance and energy results of the iMAC accelerator are presented in Chapter 14 when the software-based techniques are additionally applied to the iMAC accelerator.

8

NeuroMAX: A Dense CNN Accelerator

Convolutional neural networks (CNNs) enable embedding of artificial intelligence (AI) into devices for vision-based applications with an unprecedented accuracy. The early proposed high accuracy CNNs [30, 31, 35] required tens of millions of parameters and computations for one inference pass. This computational complexity along with high memory requirements greatly hampered their deployment on low-energy, resource-constrained devices. In addition to this, many CNN architectures used varying kernel sizes which result in reconfigurability requirement as well as low hardware utilization in accelerator designs. Separable convolution for CNNs was introduced the first time in mobilenets [33, 34] to reduce the number of multiply and accumulates (MACs). In addition, many modern CNNs use kernels of size 3×3 to promote ease of accelerator design with high hardware utilization and throughput.

Design of an efficient dataflow for scheduling data into the accelerator is equally important. An inefficient dataflow results in reduced hardware utilization which causes a decrease in throughput. Dataflow should also promote the reusability of data since, in most cases, the same kernels are being applied on the entire input feature map. It has been shown previously that the movement of data to/from double data rate (DDR) memory is 200× more costly in terms of energy consumption than a standard MAC operation [36]. Thus, the dataflow design should not only optimize the throughput and area, but also the data movement, in order to ensure reduced energy expenditure. Log-based accelerators have recently gained quite a lot of traction because of their simpler structure as compared to traditional accelerators with linear processing elements (PEs). Each PE in traditional CNN accelerator cores is essentially responsible for one multiplication in convolution operation. Log PEs replace the bulky multiplier cores with low *cost* barrel shifters without incurring a significant loss in accuracy. We clarify that cost here primarily refers to the area cost, which is determined by the number of LookUp Tables (LUTs) for field-programmable gate arrays (FPGAs) and gate count for application-specific integrated circuits (ASICs).

Accelerators for Convolutional Neural Networks, First Edition.
Arslan Munir, Joonho Kong, and Mahmood Azhar Qureshi.

This area cost is important because there are limited resources on-chip and thus this area cost also translates to monetary cost of system-on-chip (SoC). Many past approaches have designed log-based PE elements but have not exploited the low cost and overhead of such PEs. They instead rely on already established spatial architectures and 1D dataflows used for linear PEs. This chapter introduces **NeuroMAX**, a dense CNN accelerator capable of accelerating CONV operations. NeuroMAX accelerator core comprises 108 PEs arranged in a $6 \times 3 \times 6$, 3D spatial grid. The presented accelerator optimizes the most commonly used 3×3 and 1×1 kernel sizes to achieve high throughput and utilization. It can also be used for larger kernel sizes because of its grid structure and configurable 2D dataflow. The main contributions of this chapter are as follows:

- Design of a multithreaded, low-cost, log-based PE core. Using this core, we generate a spatial grid of $6 \times 3 \times 6 = 108$ PEs, capable of performing a wide variety of convolution operations commonly used in many CNNs.
- NeuroMAX utilizes a 2D dataflow that exploits the thread-based PE design to maximize the throughput and enhance the data reuse to minimize the off-chip DRAM memory accesses.
- The NeuroMAX architecture is implemented in software and its performance is compared against recent dense accelerator architectures. It is also implemented on an FPGA to show improvement in terms of resource utilization and static power consumption.

The remainder of this chapter is organized as follows: A summary of relevant works in literature is presented in Section 8.1. Section 8.2 summarizes log mapping which is utilized by NeuroMAX accelerator. Section 8.3 gives the architectural details of the NeuroMAX accelerator. Section 8.4 details the proposed dataflow on some use cases. Section 8.5 gives the implementation results and finally, Section 8.6 summarizes and concludes the chapter.

8.1 Related Work

Many hardware accelerators have been proposed recently and in the past. Chen et al. [45] proposed a nonsystolic array, reconfigurable spatial architecture along with a new dataflow scheme called *row stationary* to maximize the data reuse. However, this design incurs high PE cost owing to local storage and control in PE. It also has low hardware utilization which results in low throughput per PE. Liu et al. [138] proposes an FPGA-based CNN accelerator with integrated depthwise separable mode of operation. This accelerator, however, has low throughput because of the usage of 32-bit floating point format. Bai et al. [139] proposes an FPGA-based CNN accelerator having a dedicated matrix multiplication engine (MME) on Arria 10 SoC. It achieves a frame rate of 266 fps, however, its MME engine has a huge digital signal processing (DSP) cost of 1200+ DSP blocks. Chen et al. [52] is the improved version of [45] with higher hardware utilization and throughput. Miyashita et al. [37] introduced the concept of logarithmic data representation for neural network accelerator designs. It also gives accuracy comparison between linear and log quantization. Vogel et al. [38] proposes an accelerator design using arbitrary log base. It, however, does not utilize the low hardware overhead of the log-based PE and instead rely on linear PE arrangements. Huan et al. [140] proposes a reconfigurable design for various convolution kernels. It uses a propagated input data flow scheme but incurs high latency and low hardware utilization. Jo et al. [141] proposes a rescheduled dataflow for convolution to optimize the energy efficiency. Chang and Chang [142] proposes a vectorwise accelerator architecture with the goal of maximizing the hardware utilization. It supports various kernel sizes from 1×1 to 5×5.

Although some of the recent designs achieve high hardware utilization, they are not able to increase the peak throughput per PE count beyond unity owing to the use of single core, linear PEs with high area cost. This chapter overcomes the limitations of prior works by leveraging *log* PEs with multiple low cost threads within each log PE, and designing a 2D dataflow which promises high throughput by exploiting multilevel parallelism.

8.2 Log Mapping

Log mapping or log quantization maps an input value x to a logarithmically quantized value x'. Many trained neural nets have weights w and input activations a which are nonuniformly distributed. Mapping these 32-bit floating-point (fp32), nonuniformly distributed values over fixed-point, linearly quantized values introduces a significant amount of quantization noise for small bit width. Most hardware platforms use fixed-point arithmetic for data manipulation where the fixed point number is represented in signed $Qm.n$ format. Here, m represents the integer part whereas n represents the fractional part. The range of values which can be represented are $range_{lin} = [-2^{m-1}, 2^{m-1} - \epsilon]$ where, $\epsilon = 2^{-n}$, is the step size.

A linear quantizer rounds the fp32 value to the nearest multiple of ϵ and then clips it as follows:

$$x_q = clip\left[\left(round\left(\frac{x}{\epsilon}\right)\right) \cdot \epsilon, -2^{m-1}, 2^{m-1} - \epsilon\right] \tag{8.1}$$

where,

$$clip(x, min, max) = \begin{cases} max, & x \geq max \\ x, & min < x < max \\ min, & \text{otherwise} \end{cases} \tag{8.2}$$

A log quantizer takes as input, x, and the quantization parameters $\langle m, n, b \rangle$, where b is the logarithmic base, and produces a log-quantized value x' as output. The quantization process can be written as

$$x' = clip\left[\left(round(log_b(|x|))\right), -2^{m-1}, 2^{m-1} - \epsilon\right] \tag{8.3}$$

$$x_q = \begin{cases} 0, & x = 0 \\ sign(x) \cdot b^{x'}, & otherwise \end{cases} \tag{8.4}$$

Figure 8.1 shows some of the quantization results for the first five convolution layers of VGG16 [31] and SqueezeNet [62]. Instead of using log base-2 (log_2) for quantization, we use log base-$\sqrt{2}$ ($log_{\sqrt{2}}$) for more accurate mapping, as shown in Figure 8.1c,f. In fact, we observe that VGG16, pretrained on ImageNet dataset, with

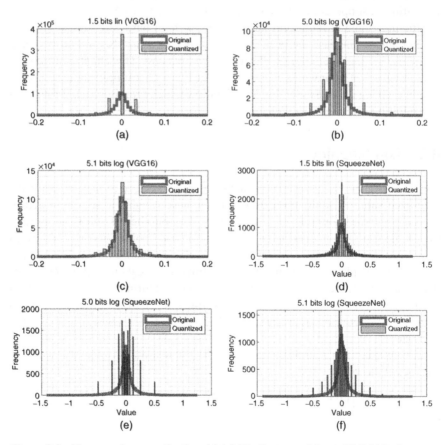

Figure 8.1 Linear vs. log quantization. (a) 1.5 bits linear vgg16 net, (b) 5.0 bits log vgg16, (c) 5.1 bits log vgg16, (d) 1.5 bits linear squeezeNet, (e) 5.0 bits log squeezeNet, and (f) 5.1 bits log squeezeNet.

fp32 data, after $log_{\sqrt{2}}$ quantization, has top-1 accuracy decrement by only ≈3.5% from 67.5% to 63.8%. This is opposed to log base-2 quantization which decreases the accuracy by ≈10%.

8.3 Hardware Architecture

8.3.1 Top-Level

Figure 8.2 shows the top-level hardware architecture of the presented Neuro-MAX CNN accelerator on Zynq-7020 SoC. The CONV core is the accelerator module containing a memory block, a state controller, PE grid, adder stages, and post-processing module. The memory block contains the weight, input, and output SRAMs with a total cumulative size of 3.8 Mb. The PE grid consists

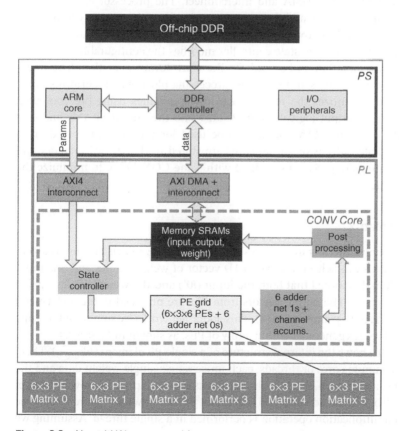

Figure 8.2 NeuroMAX system architecture.

of 108 PEs arranged in a $6 \times 3 \times 6$ 3D array. Figure 8.2 also shows the internal structure of the PE grid containing PE matrices, numbered from 0 to 5. The PE matrices are all connected to their respective input, weight, and output SRAM blocks. Each PE matrix processes independent channels in parallel for standard and separable convolutions for maximizing the throughput. The outputs from the PE matrices are provided to their respective adder nets within the PE grid. A total of six adder net 0s are present corresponding to six PE matrices. The configuration of these adder nets remain constant regardless of the type of convolution used or the filter size. The output from the adder net 0 is provided to six configurable two-stage adders whose input connections change based on the filter size and the convolution type. The first adder stage is referred to as adder net 1, and the second stage is the channel accumulation stage.

To perform a convolution operation, a tile of log-quantized input fmap and weight data is loaded from the off-chip DRAM memory into the SRAMs in the CONV core by AXI DMA and interconnect. The processor also sends the parameter information containing the values for filter size, input width, input height, output width, output height, and total channels to the state controller inside the CONV core. The state controller modifies the configurable adders and determines the dataflow to be used for the convolution operation. The linear convolution outputs are sent to the post processing block which performs ReLU operation and quantizes the results back into log values using pre computed log table. These output log values are loaded into the output SRAMs and sent back to the off-chip DRAM memory to be used for processing the next layer. No intermediate outputs or partial sums are stored in the DRAM memory and all the intermediate processing is done within the CONV core to minimize the off-chip traffic.

8.3.2 PE Matrix

Figure 8.3 shows the hierarchical design of a single PE matrix (PE matrix 0) in a bottom up view. Each PE receives a 1D vector of weight values and one input value. It should be noted that both the input ($i0'$) and the weight values ($w0'_{0-2}$) are log quantized. The output vectors from PEs are provided to the adder net 0 which generates 18 psums (o1–o18). This adder net works by summing the same color coded values generated within a row of PEs, as shown in Figure 8.4.

Figure 8.3b shows the internal structure of a single PE element ($PE_{0\_0\_0}$). There are three compute cores or threads, each processing a single weight data and the input value, and in turn, produce three outputs (p_{11}, p_{12}, p_{13}). The lowest level of the PE matrix is a thread within an individual PE, as shown in Figure 8.3a. Basic log-based multiplication operation is performed in a single thread. Assuming we have two log-quantized values, w'_q and a'_q, representing the original weight (w_q)

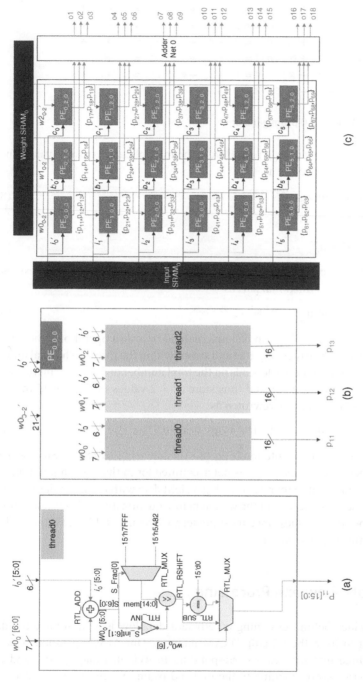

Figure 8.3 (a) Compute thread, (b) collection of threads to make a PE, and (c) 6 × 3 PE matrix 0 and adder net 0.

Row0: $o1 = P_{11} + P_{14} + P_{17}$, $o2 = P_{12} + P_{15} + P_{18}$, $o3 = P_{13} + P_{16} + P_{19}$
Row1: $o4 = P_{21} + P_{24} + P_{27}$, $o5 = P_{22} + P_{25} + P_{28}$, $o6 = P_{23} + P_{26} + P_{29}$
Row2: $o7 = P_{31} + P_{34} + P_{37}$, $o8 = P_{32} + P_{35} + P_{38}$, $o9 = P_{33} + P_{36} + P_{39}$
Row3: $o10 = P_{41} + P_{44} + P_{47}$, $o11 = P_{42} + P_{45} + P_{48}$, $o12 = P_{43} + P_{46} + P_{49}$
Row4: $o13 = P_{51} + P_{54} + P_{57}$, $o14 = P_{52} + P_{55} + P_{58}$, $o15 = P_{53} + P_{56} + P_{59}$
Row5: $o16 = P_{61} + P_{64} + P_{67}$, $o17 = P_{62} + P_{65} + P_{68}$, $o18 = P_{63} + P_{66} + P_{69}$

Figure 8.4 Adder net 0 psum generation.

and the activation input (a_q), respectively, the multiplication of these values in log domain can be carried out as

$$w_q a_q = sign(w_q) \cdot 2^{g_q'} \tag{8.5}$$

where,

$$g_q' = w_q' + a_q' \tag{8.6}$$

Equation (8.5) can be implemented in hardware by decomposing the exponent into its integer and fractional part as

$$w_q a_q = sign(w_q) \cdot 2^{INT(g_q')} \cdot 2^{FRAC(g_q')} \tag{8.7}$$

The integer part $2^{INT(g_q')}$ can be implemented by a shift operation, whereas the fractional part can be precomputed and stored within the thread. The total number of fractional computations depends on the total number of fractional bits (n) used. In our case, we have $n = 1$ and thus store $2^n = 2$ values in the thread memory. Equation (8.7) can now be rewritten as

$$w_q a_q = sign(w_q) \cdot (LUT(FRAC(g_q')) \gg \neg INT((g_q'))) \tag{8.8}$$

The hardware implementation of Eq. (8.8) is shown in Figure 8.3a. Since weights can have negative values, which is not accounted for in the log computations, we use an additional bit to represent the log weight data with the most significant bit $w_q'[6]$ representing the sign of the weight before quantization. This is not required for the input fmap values since most modern CNNs use ReLU activations which eliminate the negative outputs.

8.4 Data Flow and Processing

The main idea behind designing an efficient dataflow is to minimize the data movement to/from the off-chip DRAM memory. One MAC operation typically requires three memory reads corresponding to weight, ifmap, psum, and one memory write, corresponding to the updated psum. A neural net like AlexNet, with 724M MACs, will need ≈3000M DRAM memory accesses. Many efficient dataflows have been presented in literature to minimize this data movement. Some of these include *output stationary*, *weight stationary* and, *row stationary* [6]. Since convolution operation requires the reuse of filter weights, input, and psums, in successive operations, the dataflows are designed to optimize the re-usability without accessing the DRAM memory. We introduce a 2D weight broadcast dataflow for maximizing the re-usability of the weights, input, and psums.

8.4.1 3 × 3 Convolution

Figure 8.5 shows a 3 × 3 convolution example. Here, a 12 × 6 input is convolved with a 3 × 3 filter to produce a 10 × 4 output for stride 1 and a 6 × 3 output for stride 2. A total of 108 bits, corresponding to the 6 × 3 input tile, are received from the AXI4 interconnect and stored in the input SRAM. This input tile is modified by the state controller and provided to the PE matrix in a row shifted pattern as shown in Figure 8.6a,c for stride 1 and stride 2, respectively. We also acquire a 2D weight array and broadcast it to the PE matrix as shown in Figure 8.6b. Figure 8.7 shows the dataflow and the operation of the PE matrix for the first 6 × 3 input tile and the weight matrix at time stamp $t = 1$. The entire input tile and the 2D weight array are loaded into the PE matrix simultaneously. Because of the multithreaded

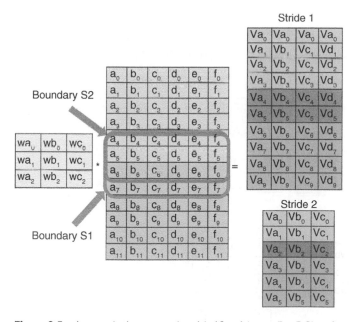

Figure 8.5 A convolution example with 12 × 6 input, 3 × 3 filter for stride 1 and 2.

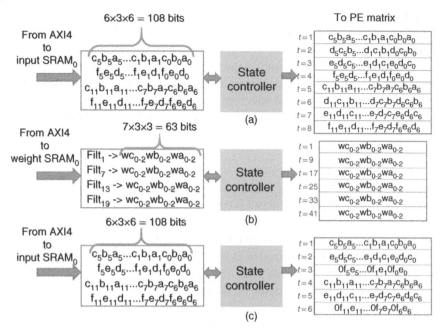

Figure 8.6 State controller operation: (a) Input, stride 1, (b) filter weights, and (c) input, stride 2.

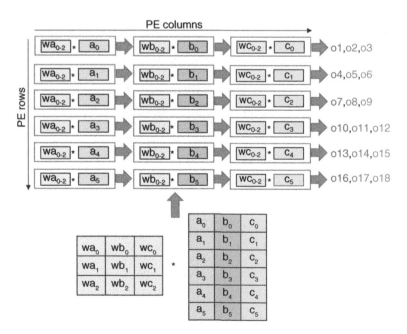

Figure 8.7 2D weight broadcast dataflow.

structure of PEs, each PE performs three multiplication operations using three threads and the outputs are rowwise summed to generate the psums (o1–o18) using adder net 0 (Figure 8.4). The dataflow chart and the processing of the entire 12×6 input is shown in Figure 8.8. The output a_0wa_{012}, in Figure 8.8, represents the three outputs a_0wa_0, a_0wa_1, a_0wa_2 generated by three threads within a PE. The adder net 0 computes the partial sum outputs (o1–o18) the same way as shown in Figure 8.4, where $p_{11} = a_0wa_0$, $p_{14} = b_0wb_0$ and $p_{17} = c_0wc_0$ are the same colored outputs along the row.

The outputs (rows 5 and 6) in Figure 8.5 for stride 1 and outputs (row 3) for stride 2 represent the boundary outputs. The boundary condition occurs when the filter overlaps two different columnwise input tile sectors. For clarity, we assume that the first input tile at $t = 1$ is processed by the PE matrix. This corresponds to the first six rows and the first three columns of the input. The PE matrix will process the last rowwise input tile at $t = 4$ which corresponds to the first six rows and the last three columns of the input as shown in Figure 8.6a. The input tile will then jump to the next columnwise 6×3 input tile which corresponds to the last six rows and the first three columns at $t = 5$ as shown in Figure 8.6a. However, it can be seen that the row 5 and 6 in the output are dependent on the overlapping results from the two concurrent columnwise input tile sectors (e.g., at $t = 1$ and $t = 5$, $t = 2$ and $t = 6$ and so on). To resolve this, the three dependent psums (o13, o17, and o16), generated from row 5 and row 6, of first columnwise tile sector of the 12×6 input, are passed through a variable length shift register with the maximum length equal to the width of the input. These psums are subsequently utilized when the next columnwise 6×3 input tile (a_6 to a_{11}) is being processed. Thus, the rows 1 to 4 in the output are generated during the time intervals $t = 1$ to $t = 4$, whereas the rows 5 to 10 are generated during the time interval $t = 5$ to $t = 8$.

The output in Figure 8.5, for stride 1, is generated by alternate colored, columnwise summation of the psums in the adder net 1 as shown in Figure 8.9a. Figure 8.9b shows the output generation for stride 2 case. The shift registers (VAR Len SR) for generating the boundary outputs are also shown in Figure 8.9. It can be observed that because of the optimized dataflow, only 2 out of 18 or 11% psums require local storage as opposed to >50% psums requiring storage (local or off-chip) in previously proposed dataflows. The throughput for the above example is 45 OPS/cycle (total OPS/total cycles = 360/8 = 45), which results in an 83.3% overall thread utilization $(45/(3 \times 6 \times 3)) \times 100$. We will simply use thread utilization as hardware utilization in this context.

8.4.2 1×1 Convolution

1×1 convolutions are very popular in modern CNNs. These convolutions, along with the depthwise separable, are replacing the normal 2-D convolutions because

$t=1$	$wa_{0\text{-}2}$	$wb_{0\text{-}2}$	$wc_{0\text{-}2}$
$c_0b_0a_0$	a_0wa_{012}	b_0wb_{012}	c_0wc_{012}
$c_1b_1a_1$	a_1wa_{012}	b_1wb_{012}	c_1wc_{012}
$c_2b_2a_2$	a_2wa_{012}	b_2wb_{012}	c_2wc_{012}
$c_3b_3a_3$	a_3wa_{012}	b_3wb_{012}	c_3wc_{012}
$c_4b_4a_4$	a_4wa_{012}	b_4wb_{012}	c_4wc_{012}
$c_5b_5a_5$	a_5wa_{012}	b_5wb_{012}	c_5wc_{012}

$t=2$	$wa_{0\text{-}2}$	$wb_{0\text{-}2}$	$wc_{0\text{-}2}$
$d_0c_0b_0$	b_0wa_{012}	c_0wb_{012}	d_0wc_{012}
$d_1c_1b_1$	b_1wa_{012}	c_1wb_{012}	d_1wc_{012}
$d_2c_2b_2$	b_2wa_{012}	c_2wb_{012}	d_2wc_{012}
$d_3c_3b_3$	b_3wa_{012}	c_3wb_{012}	d_3wc_{012}
$d_4c_4b_4$	b_4wa_{012}	c_4wb_{012}	d_4wc_{012}
$d_5c_5b_5$	b_5wa_{012}	c_5wb_{012}	d_5wc_{012}

$t=3$	$wa_{0\text{-}2}$	$wb_{0\text{-}2}$	$wc_{0\text{-}2}$
$e_0d_0c_0$	c_0wa_{012}	d_0wb_{012}	e_0wc_{012}
$e_1d_1c_1$	c_1wa_{012}	d_1wb_{012}	e_1wc_{012}
$e_2d_2c_2$	c_2wa_{012}	d_2wb_{012}	e_2wc_{012}
$e_3d_3c_3$	c_3wa_{012}	d_3wb_{012}	e_3wc_{012}
$e_4d_4c_4$	c_4wa_{012}	d_4wb_{012}	e_4wc_{012}
$e_5d_5c_5$	c_5wa_{012}	d_5wb_{012}	e_5wc_{012}

$t=4$	$wa_{0\text{-}2}$	$wb_{0\text{-}2}$	$wc_{0\text{-}2}$
$f_0e_0d_0$	d_0wa_{012}	e_0wb_{012}	f_0wc_{012}
$f_1e_1d_1$	d_1wa_{012}	e_1wb_{012}	f_1wc_{012}
$f_2e_2d_2$	d_2wa_{012}	e_2wb_{012}	f_2wc_{012}
$f_3e_3d_3$	d_3wa_{012}	e_3wb_{012}	f_3wc_{012}
$f_4e_4d_4$	d_4wa_{012}	e_4wb_{012}	f_4wc_{012}
$f_5e_5d_5$	d_5wa_{012}	e_5wb_{012}	f_5wc_{012}

$t=5$	$wa_{0\text{-}2}$	$wb_{0\text{-}2}$	$wc_{0\text{-}2}$
$c_6b_6a_6$	a_6wa_{012}	b_6wb_{012}	c_6wc_{012}
$c_7b_7a_7$	a_7wa_{012}	b_7wb_{012}	c_7wc_{012}
$c_8b_8a_8$	a_8wa_{012}	b_8wb_{012}	c_8wc_{012}
$c_9b_9a_9$	a_9wa_{012}	b_9wb_{012}	c_9wc_{012}
$c_{10}b_{10}a_{10}$	$a_{10}wa_{012}$	$b_{10}wb_{012}$	$c_{10}wc_{012}$
$c_{11}b_{11}a_{11}$	$a_{11}wa_{012}$	$b_{11}wb_{012}$	$c_{11}wc_{012}$

$t=6$	$wa_{0\text{-}2}$	$wb_{0\text{-}2}$	$wc_{0\text{-}2}$
$d_6c_6b_6$	b_6wa_{012}	c_6wb_{012}	d_6wc_{012}
$d_7c_7b_7$	b_7wa_{012}	c_7wb_{012}	d_7wc_{012}
$d_8c_8b_8$	b_8wa_{012}	c_8wb_{012}	d_8wc_{012}
$d_9c_9b_9$	b_9wa_{012}	c_9wb_{012}	d_9wc_{012}
$d_{10}c_{10}b_{10}$	$b_{10}wa_{012}$	$c_{10}wb_{012}$	$d_{10}wc_{012}$
$d_{11}c_{11}b_{11}$	$b_{11}wa_{012}$	$c_{11}wb_{012}$	$d_{11}wc_{012}$

$t=7$	$wa_{0\text{-}2}$	$wb_{0\text{-}2}$	$wc_{0\text{-}2}$
$e_6d_6c_6$	c_6wa_{012}	d_6wb_{012}	e_6wc_{012}
$e_7d_7c_7$	c_7wa_{012}	d_7wb_{012}	e_7wc_{012}
$e_8d_8c_8$	c_8wa_{012}	d_8wb_{012}	e_8wc_{012}
$e_9d_9c_9$	c_9wa_{012}	d_9wb_{012}	e_9wc_{012}
$e_{10}d_{10}c_{10}$	$c_{10}wa_{012}$	$d_{10}wb_{012}$	$e_{10}wc_{012}$
$e_{11}d_{11}c_{11}$	$c_{11}wa_{012}$	$d_{11}wb_{012}$	$e_{11}wc_{012}$

$t=8$	$wa_{0\text{-}2}$	$wb_{0\text{-}2}$	$wc_{0\text{-}2}$
$f_6e_6d_6$	d_6wa_{012}	e_6wb_{012}	f_6wc_{012}
$f_7e_7d_7$	d_7wa_{012}	e_7wb_{012}	f_7wc_{012}
$f_8e_8d_8$	d_8wa_{012}	e_8wb_{012}	f_8wc_{012}
$f_9e_9d_9$	d_9wa_{012}	e_9wb_{012}	f_9wc_{012}
$f_{10}e_{10}d_{10}$	$d_{10}wa_{012}$	$e_{10}wb_{012}$	$f_{10}wc_{012}$
$f_{11}e_{11}d_{11}$	$d_{11}wa_{012}$	$e_{11}wb_{012}$	$f_{11}wc_{012}$

Figure 8.8 Dataflow chart for 3×3 stride 1 convolution in Figure 8.5.

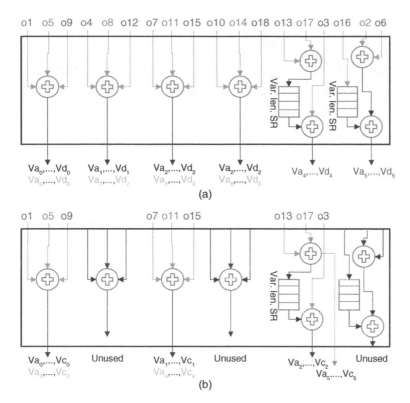

Figure 8.9 Adder net 1 configuration: (a) Stride 1 and (b) Stride 2.

of the less number of MAC operations [33]. The 1×1 CONV operation convolves $1 \times 1 \times C \times P$ filters with a $M \times N \times C$ input to produce $M \times N \times P$ outputs. Here, C is the number of channels, P is the number of filters, M is the input width and N is the input height.

Figure 8.10 shows a 1×1 CONV example where a $3 \times 6 \times 6$ input is convolved with 6, $1 \times 1 \times 6$ filters to produce a $3 \times 6 \times 6$ output. Since this convolution generates the psums by channel accumulation, the outputs from the multiple PE matrices are utilized. For the example in Figure 8.10, the state controller data scheduling for PE matrix 0 and 1 is shown in Figure 8.11. It can be seen that the first three channels of the input are convolved with the first three channels of all the filters in PE matrix 0, whereas the last three channels of the input are convolved with the last three channels of all the filters in PE matrix 1. The time stamps during specific processing of input and weights in PE matrices are also shown in Figure 8.11. It should be noted that for an input with more channels, the rest of the PE matrices will also be used. Thus, by using the dataflow in Figure 8.11, the architecture can

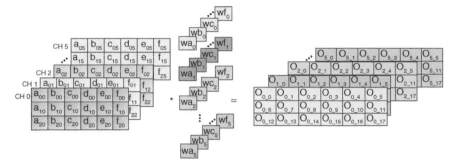

Figure 8.10 1 × 1 convolution example.

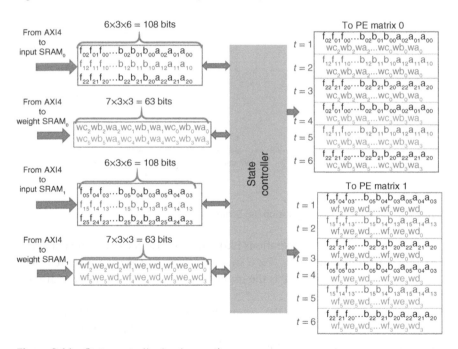

Figure 8.11 State controller load operation.

process 18 channels concurrently by using the 6 PE matrices, with each PE matrix processing 3 input and filter channels.

The dataflow chart for the PE matrix 0 for the example in Figure 8.10 is shown in Figure 8.12. The same dataflow chart can also be generated for the PE matrix 1. As mentioned earlier, the psums in 1 × 1 convolution are calculated using channel-wise accumulation. The 18 outputs (o1–o18) generated by the

$t=1$	wa_{0-2}	wb_{0-2}	wc_{0-2}
a_{00-02}	$a_{00}wa_{012}$	$a_{01}wb_{012}$	$a_{02}wc_{012}$
b_{00-02}	$b_{00}wa_{012}$	$b_{01}wb_{012}$	$b_{02}wc_{012}$
c_{00-02}	$c_{00}wa_{012}$	$c_{01}wb_{012}$	$c_{02}wc_{012}$
d_{00-02}	$d_{00}wa_{012}$	$d_{01}wb_{012}$	$d_{02}wc_{012}$
e_{00-02}	$e_{00}wa_{012}$	$e_{01}wb_{012}$	$e_{02}wc_{012}$
f_{00-02}	$f_{00}wa_{012}$	$f_{01}wb_{012}$	$f_{02}wc_{012}$

$t=2$	wa_{0-2}	wb_{0-2}	wc_{0-2}
a_{10-12}	$a_{10}wa_{012}$	$a_{11}wb_{012}$	$a_{12}wc_{012}$
b_{10-12}	$b_{10}wa_{012}$	$b_{11}wb_{012}$	$b_{12}wc_{012}$
c_{10-12}	$c_{10}wa_{012}$	$c_{11}wb_{012}$	$c_{12}wc_{012}$
d_{10-12}	$d_{10}wa_{012}$	$d_{11}wb_{012}$	$d_{12}wc_{012}$
e_{10-12}	$e_{10}wa_{012}$	$e_{11}wb_{012}$	$e_{12}wc_{012}$
f_{10-12}	$f_{10}wa_{012}$	$f_{11}wb_{012}$	$f_{12}wc_{012}$

$t=3$	wa_{0-2}	wb_{0-2}	wc_{0-2}
a_{20-22}	$a_{20}wa_{012}$	$a_{21}wb_{012}$	$a_{22}wc_{012}$
b_{20-22}	$b_{20}wa_{012}$	$b_{21}wb_{012}$	$b_{22}wc_{012}$
c_{20-22}	$c_{20}wa_{012}$	$c_{21}wb_{012}$	$c_{22}wc_{012}$
d_{20-22}	$d_{20}wa_{012}$	$d_{21}wb_{012}$	$d_{22}wc_{012}$
e_{20-22}	$e_{20}wa_{012}$	$e_{21}wb_{012}$	$e_{22}wc_{012}$
f_{20-22}	$f_{20}wa_{012}$	$f_{21}wb_{012}$	$f_{22}wc_{012}$

$t=4$	wa_{3-5}	wb_{3-5}	wc_{3-5}
a_{00-02}	$a_{00}wa_{345}$	$a_{01}wb_{345}$	$a_{02}wc_{345}$
b_{00-02}	$b_{00}wa_{345}$	$b_{01}wb_{345}$	$b_{02}wc_{345}$
c_{00-02}	$c_{00}wa_{345}$	$c_{01}wb_{345}$	$c_{02}wc_{345}$
d_{00-02}	$d_{00}wa_{345}$	$d_{01}wb_{345}$	$d_{02}wc_{345}$
e_{00-02}	$e_{00}wa_{345}$	$e_{01}wb_{345}$	$e_{02}wc_{345}$
f_{00-02}	$f_{00}wa_{345}$	$f_{01}wb_{345}$	$f_{01}wc_{345}$

$t=5$	wa_{3-5}	wb_{3-5}	wc_{3-5}
a_{10-12}	$a_{10}wa_{345}$	$a_{11}wb_{345}$	$a_{12}wc_{345}$
b_{10-12}	$b_{10}wa_{345}$	$b_{11}wb_{345}$	$b_{12}wc_{345}$
c_{10-12}	$c_{10}wa_{345}$	$c_{11}wb_{345}$	$c_{12}wc_{345}$
d_{10-12}	$d_{10}wa_{345}$	$d_{11}wb_{345}$	$d_{12}wc_{345}$
e_{10-12}	$e_{10}wa_{345}$	$e_{11}wb_{345}$	$e_{12}wc_{345}$
f_{10-12}	$f_{10}wa_{345}$	$f_{11}wb_{345}$	$f_{12}wc_{345}$

$t=6$	wa_{3-5}	wb_{3-5}	wc_{3-5}
a_{20-22}	$a_{20}wa_{345}$	$a_{21}wb_{345}$	$a_{22}wc_{345}$
b_{20-22}	$b_{20}wa_{345}$	$b_{21}wb_{345}$	$b_{22}wc_{345}$
c_{20-22}	$c_{20}wa_{345}$	$c_{21}wb_{345}$	$c_{22}wc_{345}$
d_{20-22}	$d_{20}wa_{345}$	$d_{21}wb_{345}$	$d_{22}wc_{345}$
e_{20-22}	$e_{20}wa_{345}$	$e_{21}wb_{345}$	$e_{22}wc_{345}$
f_{20-22}	$f_{20}wa_{345}$	$f_{21}wb_{345}$	$f_{22}wc_{345}$

Figure 8.12 Dataflow chart for 1×1 convolution in Figure 8.10.

individual PE matrices are summed in their respective adder net 1s. The input connections for adder net 1 (AN 1_0) and the channel accumulator (CA 0) of PE matrix 0 are shown in Figure 8.13a. Here, ol_0 is the psum output from the PE matrix 0 and ol_5 is the psum output from the PE matrix 5. Since the example in Figure 8.10 is small, it only requires the first two PE matrices and their outputs, that is, only ol_0–18_0 and ol_1–18_1 are active. The output in Figure 8.10 is generated by using all six adder net 1s and the channel accumulators as shown in Figure 8.13b. The throughput for the above example is 108 OPS/cycle (total OPS/total cycles = $(6 \times 6 \times 3 \times 6/6 = 108)$, which results in a 100% overall thread utilization $(108/(3 \times 6 \times 3 \times 2) \times 100)$.

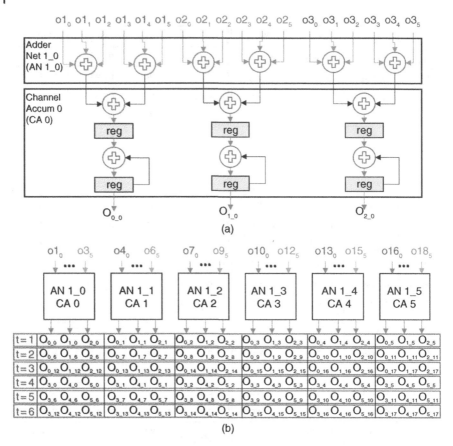

Figure 8.13 (a) Channel-wise accumulation for PE matrix 0. (b) All channel-wise accumulations.

8.4.3 Higher-Order Convolutions

The presented NeuroMAX accelerator is designed to optimize 3×3 and 1×1 convolutions. It can, however, also be used to accelerate larger kernel sizes. NVIDIA [150] proposed a kernel decomposition method such that an additional support for 4×4 and 5×5 filter is needed to implement any filter size. Figure 8.14a gives an example of 5×5 convolution. As the size of the PE matrix is 6×3, a filter of width greater than 3 and height greater than 6 needs multiple cycles to calculate the output value. This can be seen in Figure 8.14b,c where the last two columns of the input matrix and the weight matrix are loaded at time stamp $t = 2$. Figure 8.15 shows the dataflow chart which accounts for this configuration. The generated psums (o1–o18) are provided to the adder net 1 as

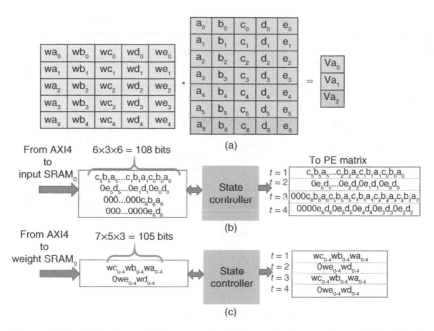

From AXI4 to input SRAM$_0$ 6×3×6 = 108 bits

To PE matrix

Figure 8.14 (a) 5 × 5 convolution example, (b) input load operation, and (c) weight load operation.

$t = 1$	wa_{0-4}	wb_{0-4}	wc_{0-4}		$t = 2$	wd_{0-4}	we_{0-4}	0
$c_0b_0a_0$	a_0wa_{012}	b_0wb_{012}	c_0wc_{012}		$0e_0d_0$	d_0wd_{012}	e_0we_{012}	0
$c_1b_1a_1$	a_1wa_{012}	b_1wb_{012}	c_1wc_{012}		$0e_1d_1$	d_1wd_{012}	e_1we_{012}	0
$c_2b_2a_2$	a_2wa_{312}	b_2wb_{312}	c_2wc_{312}		$0e_2d_2$	d_2wd_{312}	e_2we_{312}	0
$c_3b_3a_3$	a_3wa_{342}	b_3wb_{342}	c_3wc_{342}		$0e_3d_3$	d_3wd_{342}	e_3we_{342}	0
$c_4b_4a_4$	a_4wa_{342}	b_4wb_{342}	c_4wc_{342}		$0e_4d_4$	d_4wd_{342}	e_4we_{342}	0
$c_5b_5a_5$	a_5wa_{342}	b_5wb_{342}	c_5wc_{342}		$0c_5d_5$	d_5wd_{342}	0_5we_{342}	0
$t = 3$	wa_{0-4}	wb_{0-4}	wc_{0-4}		$t = 4$	wd_{0-4}	we_{0-4}	0
$c_2b_2a_2$	a_2wa_{012}	b_2wb_{012}	c_2wc_{012}		$0e_2d_2$	d_2wd_{012}	e_2we_{012}	0
$c_3b_3a_3$	a_3wa_{012}	b_3wb_{012}	c_3wc_{012}		$0e_3d_3$	d_3wd_{012}	e_3we_{012}	0
$c_4b_4a_4$	a_4wa_{312}	b_4wb_{312}	c_4wc_{312}		$0e_4d_4$	d_4wd_{312}	e_4we_{312}	0
$c_5b_5a_5$	a_5wa_{342}	b_5wb_{342}	c_5wc_{342}		$0e_5d_5$	d_5wd_{342}	e_5we_{342}	0
$c_6b_6a_6$	a_6wa_{342}	b_6wb_{342}	c_6wc_{342}		$0e_6d_6$	d_6wd_{342}	e_6we_{342}	0
000	0	0	0		000	0	0	0

Figure 8.15 Dataflow chart for 5 × 5 convolution in Figure 8.14a.

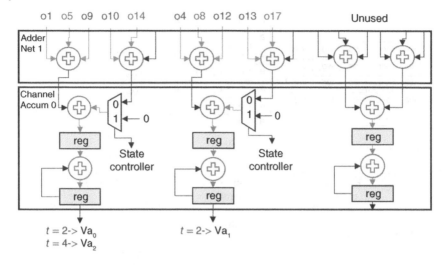

Figure 8.16 Adder configuration for 5 × 5 convolution.

shown in Figure 8.16. For this convolution, the output values are calculated as

$$Va_0, Va_2 = ((o1 + o5 + o9) + (o10 + o14))_{old} + (o1 + o5 + o9)_{new} \qquad (8.9)$$

$$Va_1 = ((o4 + o8 + o12) + (o13 + o17))_{old} + (o4 + o8 + o12)_{new} \qquad (8.10)$$

In Eqs. (8.9) and (8.10), the *old* value corresponds to the convolution output from the first three columns of the input and the weight matrix at $t = 1$, whereas the *new* value corresponds to the last two columns at $t = 2$. The adder net 1 and the channel accumulator configuration for this convolution is shown in Figure 8.16. A similar configuration and dataflow chart are used for implementing a 4 × 4 convolution. In addition to this, the CONV core can also perform pooling operation by choosing the appropriate stride and kernel.

8.5 Implementation and Results

This section discusses the implementation of the introduced NeuroMAX accelerator and presents the area cost, power consumption, performance, throughput, and hardware utilization results. The accelerator has been implemented in software and also on hardware (PL side of Xilinx Zynq-7020 SoC operating at 200 MHz). Figure 8.17 shows cost comparison between our multithreaded log PE core and an area-optimized linear multiplier core with equal output bit precision and latency.

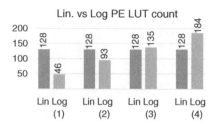
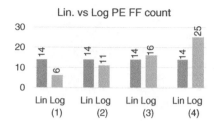

Figure 8.17 Linear vs. log PE LUT and FF cost (16-bit).

It can be seen that by choosing a thread count of 3 (shown as log (3) in Figure 8.17), the LUT and FF cost is only 1.05× and 1.14× that of the linear PE. Thus, a total of 108 linear PEs would be equivalent, in cost, to ≈122 multithreaded log PEs. For fairness, we will use the cost adjusted PE number for performance comparison.

Table 8.1 shows the resource utilization of the implemented accelerator core as well as the power consumption. Figure 8.18a–c shows the breakdown of LUT cost, FF cost and power consumption among different modules of the accelerator. The PE grid and the adder net 0 combined have the highest LUT and FF count (81% and 91%, respectively). The postprocessing block consumes negligible resources. The processing system (ARM core) dominates the power consumption (57%), while the PE grid and adder net 0 have the second highest consumption (26%) of the total.

Figure 8.19 shows layer-by-layer hardware utilization for various CNN architectures. NeuroMAX achieves an average utilization of 95%, 84%, and 86% for VGG-16, MobileNet v1, and, ResNet-34, respectively. The dip in hardware utilization in some layers of mobilenet and ResNet-34 is because of stride 2 convolutions which utilize only 50% of the available PE cores. The low utilization in the first layer of VGG16 is because it only has three channels and since each PE matrix processes one channel, the last three PE matrices remain idle which gives an exact utilization of 50%.

Table 8.1 Resource utilization.

Property	Accelerator	Utilization
LUTs	20,680	38%
FFs	17,207	16%
36 kB BRAMs	108	77%
Power	2.727 W	NA

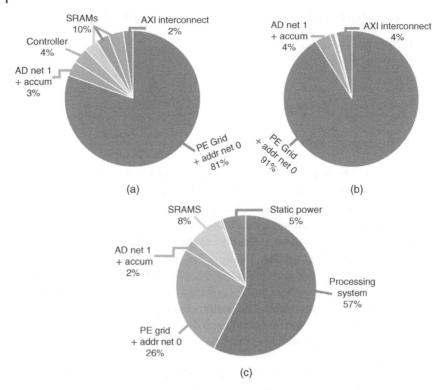

Figure 8.18 Breakdown of (a) LUT cost, (b) FF cost, and (c) power consumption for NeuroMAX.

Chang and Chang [142] recently presented an accelerator, referred to as VWA, with 1D broadcast dataflow which promises higher utilization and throughput (GOPS) than all the previous designs. NeuroMAX is, therefore, compared against VWA [142] in Figure 8.20 for various CNNs. VWA uses a total of 168 PE cores and provides a utilization of 99% with throughput 166.32 GOPS, 93.4% with throughput 156.91 GOPS, and 90.2% with throughput 151.54 GOPS for VGG16, ResNet-34 and mobilenet, respectively. We use 122 PE cores (cost adjusted), a 28% decrease from VWA, and provide a throughput of 307.8 GOPS, an 85% increase, 281.8 GOPS, a 79.4% increase, and 268.92 GOPS, a 77.4% increase, for the three CNNs, respectively. This increase in throughput with lower PE count is attributed toward our low-cost, multithreaded PE core design and an efficient 2D dataflow. We also achieve somewhat similar hardware utilization, that is, 94% for VGG16, 87.3% for ResNet-34, and, 83% for mobilenet. It should be noted that

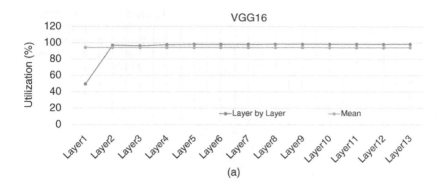

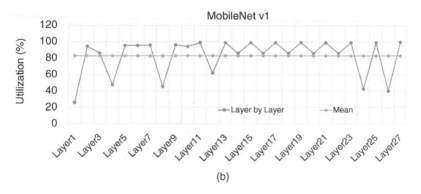

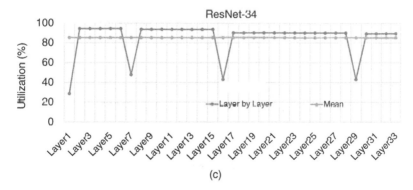

Figure 8.19 Hardware utilization of NeuroMAX for (a) VGG-16, (b) MobileNet v1, and (c) ResNet-34.

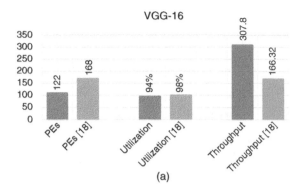

(a)

Figure 8.20 PE count vs. utilization vs. throughput comparison of NeuroMAX with VWA. Source: Adapted from [142].

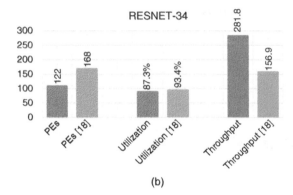

(b)

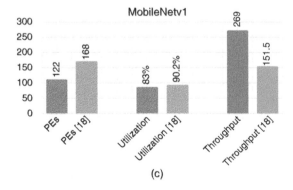

(c)

Table 8.2 Comparison of NeuroMAX with previous designs.

Property	NeuroMAX	Eyeriss [45]	Liu et al. [138]	Vogel et al. [38]	VWA [142]
Technology	Zynq-7020 SoC	65 nm	Zynq-7100	Arria 10 SoC	Virtex-7
Precision (bits)	6-bit log	16-bit	32fp	16-bit	5-bit log
PE number	122 (adjusted)	168	1926	1278	256
Processing clock (MHz)	200	200	100	133	Unreported
Peak throughput (GOPS)	324	84	17.11	170.6	Unreported
Peak throughput/PE	2.7 (adjusted)	0.5	0.008	0.13	Unreported
Cost (LUTs(a),gates(b))	20.6k(a)	1176k(b)	142k(a)	66k(a)	29k(a)
Power (W)	2.72	0.278	4.083	Unreported	3.756

VWA implements the accelerator on an ASIC, whereas we use an FPGA, thus, an accurate comparison in LUT count, FF count, and power consumption cannot be made. It is, however, evident that the design in VWA when ported into FPGA will have ≈31% more LUTs and FFs owing to more number of PEs used. Table 8.2 shows the comparison of our accelerator with previous state-of-the-art ASIC and FPGA designs. We see an improved performance in terms of PE number, peak throughput, and peak throughput/PE ratio. Only VWA has a peak throughput/PE ratio equal to unity with average around 0.85. Our peak throughput/PE is 3 with average around 2.7 after cost adjustment. The power comparison reveals that the FPGA-based designs inherently consume more power compared to ASICs. We can, however, see that NeuroMAX consumes significantly less power and has lower cost in terms of LUT count compared to other FPGA designs. Table 8.3 gives a layer-by-layer processing latency comparison for VGG16. Both Eyeriss [45] and VWA [142] benchmark the latency of their accelerators on this CNN; therefore, we also evaluate and compare NeuroMAX's performance on VGG16. It should be noted however that VWA uses 500 MHz processing clock in their design. For fair comparison, we make suitable adjustments in their reported values. Our presented NeuroMAX accelerator has 93% and 47% decrease in latency, when compared to Eyeriss and VWA, respectively, at 200 MHz clock.

Table 8.3 VGG16 latency comparison.

Layer	NeuroMAX	Eyeriss [45]	VWA [142]
CONV1_1 (ms)	1.35	38.0	2.57
CONV1_2 (ms)	28.9	810.6	55.04
CONV2_1 (ms)	14.4	405.3	27.43
CONV2_2 (ms)	29.26	810.8	55.7
CONV3_1 (ms)	14.54	204	27.7
CONV3_2 (ms)	28.6	408.1	54.5
CONV3_3 (ms)	28.7	408.1	54.6
CONV4_1 (ms)	14.4	105.1	27.42
CONV4_2 (ms)	29	210.0	55.23
CONV4_3 (ms)	29.5	210.0	56.19
CONV5_1 (ms)	7.24	48.3	13.79
CONV5_2 (ms)	7.23	48.5	13.77
CONV5_3 (ms)	7.11	48.5	13.54
Total (ms)	240.23	3755.3	457.5

8.6 Chapter Summary

This chapter explained the architectural details and working of NeuroMAX – a dense accelerator which leveraged multithreaded, log-based PE cores. Experimental results indicated that the designed PE cores are capable of providing a 200% increase in peak throughput while only increasing the area overhead by 6%, when compared to a standard multiplier-based PE core. NeuroMAX used an efficient 2D weight broadcast dataflow scheme which exploited the multilevel parallelism of the processing engine and enabled hardware utilization close to a 100%. The accelerator is capable of performing a wide variety of convolutions including standard and separable 3×3 stride 1 and 2, 4×4, 5×5, and 1×1 depthwise, required in modern CNN architectures. Experimental results showed that the NeuroMAX delivered a throughput increase of 77.4% and a latency decrease of 47% with a 28% decrease in PE count against recently proposed accelerator designs for modern CNNs. NeuroMAX also provided at least a 27% and a 29% decrease in power consumption and LUT count, respectively, against prior FPGA-based CNN accelerators.

Part IV

Sparse CNN Accelerators

9

Contemporary Sparse CNN Accelerators

This chapter provides background on sparse convolutional neural network (CNN) accelerators. Before delving into sparse CNN accelerators, this chapter first discusses why the data in CNN models are generally sparse and why considering sparsity in hardware accelerators is important. This chapter then discusses general approaches for designing sparse CNN accelerators. Since the CNNs or multilayer perceptrons (MLPs) are generally processed in the form of matrix multiplication (MM), this chapter elaborates on the sparse matrix multiplication hardware accelerators. This chapter also covers recent advancements in sparse CNN accelerators.

9.1   Background of Sparsity in CNN Models

Sparsity refers to the fraction of zeros in a CNN layer's weight and input activation matrices. Weight sparsity is static and is introduced while pruning a network during training. Han et al. [46] developed an iterative scheme for pruning a deep neural network while retraining the network's accuracy. Activation sparsity is introduced dynamically during the inference phase and is highly dependent on the input being processed. This sparsity occurs mostly because of the rectified linear unit (ReLU) activation function, most commonly used in many CNN models, which convert all the negative outputs of a layer to zero.

Figure 9.1 shows the weight and activation sparsity among two of the most commonly used CNNs. It can be seen that the weight sparsity for AlexNet and VGG-16 can reach as high as 70% and 80%, respectively, for some layers. Activation sparsity tends to be lower in the initial layers but rises considerably in later layers with some layers of VGG-16 having activation sparsity as high as 85%. This goes to show that many neural nets, though seemingly compute and memory bandwidth intensive, are incredibly sparse with huge amounts of redundant computations. An architecture which efficiently exploits this redundancy can provide immense gains in both performance and energy efficiency.

Accelerators for Convolutional Neural Networks, First Edition.
Arslan Munir, Joonho Kong, and Mahmood Azhar Qureshi.
© 2024 The Institute of Electrical and Electronics Engineers, Inc. Published 2024 by John Wiley & Sons, Inc.

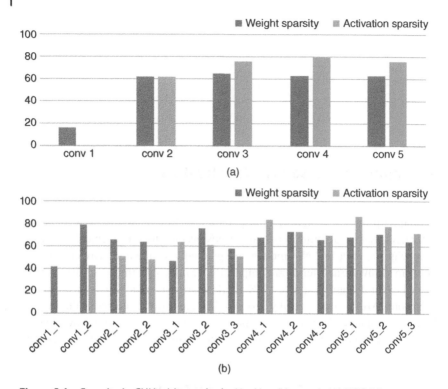

Figure 9.1 Sparsity in CNNs: (a) sparsity in AlexNet, (b) sparsity in VGG-16.

To represent the sparse weights or inputs various formats can be employed. As explained in Chapter 3, entropy-based coding such as Huffman coding or arithmetic coding can be used. In addition, run-length coding, bitmap-based coding, two-step compression [108], or compressed sparse row (CSR) format can also be used. As this book has already explained each of these methods in Chapters 3–5, we omit the explanation of these formats or coding methods in this chapter.

9.2 Background of Sparse CNN Accelerators

A sparse CNN accelerator can be defined as a CNN accelerator that accepts weights and input feature maps in the sparse format. Figure 9.2 compares sparse and dense CNN accelerators. Although in Figure 9.2, the CSR format is shown to represent a sparse matrix, the sparse format inputs can be any specialized format for representing the sparse matrices or tensors, such as bitmap-based format or run-length coding which was already presented in Chapter 3.

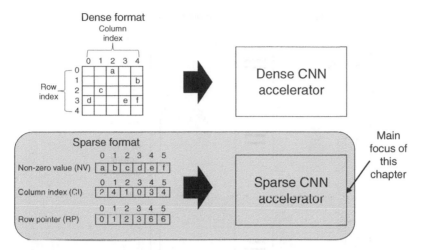

Figure 9.2 The comparison between the dense and sparse CNN accelerators. We have shown the CSR format as an example of the sparse format though other sparse format such as bitmap-based compression can also be used for sparse CNN accelerators.

Since CNN operations can be generally performed with matrix multiplication, we explain matrix multiplication accelerators, which can be used for CNN acceleration. The sparse matrix multiplication (SpMM) can be performed in typical central processing units (CPUs) or GPUs. However, CPUs do not perform data parallel workloads well while they have strengths on executing the control-intensive workloads. Although graphic processing units (GPU)s (e.g., NVIDIA V100 [150]) could be an alternative for executing the data parallel workloads, GPU cannot skip the zero multiply and accumulations (MAC)s and only provides a rigid support for sparsity, worsening the performance and energy efficiency. In addition, GPUs are typically power-hungry, making them hard to be deployed in systems that have a tight cost budget. On the other hand, systolic arrays such as Google tensor processing units (TPUs) [78] have strengths in executing matrix multiplications. However, the systolic arrays, which are explained in Chapter 6 of this book, cannot also skip the zero MACs due to their fixed dataflow. Thus, a specialized accelerator for SpMM will be a key component for performance and power efficiency of modern computer systems.

For efficient SpMM, there are two traditional and well-known approaches: inner-product and outer-product. For explanation of the inner-product and the outer-product, we assume that we perform the matrix multiplication $A \times B = C$. The dimensions of matrices A, B, and C are $M \times N$, $N \times K$, and $M \times K$, respectively. The inner-product approach performs the dot product between each row of A and each column of B. As shown in Figure 9.3, a dot product is performed for each row vector u in A and each column vector v in B to generate each scalar element

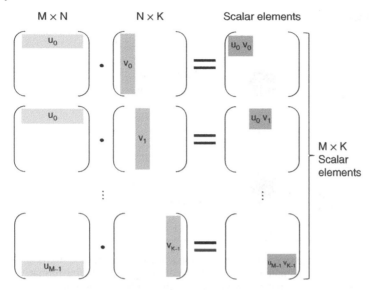

Figure 9.3 Inner product-based matrix multiplication.

in the matrix C. The outer-product approach performs the outer product between each column of A and each row of B. As shown in Figure 9.4, an outer-product between the two vectors is performed for each column vector u in A and each row vector v in B to generate $N \times N$ partial sum matrices with the dimension $M \times K$. Generation of partial sum matrices can be better understood and visualized by considering the dimensions of vector u and v. The vector u in A is of dimension $M \times 1$ and the vector v in B is of dimension $1 \times K$, so when we multiply the vector u with the vector v, we get a matrix of dimension $M \times K$, which is a partial sum matrix in the context of original matrix multiplication of matrices A and B. To generate the matrix C of dimension $M \times K$, all the partial sum matrices are added.

For sparse matrix multiplication, to remove the MAC operations with zero elements, the inner-product must match the column indices of the nonzero elements in the row vector of the matrix A and row indices of the nonzero elements in the column vector of the matrix B during the dot-product, making the hardware design complicated. Though the outer-product does not require the index matching, partial results from the cross-product require a large on-chip memory to minimize the amount of data transfer between the accelerator and the off-chip memory. In addition, in the cases of inner-product and outer-product, accessing the column of the matrices could be difficult for exploiting the locality. In order to fully exploit the locality from the matrix column, the matrix (i.e., B in the inner-product and A in the outer-product) should be stored in a transposed format, eventually causing the burden of transposing operations. To overcome the drawbacks of the inner- and outer-product, one can utilize a row-wise product-based approach as an

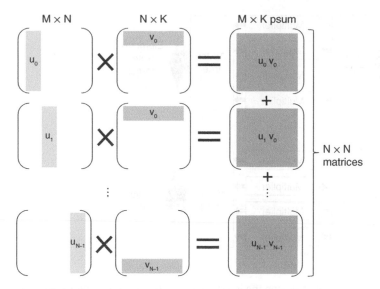

Figure 9.4 Outer product-based matrix multiplication.

alternative. The main advantages of the row-wise product matrix multiplication can be summarized as follows: First, it does not need to perform index matching. Second, it does not require a huge size of on-chip memory which is necessary for storing the partial results. Third, it does not require columnwise access to the operand matrices, making it advantageous to exploit the locality.

Figure 9.5 briefly describes generic matrix multiplication hardware architectures for (i) inner product-based, and (ii) outer product-based matrix multiplications. Before multiplication, the inner-product-based architecture performs index matching for removal of the ineffectual operations (i.e., multiplying with zero-valued operand). Nonzero index-matched values are multiplied and accumulated for generating an element[1] in the output matrix. The outer product requires multicasting of the operands in a certain column in the matrix A to the operands in a certain row in the matrix B. After performing the multiplications, the matrix merger generates a partial matrix (or multiple partial matrices) by accumulating the partial matrices.

9.3 Recent Advancements in Sparse CNN Accelerators

As the SpMM is frequently used in a wide variety of the emerging applications, many SpMM hardware architectures have been recently introduced. One of

---

1 If we have multiple multiplier hardware, we can also generate multiple elements in parallel.

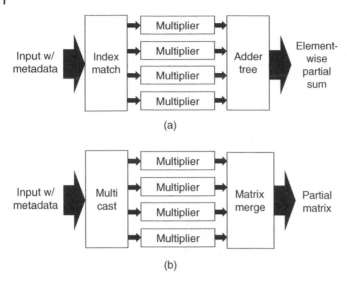

Figure 9.5 The comparison between the inner product-based and outer product-based matrix multiplication (MM) architecture. (a) Inner product-based MM architecture and (b) outer product-based MM architecture.

the most well-known and intuitive approaches for matrix multiplication is an inner-product approach. In [150], Gondimalla et al. have introduced SparTen architecture, which utilizes an inner-product based approach. They have introduced an efficient inner-join with bitmask (to mark nonzero element positions) which eventually are ANDed to identify ineffectual operations. They have also introduced a sorting-based greedy load balancing technique for the processing elements (PEs). Qin et al. [152] have also proposed an inner-product based hardware accelerator architecture, which they named as SIGMA. They have introduced a dot product engine (a.k.a., Flex-DPE) that exploits tree-based topology and forward adder network in order to support flexible interconnect. Their proposed architecture also utilizes a bitmap-based format as a compressed data format. However, only loaded operand matrix is represented by the compressed format while the streaming matrix is represented by a dense format (i.e., including both zero and non-zero elements). These inner-product based approaches inherently require index matching (or inner-join), which is not desirable for cost-efficient hardware design and implementation.

To remove the complex index matching process, several outer-product based approaches have been introduced. Zhang et al. have proposed SpArch [153] that utilizes the outer-product approach for sparse matrix multiplication. For compressed data format, SpArch utilizes condensed matrix representation that compacts non-zero elements in a row. SpArch also utilizes Huffman tree-based scheduler, which helps efficiently use memory bandwidth. When scheduling the partial result matrix generation during the outer-product, SpArch produces partial result matrices that have less nonzero elements earlier than those that have more nonzero elements. As the condensed format of the matrices with less nonzero elements will use less memory capacity, it enables an efficient use (i.e., occupying less capacity in the memory to store the partial result matrices for a longer time) of the memory and reduces memory bandwidth requirement. Hojabr et al. have proposed SPAGHETTI [154], which also utilizes the outer-product approach. SPAGHETTI uses different compressed formats for input matrices (CSR and compressed sparse column for each operand matrix) and output matrix (COO: coordinate format). Since the COO format is not a sorted format (i.e., the coordinates and values are not sorted in a format of row- or column-major order), it is hard to be utilized in an in situ manner. These outer-product based approaches typically require a large storage for partial result matrices.

In order to complement the disadvantages of the inner- and outer-product-based approaches, several row-wise product-based approaches have also been proposed. Srivastava et al. have proposed MatRaptor [155], which is a row-wise product-based approach with a new compressed format, channel cyclic sparse row (C^2SR). Exploiting that the multiplications for each row of the matrix A can be performed in parallel, MatRaptor carries out row-wise multiplication followed by sort and accumulation with the primary and helper queues. Similarly, in [156], another row-wise product-based approach has been introduced by Zhang et al., which they named as Gamma. The approach by Zhang et al. also exploits the row-level parallelism while it also employs Fiber cache, a specialized memory structure to store nonzero elements and their coordinates. In [102], Lee et al. have proposed a row-wise product-based matrix multiplication accelerator with optimal load balancing. The proposed design in [102] exploits the CSR format which is widely used for representing SpMM. The hardware accelerator performs the matrix multiplication operations with CSR-formatted operand matrices, generating the CSR-formatted output matrix. The load balancing technique proposed in [102] leads to better parallelism between the PEs. The technique considers the amount of operations assigned to each PE so that the execution time of each PE is as close as possible. In Chapters 10–12, we introduce several sparse CNN or SpMM accelerators.

9.4 Chapter Summary

This chapter explored the sparsity characteristics in CNN models and also defined sparse CNN accelerators. The chapter further provided background of sparse CNN accelerators and highlighted recent advancements in sparse

CNN accelerators. In Chapters 10–12, this book explores different sparse CNN accelerators. Chapter 10 discusses a sparse CNN accelerator that leverages in situ decompression and acceleration for compressed sparse input feature maps (IFMs) [108]. Chapter 11 and Chapter 12 discuss Sparse-PE [157] and Phantom [158], respectively, which are two sparse CNN accelerators.

10

CNN Accelerator for In Situ Decompression and Convolution of Sparse Input Feature Maps

In this chapter, an accelerator architecture that efficiently performs convolution operations with the two-step compressed data format (introduced in Chapter 4) is introduced. In addition, the introduced hardware accelerator adopts three techniques to further optimize the convolutional neural network (CNN) hardware accelerator, which is introduced in Section 10.3. The presented sparse hardware accelerator is prototyped on a field-programmable gate array-system-on-chip (FPGA-SoC). Please note that the sparse CNN acceleration technique discussed in this chapter is based on lossless compression of input feature maps (IFM)s, meaning that there is no accuracy loss by adopting the presented technique.

10.1 Overview

For CNN acceleration with data transfer overhead reduction, the presented technique exploits a HW/SW codesign methodology. Figure 10.1 shows an overall flow of the presented CNN acceleration technique for sparse input feature maps (IFMs). On the software side, the noncompressed IFM is converted into the compressed format by using the compression technique presented in Chapter 4 before it is sent to the on-chip memory in the hardware accelerator via direct memory access (DMA). The weight data are not compressed and just sent to the hardware accelerator. On the hardware side, the presented CNN accelerator performs convolution layer operations with the weight and compressed IFMs. Sections 10.2 and 10.3 present how convolution operations are performed in the hardware accelerator with the compressed IFMs.

10.2 Hardware Design Overview

Since the presented acceleration technique compresses the IFMs, it is crucial to efficiently perform convolution operations with the compressed data format.

Accelerators for Convolutional Neural Networks, First Edition.
Arslan Munir, Joonho Kong, and Mahmood Azhar Qureshi.
© 2024 The Institute of Electrical and Electronics Engineers, Inc. Published 2024 by John Wiley & Sons, Inc.

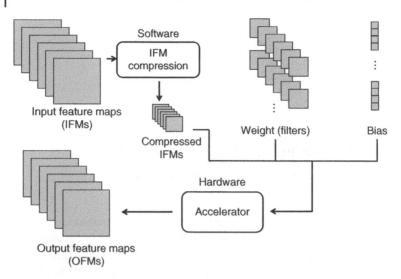

Figure 10.1 The execution flow of the presented acceleration technique.

The presented hardware accelerator performs convolution operations with only non-zero elements (NZE)s and their location information (extracted from *Indices* and *Count_table*) and avoids the multiply-accumulate (MAC) operations with the zero operands,[1] eventually resulting in performance and energy benefits proportional to the degree of input sparsity. Figure 10.2 describes the overall execution flow of the introduced hardware accelerator.

The first part of the introduced hardware accelerator is searching and weight matching. It brings the compressed IFMs (*nonzero elements*) with metadata (*indices* and *count_table*) and store them in on-chip memory in the accelerator (① in Figure 10.2). Firstly, it brings NZEs to the *nonzero element buffer* before performing the MAC operations (② in Figure 10.2). To perform MAC operations with sparse inputs, it is crucial to align the weights with the NZEs to be multiplied, which is done in the *Nonzero alignment logic*. In the *Nonzero alignment logic* (③ in Figure 10.2), there are *filter alignment logic* and *filter offset buffer*. *Filter alignment logic* (④ in Figures 10.2 and 10.3) finds the offset of the weights in the filter which will be multiplied with nonzero IFM elements. Figure 10.3 shows a detailed operation of the filter alignment logic. To perform index matching, it first restores the original IFM index in the 1D vector format by using the *Indices* and

---

1 Though we compute the MAC operations with only NZEs, it does not hurt accuracy as compared to the case without the presented compression and acceleration technique because MAC operations with the zero values are ineffectual (i.e., $N \times 0 = 0$).

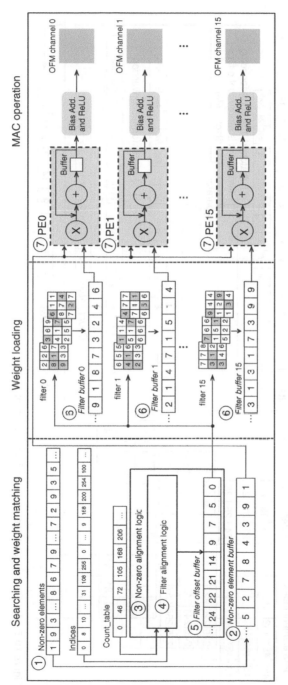

Figure 10.2 Overall architecture of the presented CNN accelerator.

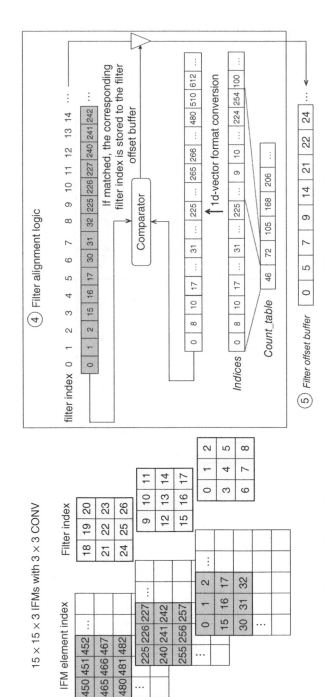

Figure 10.3 Architecture and operations of filter alignment logic.

Count_table. It then performs a comparison between the 1D vector format indices of the NZEs and the indices of the IFM area where it will perform the convolution operations (dark-gray shaded buffer in Figure 10.3). If there are matched indices, it stores the filter indices to the *filter offset buffer* (⑤ in Figures 10.2 and 10.3) in a first-in first-out (FIFO) manner.

After filling the *filter offset buffer*, the weights are loaded to the *filter buffers* (⑥ in Figure 10.2). The values in the *filter offset buffer* indicate the location of weight values in the filter. For example, Figure 10.2 shows that the weight value in the filter indices[2] 0, 5, 7, 9, 14, 21, 22, and 24 will be selected and loaded into the *filter buffers*. This process of loading filter weights into filter buffers is also depicted in weight loading part of Figure 10.2. For example, filter 0[0] corresponds to the weight value 6 in Figure 10.2, and thus it loads 6 in the *filter buffer*. The rest of the weight values are also loaded into the *filter buffer* in the same manner. Please note that the *filter buffer* holds 16 entries in the presented hardware design and implementation, although only eight entries are shown in Figure 10.2. Once 16 weight values are loaded into the *filter buffer*, it performs MAC operations with the aligned NZEs and the corresponding weights in the processing elements (PEs), followed by bias addition and activation (ReLU) (⑦ in Figure 10.2). The output feature map (OFM) elements are also stored in the on-chip memory. The presented hardware accelerator design exploits output channel-level parallelism, which means each PE performs the MAC operations for each output channel. The presented hardware accelerator design for 32-bit floating-point precision[3] uses 16 PEs though the number of PEs is also design dependent.

In the filter alignment logic, the storage for 1D vector format conversion may require the nonnegligible storage overhead. Assuming that the maximum number of NZEs is 2^{16}, we need 128KB ($2B \times 2^{16}$) on-chip buffer to temporarily store the converted indices for 1D vector format. It accounts for the on-chip buffer size of 10.3% (=128 KB/1247 KB; 1247 KB is the total block random access memory (BRAM) usage in the presented FPGA prototype with floating-point 32-bit precision support), which is not a significant overhead. To alleviate this overhead, the counter or on-demand conversion may help reduce the on-chip buffer requirements of the presented design, though it should be done with further design optimizations.

---

2 1D vector index is used instead of 3D tensor index in the filter. It means
Filter[z][y][x] = Filter[x+y*width+z*width*height].
3 We have also implemented 16-bit fixed-point precision-based accelerator with 32 PEs, which is explained in Section 10.4

10.3   Design Optimization Techniques Utilized in the Hardware Accelerator

While the back-end (MAC PEs, bias addition, and activation) logic is very similar to the conventional CNN accelerators, the front-end logic (searching and weight matching, and weight loading) is newly introduced in the presented design. Though the baseline (i.e., introduced in Section 10.2) hardware design can bring a nonnegligible performance benefit, one can further optimize the front-end of an accelerator for even better performance. The presented accelerator design leverages three design optimization techniques for the front-end part of the accelerator.

- **Parallel Searching and Weight Matching**: The most performance-critical aspect of the presented hardware accelerator is searching and weight matching that finds and aligns filter weights that will be multiplied with the NZEs in IFMs. It needs to compare the NZE indices to the original 1D vector index in the IFM, which is performed sequentially in the baseline design. For better performance, it uses multiple comparison logics (16 in the presented design) so that the searching and weight matching can be performed for multiple NZEs in parallel.
- **Input Data Reuse**: $N \times N$ kernels with $N>1$ provide an opportunity for IFM data reuse. For example, let us assume that it performs 3×3 convolution operations with the depth of 3 (i.e., $\mathbf{3 \times 3 \times 3}$ filter). For the next adjacent OFM element, instead of searching 27 ($\mathbf{3 \times 3 \times 3}$) elements and reloading all NZEs to the *nonzero element buffer*, it can search and load the data for only nine elements while the rest 18 elements are reused in the *nonzero element buffer*. This is because 3×3 convolutions (CONV) (in general, all $N \times N$ kernels with $N>1$) is carried out in a sliding window manner. Please note here that 3×3 CONV operation is performed with a sliding window-based operation [159], while it does not mean that the presented hardware uses sliding window logic. Assuming the kernel window slides in a row-major order, the IFM elements overlapped with the second and third columns of the 3×3 kernel can be reused in CONV operations for the next adjacent OFM element. On the other hand, when performing 1×1 convolution, it does not perform the input data reuse as 1×1 convolution has no opportunity for IFM data reuse in the presented design.[4]
- **Removal of Complex Operations**: Searching and weight matching require several complex operations such as division and modulo to calculate offset or index values. The presented hardware design replaces those complex operations with simpler operations such as shift operations or table lookup so that the

---

4 For 1×1 CONV, since there is no overlapped IFM element when sliding the kernel window, it cannot reuse the input data.

latency for searching and matching can be reduced. For removal of the complex operations, it does not actually affect the data (e.g., NZEs), while it only reduces the complexity of the required operations, resulting in performance improvement. According to the evaluations, the removal of complex operations results in 1.7× and 2.4× speedups for 1 × 1 and 3 × 3 CONV, respectively, as compared to the case without the removal of complex operations, implying that the removal of complex operations affects performance significantly.

10.4 FPGA Implementation

We implement the presented hardware accelerator and software (for compression) in Xilinx ZCU106 FPGA-SoC platform [160], which is equipped with a quad-core ARM Cortex-A53 CPU [161], programmable logic elements, and various hard intellectual properties (IPs). The presented hardware accelerator is implemented in the programmable logic part while the introduced compression algorithm is implemented in software and executed on the CPU on-board Xilinx ZCU106 FPGA-SoC platform.

For hardware implementation, Xilinx high-level synthesis (HLS), and Vivado design suite are used. The implemented hardware accelerator operates at 150 MHz clock frequency. Although we have explained the compression technique based on 32-bit floating-point elements, the presented hardware accelerator has been implemented with two different versions of precisions, 32-bit floating-point and 16-bit fixed-point. In the resource-constrained mobile or edge platforms, the data quantization is a common technique for efficient on-device CNN inferences. This implementation of the presented CNN accelerator with 32-bit floating-point and 16-bit fixed-point is expedient as many CNN hardware accelerators have been implemented to process 16-bit fixed-point as well as 32-bit floating-point elements for CNN inferences. Please note that the compression technique (presented in Chapter 4) can be identically employed to both versions of the accelerator. Furthermore, the IFM compression technique can be applied for other quantization levels, such as 5-bit quantization or log quantization. However, in this work, we have explained the presented approach with two different precisions (32-bit floating-point for the compression technique and accelerator and 16-bit fixed-point for the accelerator). Depending on the CNN applications, a system designer can choose an appropriate version of the accelerator. Due to the reduced resource usages of the 16-bit fixed-point version of the accelerator under the same number of PEs, we increase the number of PEs from 16 to 32 in the 16-bit fixed-point version. Table 10.1 summarizes the resource utilization of the presented hardware accelerator's implementation in Xilinx ZCU106. The results in Table 10.1 correspond to the presented hardware accelerator implementation

Table 10.1   FPGA resource utilization of the presented hardware accelerator implementations.

	32-bit floating-point	16-bit fixed-point	Available resources
BRAM 18Kb	554 (88%)	458 (73%)	624
DSP48E	136 (8%)	540 (31%)	1,728
FF	64,600 (14%)	35,458 (7%)	460,800
LUT	66,481 (29%)	132,143 (57%)	230,400

that incorporates all the optimization techniques discussed in Section 10.3. For both versions of the accelerators, the implementation can execute both 1×1 CONV and 3×3 CONV versatility. The presented accelerator design focuses on the cost efficiency, which means the main goal is to improve performance per resource usage (cost). As seen from Table 10.1, the absolute amount of the resource usage as well as usage rates of the presented implementation is very low, meaning that the presented design and implementation are well suited for resource-constrained systems. When comparing the 16-bit fixed-point version to the 32-bit floating-point version, the former uses less BRAM blocks as it uses 16-bit elements instead of 32-bit elements. However, the 16-bit fixed-point version uses more digital signal processor (DSP)s, flip-flops (FF)s, and lookup table (LUT)s because of the increased number of PEs as compared to the 32-bit floating-point version.

For both the 32-bit floating-point and 16-bit fixed-point versions, the resource utilization of 18 kb BRAM (i.e., on-chip memory) blocks is still higher than that of the other components such as LUTs and FFs. The presented implementation uses BRAM blocks to store the compressed IFMs, weights, and OFMs. To exploit the parallelism between the output channels with multiple PEs, we need to maintain as many IFMs, weights, and OFMs on-chip as possible, resulting in high resource utilization of the BRAM blocks. While hardware resource utilization of the searching and weight matching part, which is mainly composed of the LUTs and FFs, is hardly proportional to the number of PEs (because it is shared between the PEs), that of the other parts including BRAM blocks is linearly proportional to the number of PEs. For the best performance in the platform, we have implemented the presented accelerator to have as many processing elements (please note that the number of processing elements is 2^N where integer $N \geq 0$) as possible, resulting in high BRAM block utilizations in the platform.

10.5 Evaluation Results

Since we have prototyped the presented sparse CNN accelerator in FPGA-SoC, direct quantitative comparison with many of the previously proposed CNN accelerators would be infeasible as some of the previously proposed CNN accelerators have been implemented in application-specific integrated circuit (ASIC) [44, 45], which hugely differs from an FPGA in terms of the degree of logic optimizations, or some of the accelerators have been evaluated in simulators [162, 163]. Hence, Section 10.5.1 compare the introduced technique to CPU-based (i.e., fully software-based with 1.2 GHz clock frequency) CNN inference with Darknet framework [143] (by only comparing CONV layer execution time) with a single-core execution. Though the ZCU106 platform has quad-core Cortex-A53 CPU, the reason why we assume a single-core CPU execution as a baseline is that the main target for the presented technique is a resource-constrained system. For example, the resource-constrained edge devices (e.g., IoT devices) often use a single-core CPU due to resource and power constraint (e.g., Raspberry Pi Zero [164] still uses a single-core CPU, ARM1176 series CPU [165]). We have compiled the software code for two different versions: without and with single instruction multiple data (SIMD) vector instruction supports for both baseline and the presented acceleration technique. Section 10.5.2 provides quantitative comparison results of the presented hardware accelerator implementation as compared to the previous FPGA-based hardware accelerators.

For benchmarks, six convolution layers from SqueezeNet [62] have been selected: CONV layers 15, 17, 26, 28, 41, and 43. Table 10.2 summarizes the configurations of the convolution layers used for the evaluation. When executing the selected six layers, all the data (input, output, and weight) required for processing a single CONV layer can be fit into the accelerator on-chip memory (i.e., BRAM in the FPGA-SoC). Though we run the experiments with the selected six layers, we believe that it does not hurt the generality of the evaluation. For the layers in which all the data cannot be fit into the accelerator on-chip memory, we can perform the accelerator execution along with the DMA data transfer multiple times. In this case, performance can be easily estimated by adding the results of accelerator execution time and DMA data transfer time obtained from executing the accelerator and DMA transfer multiple times. For IFMs used for the evaluations, we have synthetically generated 100 random-valued IFMs for each degree of sparsity (50%, 60%, 70%, 80%, and 90%). For evaluations of performance, energy, and data transfer, 32-bit floating-point version of the hardware accelerator is

Table 10.2 The configurations of CNN layers for evaluations.

	Layer 15	Layer 17	Layer 26	Layer 28	Layer 41	Layer 43
IFM size	$29 \times 29 \times 32$	$29 \times 29 \times 32$	$15 \times 15 \times 48$	$15 \times 15 \times 48$	$15 \times 15 \times 64$	$15 \times 15 \times 64$
OFM size	$29 \times 29 \times 128$	$29 \times 29 \times 128$	$15 \times 15 \times 192$	$15 \times 15 \times 192$	$15 \times 15 \times 256$	$15 \times 15 \times 256$
Filter size	$1 \times 1 \times 32$	$3 \times 3 \times 32$	$1 \times 1 \times 48$	$3 \times 3 \times 48$	$1 \times 1 \times 64$	$3 \times 3 \times 64$
# of filters	128	128	192	192	256	256
Stride	1	1	1	1	1	1
Pad	0	1	0	1	0	1

The layers' configurations are based on SqueezeNet implementation in Darknet Framework.
Source: Adapted from [143].

used since the baseline CNN framework [143] only supports 32-bit floating-point precision while not supporting the 16-bit fixed-point precision [166].

10.5.1 Performance and Energy

Figure 10.4 summarizes performance comparison across various levels of IFM sparsity. Please note that the performance is normalized to the case of CPU-based CNN inference without the IFM compression. For fair comparison, the DMA data transfer time (both read and write) and compression time[5] are also included to the total execution time in the case of the presented design. In the cases of executing 1×1 CONV and 3×3 CONV, the presented technique leads to better performance by 3.4× to 5.4× and 11.3× to 22.6×, respectively, as compared to the CPU-based execution without SIMD supports. Even when comparing with the CPU-based execution with SIMD supports, the presented technique still leads to better performance by 1.1× to 1.7× and 3.5× to 7.1× in the cases of 1×1 CONV and 3×3 CONV, respectively. As demonstrated in the results, the presented acceleration technique shows better performance (compared to the CPU-based execution) in 3×3 CONV rather than 1×1 CONV. This is because the presented hardware design is versatile for both 1×1 CONV and 3×3 CONV. Since 3×3 CONV has more complex operations compared to 1×1 CONV, the presented hardware design is mainly optimized for 3×3 CONV rather than 1×1 CONV. Moreover, the hardware logic for data

---

5 The OFMs of the previous layer are IFMs of the current layer in CNNs, thus inherently incorporating the recompression latency for the OFMs of the previous layer in the latency evaluation. According to the evaluation, the compression latency on the software side occupies only a small portion of the entire latency (3.5%–9.5% of the entire latency).

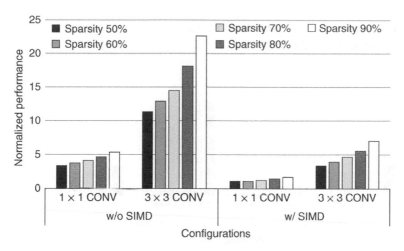

Figure 10.4 Performance comparison of the presented acceleration technique normalized to the CPU-based execution w/o and w/SIMD supports.

Table 10.3 Average power results obtained from Xilinx Vivado.

	Processor system (PS)		Programmable logic (PL)	
	Static	**Dynamic**	**Static**	**Dynamic**
Power (W)	0.100	2.701	0.602	1.133

reuse is only for 3×3 CONV, which is merely regarded as hardware overhead in the case of 1×1 CONV.

The presented acceleration technique also reduces energy consumption due to significant reduction of execution time for CNN inferences. For energy calculation, we utilize estimated average power results (shown in Table 10.3) from Vivado tool. The static power is always consumed as long as the system is turned on while the dynamic power is only consumed when the component is running. Thus, in order to obtain power consumption of the baseline (i.e., only CPU execution), we add the dynamic and static power of the processor system (PS: CPU part) and only static power of the programmable logic (PL: FPGA part). For energy calculation of the baseline, we multiply average power consumption by the execution time. To obtain the power consumption when employing the presented acceleration technique, we break down the execution into two phases: data compression and CONV which are performed in the CPU and accelerator, respectively. When performing the data compression, the total system power consumption is equal to an addition

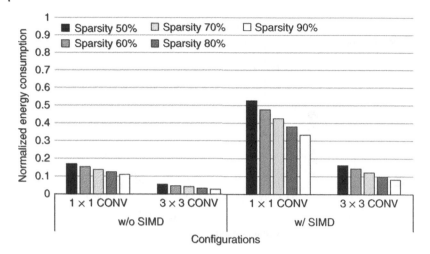

Figure 10.5 Energy comparison of the presented acceleration technique normalized to the CPU-based execution w/o and w/SIMD supports.

of dynamic and static power of the PS and only static power of the PL (excluding the dynamic power of the PL). On the other hand, when performing the CONV operations in the accelerator, the total system power consumption is equal to the addition of static power of the PS (excluding the dynamic power of the PS) and dynamic and static power of the PL. To calculate the total energy consumption, for each execution phase, we multiply the execution time by the total system power consumption and aggregate the energy consumption of the two phases.

Figure 10.5 shows the energy results normalized to the CPU-based CNN inference across various levels of IFM sparsity. As compared to the CPU-based execution without SIMD supports, the presented technique reduces system-level energy consumption by 83.4%–89.3% and 95.0%–97.4% in the cases of 1×1 CONV and 3×3 CONV, respectively. When the SIMD supports in the CPU are available, the presented technique still reduces energy consumption by 47.7%–66.9% and 84.0%–91.9% in the cases of 1×1 CONV and 3×3 CONV, respectively. As demonstrated in the energy results, the presented technique leads to a huge energy reduction, implying the presented technique is suitable for resource-constrained embedded systems such as tiny Internet of things (IoT) devices.

10.5.2 Comparison with State-of-the-Art Hardware Accelerator Implementations

We compare the two versions (32-bit floating-point and 16-bit fixed-point precision) of the presented hardware accelerator implementation with several recent

FPGA-based CNN accelerator implementations [138, 148, 167–169]. For quantifying the cost (area) efficiency, the most fair way to perform comparison would be based on the hardware implementations of [138, 148, 167–169] under the same or similar costs. However, it is not possible to implement the hardware designs in [138, 148, 167, 168], and [169] to have hardware cost (or resource usages) same or similar to the presented accelerator (i.e., our own implementations of the accelerators in [138, 148, 167, 168], and [169] that have the costs similar to the presented accelerator may distort the results due to suboptimal or different implementations compared to those in [138, 148, 167, 168], and [169]). Thus, we introduce the metric, giga operations per second per unit cost (GOPs/cost), which quantifies the performance of the accelerator at iso-cost. We clarify that the cost here estimates the area required for implementing the accelerator in an FPGA fabric and BRAM blocks.

The cost is estimated based on resource usage and the number of the transistors required for each hardware resource component. Firstly, we calculate the number of metal-oxide-semiconductor (MOS) transistors required for implementing each type of components. For calculation of the 18kb BRAM block, we multiply 6 (6T SRAM cell) by the number of cells (18*1024) in the block. For FFs, we assume that the FF is composed of two cascaded latches (SRAMs), requiring 12 transistors for each FF. For lookup tables (LUTs), we assume 5×1 LUTs which are commonly used in the modern FPGAs. A single 5×1 LUT can be implemented with 32 SRAMs and 31 2×1 MUXes [171]. For LUT cost calculations, we only consider the SRAM cost because SRAM cells typically occupy large area (due to the sizing of the transistor) than 2×1 MUXes. Please note that excluding the 2×1 MUX area is still a conservative assumption as the implementation uses the smaller number of the LUTs (see Table 10.4). Due to the lack of the detailed design and implementation of DSPs, we omit the cost of the DSPs. For the technology-dependent (TD) cost, we multiply the square of the process technology (T^2) [171] (e.g., 16 nm, 28 nm) with the number of required MOS transistors (N_{Tr}) for each type of components. After that, by multiplying the number of used blocks or elements in the FPGA with $T^2 \times N_{Tr}$, we can estimate the relative cost (area) of the three different components (i.e., BRAM blocks, FFs, and LUTs) in the FPGA. By aggregating the relative costs of the three types of the components, we can figure out the entire relative cost of a certain accelerator implementation. Finally, we normalize the relative cost of each implementation to that of the presented 16-bit fixed point implementation.

As shown in Table 10.4, although the presented implementations attain lower absolute GOPs as compared to the implementations in [138, 148, 167, 168], and [169], the 16-bit fixed-point version of the presented hardware implementation achieves 1.9× (on average) better technology-dependent performance per unit cost as compared to [138, 148, 167, 168], and [169]. Similarly, 32-bit

Table 10.4 Quantitative comparison of the presented hardware accelerator with the state-of-the-art designs.

Comparison metrics	[167]	[168]	[138]	[169]	[148]	Presented accelerator (32-bit floating point)	Presented accelerator (16-bit fixed point)
Platform	Zynq7100-based	Virtex7-based	Zynq7100-based	VC709	VC707	ZCU106	ZCU106
Process technology	28 nm	28 nm	28 nm	28 nm	28 nm	16 nm	16 nm
Precision	16-bit fixed	32-bit float	32-bit float	32-bit float	32-bit float	32-bit float	16-bit fixed
Clock (MHz)	60	200	100	200	100	150	150
BRAM blocks (18 Kb)	772	1,515	708	1,121	1,024	554	458
FF	107K	383K	187,146	292,016	205,704	64,600	35,458
LUT	229K	252K	142,291	192,493	186,251	66,481	132,143
DSP	128	1,123	1,926	1,032	2,240	136	540
GOPs	17.2	78.3	17.1	66.4	61.6	6.8	10.9
Power (W)	2.3	6.0	3.3	5.3	3.6	2.4	2.7
TD Relative estimated cost except DSP	5.23	8.83	4.32	6.59	6.07	0.98	1.00
TD GOPs/cost	3.29	8.87	3.96	10.07	10.15	6.94	10.90

Comparison with [167] is provided for FPGA-based accelerator introduced in [167]. Comparison with [168] is provided for the 32-bit floating-point accelerator introduced in [168] because 16-bit fixed-point version accelerator in [168] has huge resource usage (e.g., LUTs and FFs usage over 460K and 640K, respectively, and a 99.6% BRAM usage in Virtex7 FPGA), which would not be suitable for resource-constrained systems. "TD" means the technology-dependent, considering the process technology impact.
Source: Adapted from [138, 148, 167–169]

floating-point version of the presented hardware implementation also attains better technology-dependent performance per unit cost as compared to [138] and [167]. On the other hand, the presented implementations use much less DSP blocks compared to the other designs. Considering that the cost estimated here excludes the cost of the DSP blocks, the actual (i.e., DSP-included) technology-dependent cost efficiency of the presented implementations will be much better as compared to [138, 148, 167, 168], and [169]. In summary, the presented hardware accelerator is very suitable for resource-constrained systems where performance under the limited hardware cost is the most important design metric. Moreover, in terms of power consumption (obtained from Xilinx power estimator tool [172]), Table 10.4 indicates that the presented implementations show lower power consumption than [138, 148, 168], and [169] assuming that the accelerators are implemented in the same FPGA device (i.e., the implementation is technology-independent). These power results verify that the presented acceleration is more suitable for low-power, low-energy, and resource-constrained systems as compared to the contemporary CNN accelerators. Though the presented accelerator shows a little higher power consumption than [167], the TD GOPs/cost of the presented accelerator is much better than [167], leading to a better tradeoff between cost efficiency and power consumption.

Unlike the works which only present hardware accelerators, the presented technique also have additional benefits for end-to-end system performance and energy (i.e., considering not only hardware but also software stack) by using the software-based compression. The end-to-end performance and energy comparison of the presented work with other works is not presented in Table 10.4 because the presented technique combines the software-based compression with the tailored hardware accelerator design, whereas the other works only present hardware accelerators. It also means end-to-end performance comparisons to the other accelerators [138, 148, 167–169] with the same software optimizations would result in misleading because the software optimizations would affect differently to the various accelerators. Meanwhile, as presented in Chapter 4, the IFM compression technique reduces memory access latency and the data size to be transferred between the accelerator and the off-chip memory, which leads to significant performance and energy efficiency benefits.

10.6 Chapter Summary

This chapter introduced a novel CNN accelerator that exploited sparsity in IFMs to enhance performance, reduce energy consumption, and curtail data transfer between the accelerator and the off-chip main memory. The introduced hardware accelerator performed convolution layer operations with the compressed IFM engendering performance improvement and energy reduction. The discussed sparse CNN accelerator was implemented on an FPGA-SoC platform (Xilinx ZCU106). Evaluation results from the prototype implementation demonstrated that the presented technique improved performance by 1.1× to 22.6× depending on the degree of the sparsity and filter size as compared to the CPU-based convolution layer execution. In terms of energy, the presented technique led to 47.7%–97.4% energy reduction as compared to the CPU-based execution. Moreover, the presented hardware accelerator design attained 1.9× (on average) better cost efficiency with less or comparable power consumption as compared to several state-of-the-art CNN accelerator designs. Results verified the suitability of the presented accelerator for resource-constrained artificial intelligence (AI) systems such as intelligent embedded and Internet of things (IoT) devices that require performance- and energy-efficient CNN inference.

11

Sparse-PE: A Sparse CNN Accelerator

High-accuracy convolutional neural network (CNN) models [30–32] proposed in recent years have further strengthened the notion of employing CNNs for various vision-based AI applications. These CNN models require massive amounts of convolution operations over a series of network layers to perform a classification task during the inference phase. These tremendous number of computations (typically in tens of millions) present a huge challenge for the devices employing these CNN models. In addition, because of the large number of network layers and varying layer dimensions, the massive CNN model cannot be stored in the on-chip memory of the device, and, therefore, requires off-chip dynamic random access memory (DRAM) which presents high DRAM access cost. To put this in perspective, the energy cost per fetch for 32b coefficients in an off-chip LPDDR2 DRAM is about 640 pJ, which is about 6400× the energy cost of a 32b integer ADD operation [36]. The energy cost from just the DRAM accesses would be well beyond the limitations of an embedded mobile device employing the CNN.

Various techniques have been developed to address the compute and memory bandwidth issues of a neural network accelerator, running a CNN. *Mobilenets* [33, 34] were developed to reduce the total number of computations by splitting a regular convolution operation into separable convolutions (depthwise and pointwise), without incurring a loss in accuracy. Another widely used approach for decreasing the model size is the reduction in precision of both weights and activations using various quantization strategies [37–39]. This again does not result in a significant loss in accuracy and reduces the model size by a considerable amount. Hardware implementations such as Envision [40], NeuroMAX [96], UNPU [41], and Stripes [42] show how reduced bit precision, and quantization, translates into increased throughput and savings in energy.

Nonlinear activation functions [6], in addition to deep layers, are one of the key characteristics that improve the accuracy of a CNN model. Typically, nonlinearity is added by incorporating activation functions, the most common being the rectified linear unit (ReLU) [6]. The ReLU converts all negative values in a

Accelerators for Convolutional Neural Networks, First Edition.
Arslan Munir, Joonho Kong, and Mahmood Azhar Qureshi.

feature map to zeros. Since the output of one layer is the input to the next layer, many of the computations, within a layer, involve multiplication with zeros. These feature maps containing zeros are referred to as *one-sided* sparse feature maps. The multiplications resulting from this one-sided sparsity wastes compute cycles and decreases the *effective* throughput and hardware utilization, thus, reducing the overall performance of the accelerator. It also results in high-energy cost as the transfer of zeros to/from off-chip memory is a wasted memory access. In order to reduce the computational and memory access volume, previous works [43–45] have exploited this one-sided sparsity and displayed some performance improvements.

The ReLU, being one of the most commonly used activation function, converts all negative values in a feature map to zeros, thereby, introducing the notion of *one-sided* sparsity. *Two-sided* sparsity is introduced when, in addition to the feature maps, the weight data also consists of zeros. Han et al. [46] presented an iterative method of CNN compression that resulted in a *two-sided* sparsity, that is, sparsity in both weights and activations, leading to an approximate 9× and 13× reduction in model size for AlexNet and VGG-16, respectively. A compute reduction of 4–9×, depending on the model, was also observed. These compute and memory gains, in theory, are very encouraging; however, designing an accelerator that leverages the two-sided sparsity is quite challenging as it results in inconsistency in data accesses and load imbalance.

Compression of deep neural network (DNN) models was introduced the first time in [46]. Han et al. [46] iteratively pruned the connections based on parameter threshold, and performed retraining to retain accuracy. This process resulted in *two-sided* sparsity, i.e., sparsity in both weights and activations, which led to approximately 9× model reduction for AlexNet, and 13× reduction for VGG-16. It also resulted in 4–9× *effective* compute reduction (depending on the model). These gains seem very promising; however, designing an accelerator architecture to leverage them is quite challenging because of the following reasons:

(1) Data Access Inconsistency: Computation gating is one of the most common ways by which sparsity is generally exploited. Whenever a zero in the activation or the weight data is read, no operation is performed. This results in energy savings but has no impact on the throughput because of the wastage of compute cycle. Complex read logic needs to be implemented to discard the zeros, and instead, perform effective computations on nonzero data. Some previous works [52, 53] use sparse compression formats like compressed sparse column (CSC) or compressed sparse row (CSR) to represent sparse data. These formats have variable lengths and make *looking ahead* difficult if both the weight, and the activation sparsity is being considered. Other than that, developing the complex control and read logic to process these formats can be quite challenging.

(2) Low Utilization of the Processing Element (PE) Array: Convolution operations for CNN inference are usually performed using an array of two-dimensional PEs in a CNN accelerator. Different dataflows (input stationary, output stationary, and row stationary) have been proposed that efficiently map the weight data and the activation data on to the PE array to maximize the throughput [6]. Sparsity introduces inconsistency in the scheduling of data thereby reducing the hardware utilization. The subset of PEs provided with more sparse data have idle times while those provided with less sparse (or more dense) data are fully active. This bounds the throughput of the accelerator to the most active PEs, and therefore, leads to the under utilization of the PE array.

Considering the abovementioned issues, many accelerators have been proposed in the past that attempt to strike a balance between hardware resource complexity and performance improvements. Cnvlutin [43] attempts to exploit sparsity by skipping the computations during *zero* activation data. It, however, does not avoid transfer of zeros and only skips cycles for zero-activations but not zero-weights. This results in exploitation of only *one sided* sparsity. Eyeriss [45] only gates computations for sparse activations. Eyeriss v2 [52] attempts to address the two-sided sparsity by using CSC format for both the activations and weights. It, however, requires complex read logic embedded within a PE that drastically increases the area by $\sim 93\%$ when compared to the original Eyeriss [45]. Cambricon-X [44] does not store activations in compressed format, while Cambricon-S [173] forces regularity by employing coarse grain pruning that affects accuracy. Even though it discards zeros during computation, it still retrieves and stores them. EIE [53] exploits the two-sided sparsity, albeit *only* in fully connected (FC) layers. EIE's performance is equivalent to one-sided sparsity as it discards zeros in the filter but wastes compute cycles due to being idle. Sparse CNN (SCNN) [162] targets two-sided sparsity but suffers heavily from inefficient microarchitecture and systematic load imbalance as explained in [151]. It, also, can not handle nonunit stride convolutions and FC layers. To address the complexity associated with the CSC compression format, SparTen [151] uses sparse bit mask to represent the location of zeros and nonzero data values. SparTen, however, needs an offline load balancing strategy, which it refers to as *Greedy Balancing*, to address the systematic load imbalance. The balancing is performed based on the filter density using either a software-only approach (GB-S), or a software-hardware hybrid (GB-H). This form of balancing adds extra latency and complicates the synchronization of various compute threads. SparTen also employs *Permuter* and *Output Collector Units* for the computation clusters to merge and/or accumulate the outputs from *independently* running compute units. These circuits require rather complex hardware and the complexity grows exponentially as the number of compute units are increased. In addition, SparTen, like SCNN, has no support for FC layers.

This chapter introduces Sparse-PE, a high performance, multithreaded, generic processing engine (PE) core for sparse CNN computations [157]. Unlike many previous works, this PE design can exploit full or *two-sided* sparsity and can be used for sparse computations in any layer in a typical CNN model. While the previous approaches use complex PE designs targeted toward their specific accelerator architectures, the Sparse-PE core is generic in nature and can be used as a general purpose, sparse dot product compute core. The main contributions in this chapter can be summarized as follows:

- Presenting Sparse-PE, a multithreaded, high performance, processing engine core, ideal for *two-sided* sparse computations. The core works by actively skipping a huge number of *ineffective* computations ($zero_w \times zero_a$, $zero_w \times nonzero_a$, $nonzero_w \times zero_a$) involving zeros, while only favoring *effective* computations ($nonzero_w \times nonzero_a$). This is accomplished by the use of novel selection, computation, and accumulation blocks to dynamically allocate maximum, *nonzero* computations, on to a thread matrix inside the core to drastically improve the hardware utilization. The presented PE core does not target a specific architecture, and thus, can be modified for any accelerator design.
- Unlike previous approaches that use CSC format for their PEs, the Sparse-PE core uses bit mask (BM) representation for sparse computations. We show that, on average, the CSC format has 3× higher DRAM memory accesses compared to the BM representation which directly translates into higher energy requirements for the CSC format.
- Developing a cycle-accurate performance simulator for an accelerator that uses the Sparse-PE cores and show drastic performance improvement over various recently proposed dense and sparse CNN accelerators, and high hardware utilization over a range of sparsity levels. Experiments show that the Sparse-PE core-based accelerator has a performance gain of 12× over a recently proposed dense accelerator NeuroMAX (discussed in Chapter 8 of this book). For sparse accelerators, it provides a performance gain of 4.2×, 2.38×, and 1.98× over SCNN, Eyeriss v2, and SparTen, respectively. An register transfer level (RTL) implementation of the core on Xilinx Z-7100 SoC is also done and a detailed module level breakdown of the field-programmable gate array (FPGA) primitives cost, static random access memory (SRAM) cost, and power consumption of the core is shown.

The remainder of the chapter is organized as follows: Section 11.1 gives a background on CNN sparsity and layer-by-layer sparsity associated with various popular CNN models. Section 11.2 presents the introduced Sparse-PE core and its inner workings. Experimental methodology, simulation results, comparisons, and implementation cost are given in Section 11.3. Lastly, Section 11.4 concludes this chapter.

11.1 Related Work

Many dense architectures have been introduced in the past for acceleration of CNN inferences. Accelerators proposed in [39, 126, 127] optimize compute, whereas [131, 132] optimize memory bandwidth. Quantization (linear [39, 175] and log [37, 38]) of weights and activations provides additional benefits for memory footprint and compute reductions. Accelerators such as NeuroMAX [96], VWA [142], UNPU [41], and Stripes [42] show how reduction in bit precision, improved dataflow, and quantization, increases throughput and saves energy. Another set of accelerators [138, 139] provide efficient implementation of separable convolutions on FPGA hardware. These, however, cannot handle regular convolution and FC layers which are almost always a part of CNN models. Accelerators proposed in [133, 134] use Booth encoding to avoid the use of zeros to reduce the total computations. They, however, still transfer zeros to and from memory which incurs SRAM area and energy. Block circulant matrices for weights were introduced in CirCNN [135]. CirCNN, however, requires complex fast Fourier transform (FFT) operations in its PE design. It also does not capture two-sided sparsity. In-memory accelerators [136, 137] have also been presented that use analog logic design to perform matrix multiplications within memory. Sparse multiplications, however, cannot be performed in these accelerators as they require complex arithmetic logic unit (ALU) and buffering logic. Analog circuits are also impacted by noise and variations during manufacturing process which can significantly impact the CNN model accuracy during inference.

Sparse architectures reduce the compute and memory access volume by exploiting the zeros in activations (one-sided), or both activations and weights (two-sided). Cnvlutin [43] and Cambricon-X [44] exploit one-sided sparsity by ignoring zeros in weights or input maps, but not both. Cnvlutin also does not avoid transferring of zeros and only skips cycles for activations. Tensaurus [175] accelerates sparse and dense tensor factorizations by introducing compressed interleaved sparse slice (CISS) dataflow. It, however, only supports one-sided sparsity. Recent sparse general matrix multiplication (GEMM) (SpGEMM) accelerators [152, 153, 155, 176, 177] target generalized sparse-matrix, sparse-matrix multiplications. Sigma [152] and ExTensor [176] use inner-product (output stationary) dataflow for sparse matrix multiplications. Inner product, however, is inefficient for highly sparse matrices because every element of the rows and the columns must be traversed even though there are less effectual computations (nonzero × nonzero). This leads to a significant amount of wasted computations. SpArch [153] and OuterSPACE [177] use outer-product (or input stationary) dataflow to avoid the inefficiencies associated with the traversals inherent in the inner-product dataflow. Outer-product, however, gives poor output reuse as the partial outputs generated are much more than the final outputs causing significant memory traffic. Finally, MatRaptor introduces a modified version of the CSR format referred to as channel cyclic sparse row (C^2SR) for better reuse and memory efficiency but requires complex encoding for output matrices. Eyeriss v2 [52] uses the CSC format for both weights and activations to address the two-sided sparsity. It, however, suffers from systematic load imbalance due to variations in the density of the sparse matrices. The PE design of Eyeriss v2 also requires complex buffering logic that drastically increases the area by ~93% when compared to the original Eyeriss [45]. EIE [53] exploits the two-sided sparsity in FC layers and does not address the CONV layers. EIE essentially discards zeros in weights but remains idle, thus, wasting compute cycles. Sparse CNN (SCNN) [162] targets two-sided sparsity, but its PEs suffer from inefficient microarchitecture and system-level load imbalance (also pointed out in [151]). SCNN, also, is incapable of handling nonunit stride convolutions and FC layers. Although some previous accelerator architectures attempt to exploit sparsity in CNNs, they do not address the issues related to high PE cost, inefficient microarchitecture, and dependence of PE on accelerator design. We design a multithreaded PE, referred to as Sparse-PE, which not only addresses the issues present in the previous designs but also can carry out general sparse dot product computations for any application.

11.2 Sparse-PE

Figure 11.1 shows a typical convolution operation in a CNN. Here, a 3×8 sparse input is convolved with a 3×3 sparse weight to generate a 1×6 output. The input and weight matrices have sparsity of 42% and 45%, respectively. The convolution operation can be broken down into six smaller convolution chunks (C0–C5), as shown in Figure 11.1. Each of the nine multiplications in a single convolution chunk are performed by a compute thread within a 3×3 compute thread matrix. The multiplications in dark gray are ineffective computations which mean that either one or both the multiplication operands are zeros, resulting in a wasted computation, whereas the multiplications in black are effective. It can be seen that, on average, 66% multiplications in a convolution chunk are ineffective (Output Sparsity OS = 6/9) which corresponds to an *effective* hardware utilization of only 33%. This represents a significant loss in computational efficiency as most of the compute cycles are wasted on ineffective computations. The Sparse-PE core addresses this issue and increases the hardware utilization, consequently the throughput, by minimizing the total number of ineffective computations performed by the 3×3 compute matrix. It does this by *looking-ahead* into the computations beforehand and scheduling only the valid computations to minimize the total compute cycles.

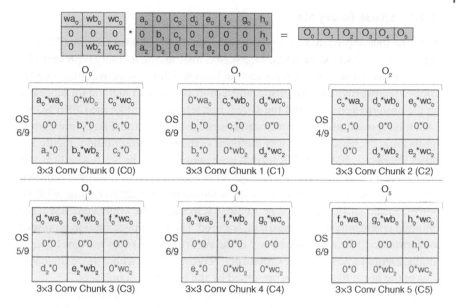

Figure 11.1 Dense convolutions.

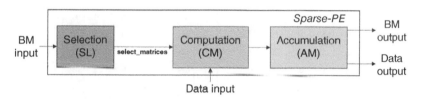

Figure 11.2 Sparse-PE architecture.

Figure 11.2 shows the high-level block diagram of the Sparse-PE core. The core takes the binary mask (BM) and data input and performs sparse computations to generate output data and binary mask. The Sparse-PE core consists of three main components: Selection (SL), Computation (CM), and Accumulation (AM). The SL block uses the sparse binary masks of input data/feature maps and weights to perform selection of valid computations ($nonzero_w \times nonzero_a$). These valid computations are represented by a set of binary matrices referred to as select matrices. The CM block uses the select matrices to map the sparse input and weight data on to a 3×3 matrix of compute threads. The mapping is performed in such a way as to maximize the utilization of individual compute threads. The AM block accumulates the CM outputs to produce valid output results. The output sparse binary mask (BM) is also generated which will be used for the next CNN layer.

11.2.1 Sparse Binary Mask

Many previous approaches use compressed sparse row (CSR) or column (CSC) formats to represent sparse data [43, 44, 53]. We, instead, use a binary representation referred to as sparse BM for representing both weights and activations. The BM representation provides a simplistic, and a more convenient method for representing the *unstored* zero data and the *stored*, nonzero data. Unlike the CSR/CSC formats, this representation does not require storage of *count* and *data pointers* which significantly decrease the memory footprint of the BM representation. Figure 11.3 shows the dense, BM and CSR format representation of the 3×3 weight matrix and the 3×8 input data/feature map given in Figure 11.1. In the dense representation, both the zero and nonzero data is stored in the memory along with the indices, as shown in Figure 11.3a. Figure 11.3b shows the equivalent BM representation where only the nonzero data is stored. The BM representation represents nonzero (stored) data with the binary 1, and zero (unstored) data with the binary 0. Finally, Figure 11.3c shows the CSR format representation, where the relative locations of the nonzero data are represented by the row and col pointers.

To process the input sparse data, the Sparse-PE core is provided the BM and the associated data in the form of chunks for processing of a particular CNN layer.

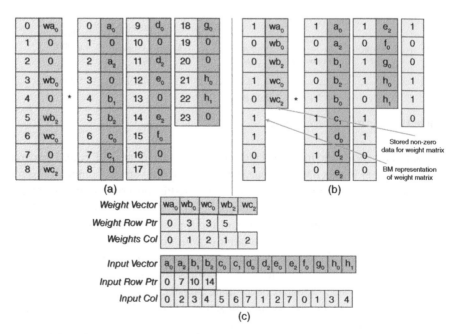

Figure 11.3 Sparse data representations (a) Indexed-based representation, (b) BM-based representation, and (c) CSR format.

Although, the Sparse-PE core can work on any type of convolution or FC layer, for convenience and ease of understanding, we will show the working of the core using the input and the weight matrix in Figure 11.1. We also assume that the input and the weight data are 8 bits wide.

11.2.2 Selection

The convolution operation works by performing dot product between two vectors. In a *two-sided* sparse CNN model, the dot product can result in four possible multiplication outputs.

(i) $zero_0 = zero_w \times zero_a$
(ii) $zero_0 = zero_w \times nonzero_a$
(iii) $zero_0 = nonzero_w \times zero_a$
(iv) $nonzero_0 = nonzero_w \times nonzero_a$

It can be seen that the only valid multiplication is the $nonzero_0$ which results when a nonzero weight ($nonzero_w$) is multiplied by a nonzero input/activation ($nonzero_a$). The SL block has two user-defined parameters, n and k. The main purpose of the SL block is to determine k, $nonzero_0$ computations in a set of n convolution chunks. The value of k represents the total number of multiplier threads in the CM block. In this design, we have a 3×3 matrix of multipliers, making the value of $k = 9$. We define n as the *lookahead factor*, which represents the number of convolution chunks the core looks into to determine k multiplications. There are a total of six convolution chunks (C0–C5) in the example input, as shown in Figure 11.1. For this design, we consider the value of n to be 3. This means that during one cycle, the core looks into $k = 9$ valid multiplications in a set of $n = 3$, 3×3 convolution chunks. The SL block does this by using a series of n, $2k$-input AND gates followed by a selector, as shown in Figure 11.4. Figure 11.5 shows the process of

Figure 11.4 Selection (SL) block diagram.

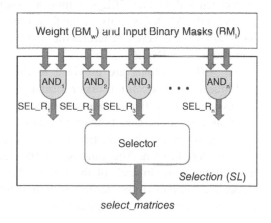

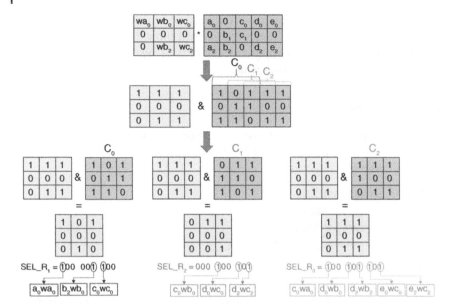

Figure 11.5 Process of ANDing between the weight binary mask and the input binary mask chunks in the SL block.

ANDing. During the first cycle, the sparse masks of the weight and $n = 3$ chunks of the input matrix are loaded into the core. Bit by bit ANDing is performed between the sparse masks of the weight and the input to generate SEL_R1, SEL_R2, and SEL_R3, representing the ANDed output of the first, second, and third, convolution chunks, respectively. The ones in the SEL_R outputs represent the location of valid nonzero multiplications, whereas zeros represent in-effective computations involving zero operands. To process the six convolution chunks, two cycles are needed and the final SEL_R outputs are shown in Figure 11.6. The first cycle generates the ANDed outputs for the first three convolution chunks (C0, C1, C2), whereas the second cycle generates the ANDed outputs for the last three convolution chunks (C3, C4, C5).

The ANDed outputs are provided to the selector which selects the valid multiplications in a column major format. There are a total of n selectors each processing a particular *comma-separated* column. For this design, the three columns Col_0, Col_1, Col_2 (shown in Figure 11.6) are processed in parallel by the three selectors. The selection process occurs iteratively in a nonlinear (or out-of-order) fashion. The purpose of the selector is to schedule the effective computations in each of the input columns (Col_0, Col_1, Col_2) on to the respective columns of the multiplier matrix. Since, at any point, the maximum number of scheduled multiplications per column can not exceed the total

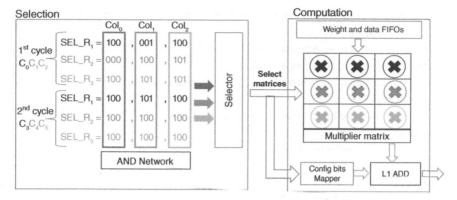

Figure 11.6 Selection for maximum multiplier utilization.

number of multipliers per column of the multiplication matrix, the selector has to make sure that during any cycle the total number of selected multiplications are equal to multiplier threads per column of the multiplier matrix $((k = 9)/3 = 3)$ to ensure maximum hardware utilization. Since every 1 in the input columns (Col_0, Col_1, Col_2) represents a valid computation, the selection algorithm works by counting the number of ones in the individual entries and selecting the entries that maximize the utilization of the multiplier matrix. Consider the second column (Col_1) in Figure 11.6 on which the second selector operates. The selection algorithm is shown in Figure 11.7. The selector iterates over the first $n = 3$ values (val_1, val_2, val_3) and generates three accumulation values ($accum_1$, $accum_2$, $accum_3$). # **ones** function calculates the total number of ones in a particular val. The first iteration comprises of the first three values 001 (val_1), 100 (val_2), 101 (val_3). The first value, i.e., 001 is assigned the highest priority and the selector counts the total number of ones in this entry and stores the result, which in this case is 1, in the *init* variable. It then computes the accumulator variables ($accum_1$, $accum_2$, $accum_3$) using the next two values (val_2, val_3). The selector then selects the values based on whether the total number of ones in accumulated values exceed the total number of compute threads in one column of the thread matrix (i.e., 3). The working of the algorithm for Col_1 is shown in Figure 11.8. In the first iteration (cycle 1), the selector selects val_1 and val_2, based on the algorithm in Figure 11.7. The selector generates the output (out_0) by creating a single row of the selected values. Since a total of three values were considered, the selector replaces the last unselected value (val_3) by zeros in the out_0 output. In the next iteration (cycle 2), the selector prioritizes the unselected value (val_3) from the previous cycle and repeats the same process to generate out_1. It takes a total of three cycles for the selector to process the entire input column.

```
init  = #ones(val₁)
accum₁ = init + #ones(val₂)
accum₂ = init + #ones(val₃)
accum₃ = init + #ones(val₂) + #ones(val₃)
if (accum₃)<=k/3
            select val₁, val₂, val₃
elseif (accum₁) <= k/3
            select val₁, val₂
            init = val₃
elseif (accum₂) <= k/3
            select val₁, val₃
            init = val₂
else
            select val₁
            init = val₂
```

Figure 11.7 Selection algorithm employed by the Selector to maximum the utilization of the multiplier matrix.

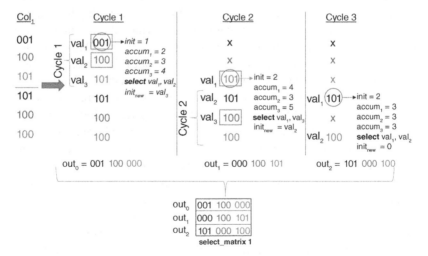

Figure 11.8 Selection process for column 1 (Col₁ in Figure 11.6) after running the Algorithm in Figure 11.7.

Figure 11.9 Generation of selection matrices.

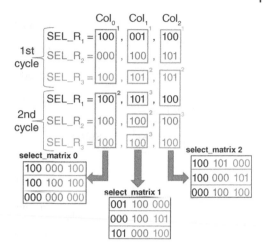

At the end, a total of three select matrices are generated by the three selectors operating in parallel, as shown in Figure 11.9.

As indicated earlier, in this design example, we have considered the value of n to be 3. Therefore, in Figure 11.8, the selector considers three values (val_1, val_2, val_3) for selection in a particular cycle and uses three accumulators ($accum_1$, $accum_2$, $accum_3$ in Figure 11.7). For a higher value of n, let us say 6, the selector will consider all the values in Col_1 in Figure 11.8. At higher levels of sparsity, the increased n will result in an increase in throughput as more valid, nonzero computations will be scheduled and more invalid, zero computations will be skipped by the core. We should also mention that increasing the value of n will also result in an increase in the hardware resource count as more logic will be required for the selector implementation. For $n > 3$, $(2n - 2)$ accumulators and conditional statements will be required by the algorithm in Figure 11.7 for the selector implementation. Therefore, the value of n is chosen in such a way as to keep a balance between performance and area overhead.

Figure 11.10 shows the implementation of the selection process for Col_1 in Figure 11.6. The outputs from the AND network are stored in a local SRAM memory. On every cycle, a new value is written into the memory, and values are read based on the priority of selection, with P1 being the higher priority. The selector block implements the algorithm presented in Figure 11.7. After every iteration, the read address (rd_addr) gets incremented to read the next value in the memory and the priorities are reversed. The outputs get stored into the selection matrix based on the row numbers. The tag bits are a crucial part of this process since they are used by the CM and the AM block for accumulation of data (explained in Sections 11.2.3 and 11.2.4). Whenever a particular value is

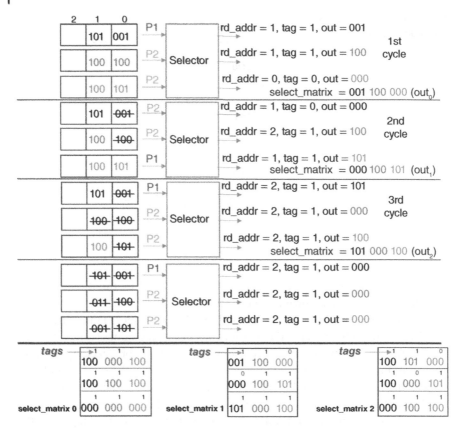

Figure 11.10 First-in first-out (FIFO)-based selector implementation in hardware for generating select_matrices.

not selected during a selection run, the tag bit associated with that value is reset to 0. The selection process ends when no more values need to be read from the memory, the read addresses for all the memories are equal, and all the tag bits are set to 1. These conditions raise a termination flag which ends the process of selection. The final select matrices, along with the associated tag bits for every value are shown in Figure 11.10.

11.2.3 Computation

Figure 11.11 shows the process of computation in the CM block. The actual sparse data and their BM representation for a particular layer is loaded into the on-chip SRAM. Based on the BM of the input and the weight matrix, zeros are inserted at various locations for length equalization and proper indexing, as shown in

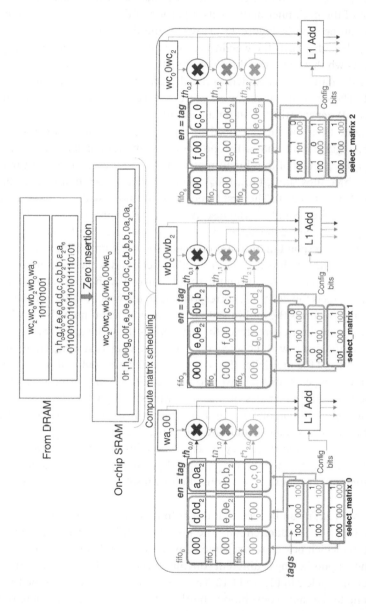

Figure 11.11 Process of computation in the first row of the multiplier matrix (Figure 11.6). The select_matrices (generated in Figure 11.10) are used to schedule the computations on to the multiplier threads.

Figure 11.11. The CM block consists of a series of fifos connected to the multiplier threads of the thread matrix. Since the size of multiplier matrix is 3×3, a total of 9 fifos ($fifo_0$-$fifo_8$) are connected to the nine individual multiplier threads. Each column of the multiplier matrix gets a portion of the zero-inserted weight matrix. This can be seen in Figure 11.11, where the first column of multiplier threads ($th_{0,0}$, $th_{1,0}$, $th_{2,0}$) gets the weight vector $wa_0 00$, the second column ($th_{0,1}$, $th_{1,1}$, $th_{2,1}$) gets $wb_0 0wb_2$ and the third column ($th_{0,2}$, $th_{1,2}$, $th_{2,2}$) gets $wc_0 0wc_2$. Zero-inserted data are also scheduled to the threads from the fifos as shown in Figure 11.11. The enabled pin of the fifos are connected to the tag bits of the select matrices. Whenever the tag bit for a particular entry is 1, the fifo is enabled and a new value from the fifo is passed to the multiplier which performs the computation. Figure 11.12 shows the process of computation for the second column ($th_{0,1}$, $th_{1,1}$, $th_{2,1}$) of the thread matrix. In the first cycle, the first three values in the three fifos ($fifo_3$, $fifo_4$, $fifo_5$) are controlled by the first row of the select_matrix 1 (001 100 000). The first three bits (001) along with the associated tag bit (1) controls $fifo_3$. Similarly the next two sets of the three bits control $fifo_4$ and $fifo_5$, respectively. Since the tag bits for the first two values (001 and 100) are set to 1, the two corresponding fifos are enabled, and the data are moved to the corresponding multiplier threads. The multiplier determines the valid nonzero computation based on the values from the select matrix. For the first value (001), the multiplier extracts the last 8 bits corresponding to the weight value (wb_2) and the data (b_2) and performs the multiplication to generate the output value $b_2 wb_2$. Similarly, the second multiplier thread ($th_{1,1}$) generates the value $c_0 wb_0$. Since the last three bits of the first row of the select matrix 1 have a tag 0 associated to it, the $fifo_5$ enable is off and the multiplier $th_{2,1}$ does not perform a valid multiplication. The same process repeats for the next two rows of the select matrix for cycles 2 and 3. The light gray rectangles on the fifo entries in Figure 11.12 represent the fifo entries that have tag bits of 1 and are thus utilized in the current cycle, whereas the dark gray rectangles indicate the entries that have tag bit of 0, and thus, are not utilized in the current cycle. Parallel to this multiplier column, the first ($th_{0,0}$, $th_{1,0}$, $th_{2,0}$) and the third ($th_{0,2}$, $th_{1,2}$, $th_{2,2}$) multiplier columns process the data in their own respective fifos using their own select matrices to generate the outputs.

From Figure 11.11, it can be seen that the output of the multiplier threads are fed into the level 1 (L1) Adder circuit. The purpose of this adder is to accumulate the outputs which belong to the same convolution chunk and to bypass the addition if the outputs belong to different convolution chunks. To further illustrate this, consider the Cycle 2 in Figure 11.12. The outputs from $th_{1,1}$ ($d_0 wb_0$) and $th_{2,1}$ ($d_2 wb_2$) belong to the same convolution chunk (C2 in Figure 11.1) and therefore need to be accumulated, whereas the output from $th_{0,1}$ ($f_0 wb_0$) belongs to a completely different convolution chunk (C4 in Figure 11.1) and has no relevance to

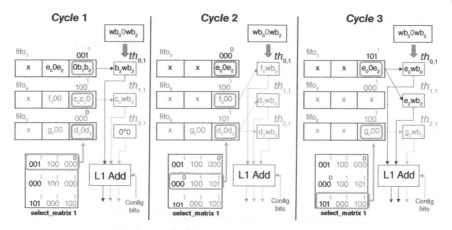

Figure 11.12 Cycle-by-cycle computation of the partial products from the second column thread matrix ($th_{0,1}$, $th_{1,1}$, $th_{2,1}$) in Figure 11.11.

the outputs from $th_{1,1}$ and $th_{2,1}$. This happens because the selector in the previous step is selecting the valid nonzero computations in a nonlinear fashion to maximize the multiplier utilization and does not necessarily care about maintaining a proper flow of multiplications. To circumvent this issue and to determine which multiplier outputs need to be accumulated, the L1 adder uses a bit mapper that encodes the select matrix rows to appropriate values, as shown in Figure 11.13a. The two bits at the output encode the following information:

00 -> The thread outputs within the multiplier column are not added and passed as is.
01 -> The outputs of $th_{0,x}$ and $th_{1,x}$ are added, whereas, the $th_{2,x}$ output is passed as is.
10 -> The outputs of $th_{1,x}$ and $th_{2,x}$ are added, whereas, the $th_{0,x}$ output is passed as is.
11 -> The outputs of all the threads within a multiplier column are added.

The mapping from the 9 bits of select matrix to 2 bit output is straightforward. Since every color coded set of three bits represent a multiplication within a particular convolution chunk, whenever there are multiple ones within the same set (black, dark gray, or light gray), the thread outputs associated to those values need to be added together. This can be seen from entry 4 of Figure 11.13a (000 000 011 -> 01). The light gray set has value 011, so according to the above mapping, the first two thread outputs are added together because they belong to the same convolution chunk. Similarly, the last entry (111 000 000) is mapped to 11, meaning that all three thread outputs within a multiplier column belong to the same convolution

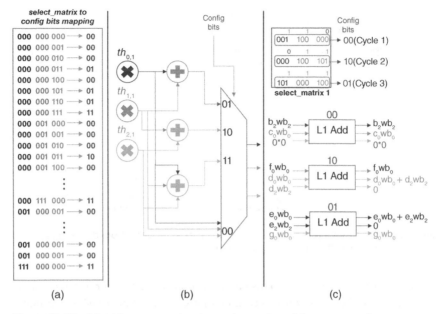

Figure 11.13 L1 Adder computational mapping and partial sum generation (a) select_matrix to configer bits mapper, (b) L1 Adder internal structure, and (c) Partial sum generation through accumulation from the L1 Adders.

chunk, and therefore, need to be accumulated. Using this mapping, the L1 adder can keep track of which thread outputs need to be accumulated and which do not. Figure 11.13b shows the internal structure of the L1 Adder. It comprises three adders which add different combinations of the thread outputs. It also comprises an output multiplexer whose select line is connected to the mapper output (2 bits). The multiplexer has three outputs which are determined by the mapper output bits. The L1 Adder operation for the second column of the thread matrix ($th_{0,1}$, $th_{1,1}$, $th_{2,1}$) is shown in Figure 11.13c. The mapper maps the individual rows of the select matrix to 2 configuration bits. Using the configuration bits, the L1 Adder generates the outputs. In the first cycle, all three outputs (b_2wb_2, c_0wb_0, 0) belong to different convolution chunks and therefore the config bits are 00, which passes the inputs to outputs without accumulation. In the second cycle, the select matrix row maps to 10, which adds the last two thread outputs (d_0wb_0, d_2wb_2) together because they belong to the same convolution chunk and forward the first thread output (f_0wb_0) as is because it belongs to a different convolution chunk. In the last cycle, the first two thread outputs are added and the last is passed as is. It should be noted that there are a total of three identical mappers (Figure 11.13a), each belonging to a particular L1 adder in Figure 11.11.

Even though the row length of the select matrix is 9 which produces $2^9 = 512$ combinations, the mapper only needs to store those combinations for which the total number of ones in the select matrix rows are less than or equal to the multiplier threads per column of the multiplier matrix (3 in this case). Therefore, the total combinations that need to be stored are only 130. Generally, the total combinations that need to be stored can be found using the following equation:

$$Combinations = \binom{k}{0} + \binom{k}{1} + \binom{k}{2} + \cdots + \binom{k}{n} \qquad (11.1)$$

Where k represents the length of a select matrix row (9 in this case) and n represents the total multiplier threads per column of the thread matrix (3 in this case). Therefore, the total memory required for storing the three mappers is only 780 bits ($130 \times 2 \times 3$).

Figure 11.14 shows the scheduling of threads for computation of the output for the example in Figure 11.1. All the threads are connected to their respective fifos and receive the data. The select matrices are used to schedule the data and for generating the 2-bit L1 Adder configuration bits (also shown in Figure 11.14). To compare the performance of a dense design which does not exploit sparsity, we can see from Figure 11.1 that a dense approach would take a total of six cycles to generate the output using the same number of multipliers (9 arranged in a 3×3 matrix). The approach presented here utilizes just three cycles to process the entire output by exploiting the sparsity and maximizing the scheduling of valid, nonzero

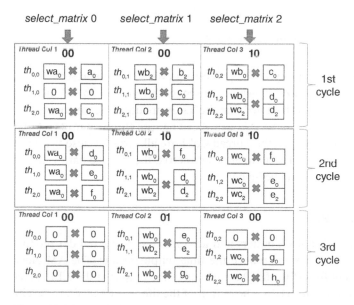

Figure 11.14 Multiplier matrix thread scheduling for the example in Figure 11.1.

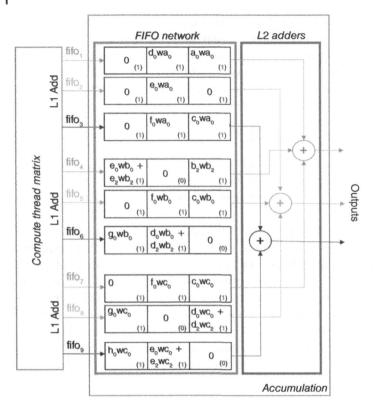

Figure 11.15 Accumulation for the example in Figure 11.1.

multiplications during majority of the processing cycles. This represents a 50% increase in the hardware utilization which consequently represents a 50% increase in throughput. It should also be noted that the hardware utilization increases further when the input sparse matrix is larger. It can be seen from Figure 11.14 that the last three multiplications in the Thread Col 1 are all zeros because the input matrix has been exhausted. For a larger input matrix, the average hardware utilization and throughput would be higher.

11.2.4 Accumulation

The accumulation (AM) block buffers and accumulates the partial dot product outputs from the CM block to produce the final output results. The AM block consists of a series of fifos (fifo$_1$-fifo$_9$) connected at the output of the 3 L1 Adder circuits, as shown in Figure 11.15. The output of the fifos is provided to a level 2

(L2) adder which accumulates the dot products for a particular convolution chunk to generate the final output. The CM block outputs the partial dot products as well as the tag values associated with every product. The tag bits are shown in parenthesis in Figure 11.15. The process of accumulation occurs in two stages by the same color coded fifos ($fifo_1$ + $fifo_4$ + $fifo_7$), ($fifo_2$ + $fifo_5$ + $fifo_8$), and ($fifo_3$ + $fifo_6$ + $fifo_9$). The outputs are either valid or partial, based on the tag values associated to each accumulation stage. If the tag values for all the inputs are equal to 1, the output is considered *valid*, otherwise, it is considered *partial*. Figure 11.16 shows the accumulation stage map for the example in Figure 11.1. On every cycle there are two accumulation stages. In the first stage, the previously generated partial outputs are added to the new entries to make the output *valid*. To do this, the AM block checks the tag bits in the partial output and adds the missing tag 1 input to make the partial output complete/valid. In the second stage, the AM replaces the already used tag 1 values with zeros and generates new partial outputs by summing the unused tag 1 values. This process can be seen in Figure 11.16. The O_3 partial value is generated by summing the fifos F3, F6, F9 in cycle 1. The output is partial because the $Input_2$ and $Input_3$ tag values are 0. O_3 is made valid by summing the O_3(partial) with the now available $Input_2$ and $Input_3$ tag 1 values in the stage 1 during the second cycle. In the second stage, during the same cycle, the already

Cycle #	Accumulation Fifos	Input$_1$/tag	Input$_2$/tag	Input$_3$/tag	Accumulation Stage	Output
1	F1 + F4 + F7	$(a_0 wa_0)/1$	$(b_0 wb_0)/1$	$(c_0 wc_0)/1$	Stage 2	O_0(valid)
1	F2 + F5 + F8	(0)/1	$(c_0 wb_0)/1$	$(d_0 wc_0 + d_2 wc_2)/1$	Stage 2	O_3(valid)
1	F3 + F6 + F9	$(c_0 wa_0)/1$	(0)/0	(0)/0	Stage 2	O_3(partial)
2	F1 + F4 + F7	$(d_0 wa_0)/1$	(0)/0	$(f_0 wc_0)/1$	Stage 2	O_4(partial)
2	F2 + F5 + F8	$(e_0 wa_0)/1$	$(f_0 wb_0)/1$	(0)/0	Stage 2	O_5(partial)
2	F3 + F6 + F9	O_3(partial)	$(d_0 wb_0 + d_2 wb_2)/1$	$(o_0 wc_0 + e_2 wc_2)/1$	Stage 1	O_3(valid)
2	F3 + F6 + F9	$(f_0 wa_0)/1$	(0)/0	(0)/0	Stage 2	O_6(partial)
3	F1 + F4 + F7	O_4(partial)	-	$(e_0 wb_0 + e_2 wb_2)/1$	Stage 1	O_4(valid)
3	F2 + F5 + F8	(0)/1	(0)/1	(0)/1	Stage 2	Outputs Exhausted
3	F2 + F5 + F8	O_5(partial)	$(g_0 wc_0)/1$	-	Stage 1	O_5(valid)
3	F2 + F5 + F8	(0)/1	(0)/1	(0)/1	Stage 2	Outputs Exhausted
3	F3 + F6 + F9	O_6(partial)	$(g_0 wb_0)/1$	$(h_0 wc_0)/1$	Stage 1	O_6(valid)
3	F3 + F6 + F9	(0)/1	(0)/1	(0)/1	Stage 2	Outputs Exhausted

Figure 11.16 Accumulation stage map.

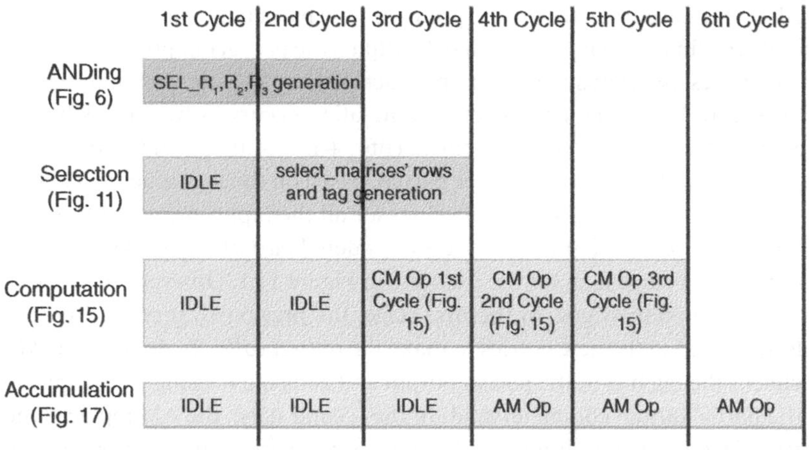

	1st Cycle	2nd Cycle	3rd Cycle	4th Cycle	5th Cycle	6th Cycle
ANDing (Fig. 6)	SEL_R$_1$,R$_2$,R$_3$ generation					
Selection (Fig. 11)	IDLE	select_matrices' rows and tag generation				
Computation (Fig. 15)	IDLE	IDLE	CM Op 1st Cycle (Fig. 15)	CM Op 2nd Cycle (Fig. 15)	CM Op 3rd Cycle (Fig. 15)	
Accumulation (Fig. 17)	IDLE	IDLE	IDLE	AM Op	AM Op	AM Op

Figure 11.17 Initial latency of the Sparse-PE core operations.

used tag 1 inputs are replaced by 0 and the new partial product (O_6) is generated. This process is repeated in subsequent cycles until all the inputs are utilized and all the outputs are *valid*.

Figure 11.17 shows the cycle-by-cycle processing latency of the various blocks of the Sparse-PE core for the example in Figure 11.1. The process of ANDing takes a total of two cycles for the generation of a pair of three-tuples (SEL_R$_1$, SEL_R$_2$, SEL_R$_3$). After the generation of the first tuple of the SEL_R$_1$, SEL_R$_2$, and SEL_R$_3$ values, the selection block starts processing and takes a total of three cycles to generate the select_matrices and the associated tag values (Figure 11.10). The computation block gets triggered after the first row of the select_matrices is generated and takes a total of three cycles to process the three rows of the select_matrices (Figure 11.14). Finally, the accumulation block takes a total of three cycles to process the partial product outputs from the computation block (Figure 11.16) to generate the final outputs. Therefore, the initial processing latency to generate the first output is six cycles. This initial latency, however, is amortized over processing over a larger input.

11.2.5 Output Encoding

Figure 11.18 shows the process of output sparse binary mask encoding. Unlike the weight masks, the output binary mask needs to be generated on-the-fly because of its dynamic nature. From Figure 11.5, we can see that the SEL_R outputs show the presence of the nonzero partial products for a particular convolution chunk.

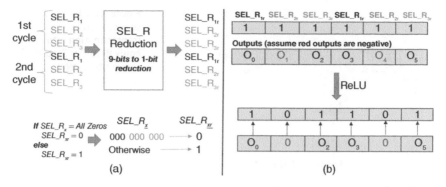

Figure 11.18 Output sparse mask generation. (a) Reduction of the individual SEL_R outputs to a single bit (SEL_R$_{xr}$), based on an all-zero check and (b) sparse binary mask after ReLU where the negative outputs and their corresponding sparse mask locations are converted into zeros.

The presence of even a single *one* in the SEL_R outputs show that the output is nonzero. To determine the output binary mask, we can use the same metadata. The first step involves reduction of the individual SEL_R outputs to a single bit (SEL_R$_{xr}$), based on an *all-zero* check, as shown in Figure 11.18a. This generates the sparse binary mask for the outputs before ReLU. Note that the SEL_R values are taken from the test example (Figure 11.1). Figure 11.18b shows the second step after ReLU, where the negative outputs, and their corresponding sparse mask locations, are converted into zeros. This final sparse mask is stored as is, whereas the output is shifted first to omit zero data entries, and then stored.

This concludes the processing that goes on in a single Sparse-PE core when convolution is performed using a 3×3 filter. For a filter of size 5×5, 7×7, or higher, the kernel factorization [178] is employed to convert larger filters into a set of smaller 3×3 filters. This factorization makes it possible to keep the design of PEs relatively simple and not incorporate complex flow control to support larger filters. It should be noted that the kernel factorization is done during model generation and training. The final generated model with 3×3 filters is then used during the inference. Sparse-PE, however, also supports 5×5 filters by using a multiplier matrix of 5×5, instead of the current 3×3.

1×1 convolution, used in many modern CNN models, is performed the same way as the 3×3 convolution. Figure 11.19 shows an example of 1×1 convolution. Here, a $1 \times 1 \times 9$ filter is convolved with a $3 \times 1 \times 9$ input matrix to produce a 3×1 output. Figure 11.19 also shows the transformation employed by the architecture to transform the 1×1 convolution operation into an equivalent 3×3 stride 3 convolution. Here, individual channels of the filter and the input matrix are

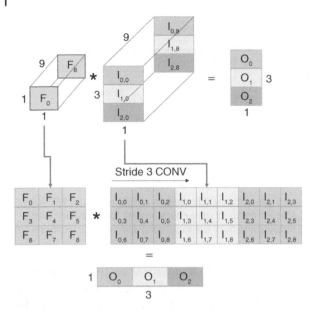

Figure 11.19 1×1 convolution layer transformation into an equivalent 3×3, stride 3 convolution layer.

transformed into a 3×3 matrix and scheduled to the core for processing. The core then performs the selection, computation, and accumulation in the same manner as explained previously. For an input and a kernel with higher channel count, as is the case for most commonly used CNN models, the channels are broken down equally and scheduled among different Sparse-PE cores (Figure 11.21).

Sparse-PE architecture also allows the processing of FC layers. Figure 11.20 shows an example of FC layer processing. Here, a 9×1 input array and a 9×3 filter matrix produces a 1×3 output. The input and the filter matrices are again transformed into an equivalent 3×3 stride 3 convolution. Sparse-PE then processes the transformed input to generate the final outputs.

In Section 11.3, we will show the performance improvement offered by an accelerator that uses a system of Sparse-PE cores to accelerate the CNN inference process.

11.3 Implementation and Results

This section describes the performance modeling and the implementation of the Sparse-PE core. An individual Sparse-PE core works by computing dot products between a subsection of the sparse input data and the sparse weight data to produce a subsection of the output data. To process multiple subsections, we envision an $R \times C$ matrix architecture of the Sparse-PE cores, where, R represents the rows and C represents the columns. From Figure 11.21, we can see that the value of R

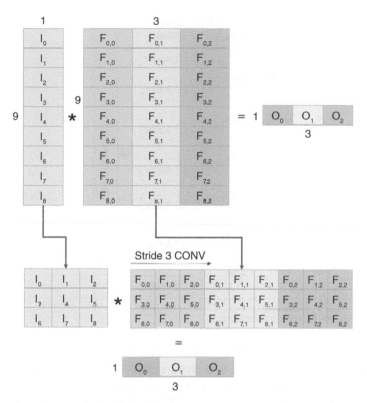

Figure 11.20 FC layer transformation into an equivalent 3×3, stride 3 convolution layer.

and C is 7 and 4, respectively, making the total number of Sparse-PE cores equal to $7 \times 4 = 28$. Since, a single Sparse-PE core has $3 \times 3 = 9$ multiplier threads, the matrix of cores in Figure 11.21 have a total of $9 \times 28 = 252$ multiplier threads. The cores get the sparse data and the binary masks from input SRAMs. The outputs of the cores are connected to level 3 (L3) adders that accumulate individual channel outputs to generate the final output. These outputs are stored in the output SRAMs and subsequently sent to the DRAM for next layer processing. We simulate the architecture using our cycle-accurate simulator and extract the throughput and hardware utilization results. We also implement the Sparse-PE core in RTL Verilog and provide an estimate of resource and power consumption.

11.3.1 Cycle-Accurate Simulator

To evaluate the performance of an individual Sparse-PE core and the 7×4 matrix of Sparse-PE cores as a whole, we develop a cycle-accurate performance simulator.

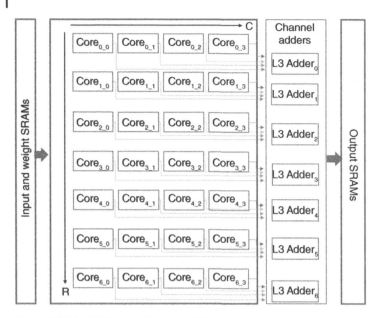

Figure 11.21 3D Sparse-PE core architecture.

The simulator generates the results using different values of n for the Sparse-PE cores in Figure 11.21. The simulator was built using MATLAB R2020a and the Sparse-PE functionality was implemented in software. The Sparse-PE cores in Figure 11.21 are implemented using a MATLAB function which is provided different data based on the current layer dimensions. The evaluation files in the simulator use the data outputted by the individual cores and schedulers to generate the throughput and the speedup results for various dense and sparse CNN models. The simulator has modifiable n parameter for the individual cores. Recall that n (look-ahead factor) represents the total number of convolution chunks the core looks into during an input processing. For the design example previously presented, we considered the n value to be 3, which indicates that at any particular cycle, the core looks into three convolution chunks to determine valid computations. To evaluate the performance, we use different values of the n parameter which allows us to *look-ahead* into a different number of convolution chunks for processing in a particular cycle. The simulator also contains routines for SparTen [151], SCNN [162], and Eyeriss v2 [52] for performing comparisons.

The performance is evaluated on many widely used CNN models including Alexnet [30], VGG16 [31], MobileNet [33], and GoogleNet [35]. We use the sparse versions of VGG16 and MobileNet for comparison purposes. To create sparse versions of the CNNs, we use the approach presented in [46] for pruning using the MATLAB's *Deep Learning Toolbox*. For fair comparison, we achieve the same level of the weight and the input sparsity as the previous approaches and then evaluate the nets for performance comparisons. The activation sparsity changes dynamically during the inference process; therefore, we average out the input sparsity for a batch of 100 randomly selected inputs. After pruning of the network, we generate the sparse binary masks for every layer and generate a network containing only the binary masks, since only this information is needed to efficiently represent the multiply-accumulate (MAC) operations needed per layer for the accelerator.

11.3.1.1 Performance with Varying Sparsity

Our core simulator has the ability to sweep both input activation/weight sparsity from high (95%/95%) to low (10%/10%). This gives us an accurate measure of how much performance improvement, in terms of speedup and hardware utilization, can be achieved using the Sparse-PE core. Figures 11.22 and 11.23 show the speedup results and the average thread utilization for VGG16 and MobileNet, respectively, under varying sparsity. These results are obtained by running the sparse neural nets layer by layer and then averaging out the speedup and the thread utilization for one complete run. It should be noted that all the layers, including

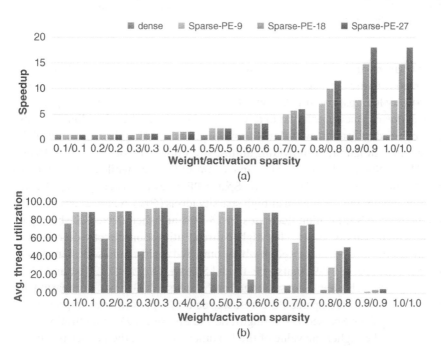

Figure 11.22 VGG16 performance with varying sparsity: (a) Speedup results and (b) average thread utilization.

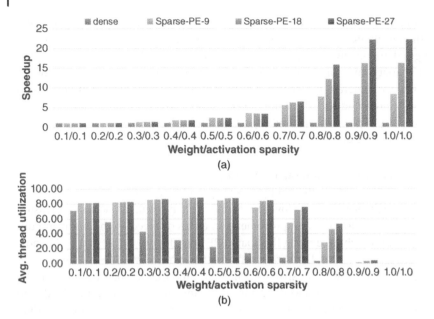

Figure 11.23 MobileNet performance with varying sparsity: (a) Speedup results and (b) average thread utilization.

the FC layers, are accounted for in this test. Three Sparse-PE core configurations (Sparse-PE-n) are considered with n (lookahead factor) changed from 9 to 18 to 27. At very low sparsity (0.1/0.1), we observe that a dense core and the Sparse-PE core perform somewhat similar in terms of performance. There is a slight increase in the thread utilization, with dense providing almost 80% utilization while all the Sparse-PE configurations providing almost 90% utilization for sparse VGG16 net. For MobileNet, the dense provides almost 70% utilization, while Sparse-PE cores provide almost 80%. For VGG16, the Sparse-PE cores consistently keep the utilization greater than 90% even at high sparsity levels (60%), whereas, as expected, the dense core's utilization decreases by 25–30% and then decreases sharply by 50% at high sparsity levels. This higher thread utilization directly correlates to improved throughput and speedup when compared against a dense design. At 80% sparsity, the Sparse-PE-9, Sparse-PE-18 and Sparse-PE-27 are 7×, 10×, and 11.5× faster, respectively, than a dense design for the sparse VGG16 net. Comparing different versions of the Sparse-PE cores, we see a 57% performance improvement when going from Sparse-PE-9 configuration to Sparse-PE-27 configuration. This shows that the higher the value of the lookahead factor n, the greater is the performance improvement delivered by our Sparse-PE core for sparse input activations/weights.

11.3.1.2 Comparison Against Past Approaches

We compare our core design against three previously proposed sparse CNN accelerators (SCNN [162], SparTen [151], Eyeriss v2 [52]), and one dense accelerator (NeuroMAX [96]). Among these designs, SCNN, SparTen, and NeuroMAX do not support FC layers, so we omit our FC layer results for fair comparison. SCNN, in addition, also does not support nonunit stride convolutions. We use the Sparse VGG16 net for comparison with these three accelerators. The average sparsity achieved without a significant loss in accuracy for the weights and activations is 77% and 68%, respectively. Figure 11.24 shows the comparison results obtained using our simulator. We observe that Sparse-PE-27, on average, performs 11.2×, 4.3×, and 1.96× better than NeuroMAX, SCNN, and SparTen, respectively.

Figure 11.25 shows the comparison of the Sparse-PE core configurations against Eyeriss v2 on selected layers of MobileNet. The average sparsity for the weights and activations is 73% and 64%, respectively. We observe that, on average, Sparse-PE-9, Sparse-PE-18, and Sparse-PE-27, perform 1.04×, 1.71×, and 2.85×,

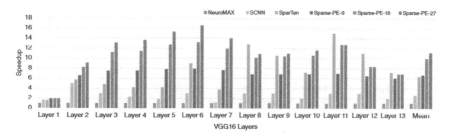

Figure 11.24 VGG16 speedup comparison.

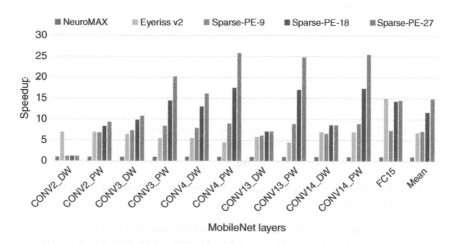

Figure 11.25 MobileNet speedup comparison.

better, respectively, than Eyeriss v2. Comparing different configurations show that the Sparse-PE-27 configuration offers 108.8% increase in speedup over Sparse-PE-9 configuration for sparse MobileNet.

Energy comparison among different accelerators is somewhat challenging as it requires working RTL implementations. Since the energy consumption is dominated by the total number of DRAM accesses, therefore, by estimating the DRAM accesses, energy difference among the accelerators can be approximated. Many of the recent works rely on the CSC/CSR formats for the storage of the nonzero data. We, therefore, compare the accessed memory for the CSC format against the sparse binary mask format. Figure 11.26 shows the intermediate activations' memory access comparison for selected sparse VGG 16 and MobileNet layers.[1] The activation sparsity for different layers is also shown. In the initial layers with

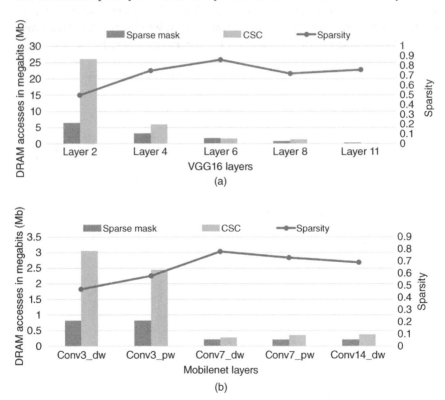

Figure 11.26 Sparse binary mask vs. CSC DRAM access for (a) Sparse VGG16 and (b) Sparse MobileNet.

---

1 The memory requirement for the nonzero data is not shown since it is the same for both the CSC format and the sparse binary mask. The accessed memory comparison is made for the sparse binary mask and the location vectors (column, index) of the CSC format.

low activation sparsity, the CSC format has approximately 4× and 3.7× higher DRAM memory accesses than the sparse mask for sparse VGG16 and Mobilenet, respectively. In the deeper layers with moderate-to-high sparsity, the memory requirement for the CSC format is around 1.7× that of the sparse mask.

This shows that the sparse binary mask format not only needs less encoding/ decoding logic, but is also efficient when it comes to memory requirements when compared against the CSC format. This translates directly to higher energy, area, and compute savings for our accelerator which employs the sparse binary mask.

11.3.2 RTL Implementation

We use Xilinx Z-7100 SoC to implement the Sparse-PE core design. The SoC is divided into two parts, the programmable logic (PL), containing the FPGA fabric, and the processing system (PS), containing ARM cores. The two are connected using an AXI on-chip communication subsystem. We implement the Sparse-PE core on the PL and use the PS to transfer data to/from a desktop computer to PL. The test design is implemented for the Sparse-PE-27 configuration and runs at 200 MHz. Table 11.1 shows the resource utilization results for a single Sparse-PE core with $n = 27$. Figure 11.27 shows the breakdown of the utilization among

Table 11.1   Resource utilization for a single Sparse-PE-27 core.

Property	Available	Used	Utilization (%)
LUTs	277k	3.4k	1.23%
FFs	554k	6k	1.1%
On-chip SRAM	26.5Mb	2.1kB	0.01%

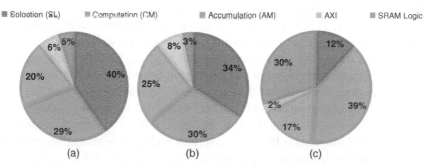

Figure 11.27   Breakdown of resource utilization for (a) LUTs, (b) FFs, and (c) SRAM memory.

various sub-blocks of the Sparse-PE core. The lookup table (LUT) and the flip-flop (FF) cost is dominated by the selection (SL) block with SL taking almost 40% and 34% of the overall LUTs and FFs used, respectively. The SRAM utilization is dominated by the computation (CM) block because of the bit mapping and the buffering fifos (Figure 11.12). The design has a power consumption of 2.48W with the PS dominating the consumption (55%).

Table 11.2 shows the implementation details of the Sparse-PE accelerator (Figure 11.21) comprising of the Sparse-PE-27 cores. It should be noted that the PE number in Table 11.2 refers to the total number of multipliers in the design. Since a single Sparse-PE-27 core has $3 \times 3 = 9$ multipliers, the total PEs (or multipliers) in the design are $R \times C \times 9 = 252$. The $R \times C$ matrix of the accelerator consumes roughly 85% of the available LUT resources, whereas the rest 15% are consumed by the additional control logic. Table 11.2 also lists the details of some recently proposed sparse CNN accelerators. Eyeriss v2, implemented on a 65 nm application-specific integrated circuit (ASIC), supports two-sided sparsity (sparse$_{wa}$), i.e., sparsity in both weights and activations. Eyeriss v2, however, uses a total of 2695 k gates which represent a 108% increase in area cost when compared to the original Eyeriss [45]. This is because of the relatively complex design of the PEs of Eyeriss v2. SparTen accelerator [151] is implemented on Intel Cyclone IV FPGA and operates at 50 MHz. It also supports two-sided sparsity but has no support for FC layers. Although the implementation cost of SparTen is not reported, the architecture of SparTen requires complex inter-PE synchronization circuits which would greatly increase its cost. Zero-Activation-Skipping Convolutional Accelerator (ZASCA) [179], implemented on a 65 nm ASIC, uses a total of 192 PEs and runs at 200 MHz. Just as Sparse-PE, ZASCA accommodates both the CONV and the FC layers in its architecture. However, unlike Sparse-PE, ZASCA only exploits activation sparsity (sparse$_a$). In addition, because of architectural limitations, ZASCA can not fully exploit its resources for 1×1 convolution, resulting in a significant decrease in hardware utilization for such convolutions. Zhu et al. [180] proposed a structured sparse CNN accelerator, implemented on Xilinx ZCU102 FPGA. The proposed accelerator uses structured pruning to reduce irregularities in sparse weights and employs a sparse wise dataflow scheme for high data reuse. The accelerator proposed in [180], however, only exploits sparsity in weights (sparse$_w$) and can not exploit activation sparsity. Because of the complex design and the dataflow scheme, the accelerator proposed in [180] has a huge logic utilization cost (390 k LUTs). Sparse-PE accelerator, even though, employs 32% more PEs than [180], it, however, utilizes 71% lesser resources. Xie et al. [181] proposed a flexible accelerator architecture that supports both structured and unstructured weight sparsity. The accelerator is implemented on Intel Aria 10 SoC and uses a hybrid parallel (HP) dataflow. Even though, the resoure count of the accelerator is lower than Sparse-PE, the dataflow employed

Table 11.2 Comparison of Sparse-PE-based accelerator with previous designs.

Property	Sparse-PE accelerator	Eyerissv2 [52]	SparTen [151]	ZASCA [179]	Zhu et al. [180]	Xie et al. [181]	Lu et al. [182]
Technology	Z-7100	65nm	Cyclone IV	65nm	ZCU102	Aria 10	ZCU102
Precision(bits)	8-bit	8-20 bits	8-bit	16-bit	16-bit	8-bit	16-bit
PE number	252	192	256	192	192	512	288
Frequency (MHz)	200	200	50	200	200	170	200
Accelerator type	sparse$_{wa}$	sparse$_{wa}$	sparse$_{wa}$	sparse$_a$	sparse$_w$	sparse$_w$	sparse$_w$
Resources (LUTs(a), Gates(b))	112k(a)	2695k(b)	unreported	1036k(b)	390k(a)	102.6k(a)	132k(a)
Core only Power (W)	3.7	0.460	unreported	0.301	unreported	4.6	unreported
Supported layers	CONV + FC	CONV + FC	CONV only	CONV + FC	CONV + FC	CONV only	CONV only

in the accelerator does not support FC layers. It, also, can only exploit weight sparsity (sparse$_w$) and has no support for activation sparsity. The accelerator proposed in [182] uses a weight-oriented dataflow that performs element-matrix multiplication. It also uses a tile lookup table (TLUT) to match the sparse weight with the input pixel to exploit weight sparsity (sparse$_w$). Similar to [181], the accelerator proposed in [182] is also a CONV only accelerator and has no support for FC layers. It also can not exploit activation sparsity (sparse$_a$).

11.4 Chapter Summary

This chapter presented Sparse-PE, a multithreaded, general purpose, dot product core for sparse convolutional neural networks. The designed core exploited *two-sided* sparsity, that is, sparsity in both the weights and activations to maximize the throughput and hardware utilization. Unlike contemporary approaches that use the CSC format and the associated complex PE design, the Sparse-PE core uses the sparse binary mask format and has a relatively low complexity. The chapter also presented novel, low-cost circuits, including selection, computation, and accumulation, which, when used in conjunction, allows the core to skip huge number of computations involving *zero* data and only favor computations involving *nonzero* data to maximize the throughput. Results showed that the Sparse-PE core could effectively keep the hardware utilization above 85% at sparsity as high as 60%, for both the input activations and weights. The chapter also compared the performance of Sparse-PE core-based accelerator against previous state-of-the-art dense and two-sided sparse CNN accelerators. Experimental results showed that the Sparse-PE offered, on average, 12×, 4.2×, 2.38×, and 1.98×, speedup over NeuroMAX (dense), SCNN (sparse), Eyeriss v2 (sparse), and SparTen (sparse), respectively.

12

Phantom: A High-Performance Computational Core for Sparse CNNs

Neural nets have been around since the 1940s; however, the first practically applicable neural network, referred to as the LeNet [5], was proposed in 1989. This neural network was designed to solve the problem of digit recognition in handwritten numeric digits. It paved the way for the development of neural networks responsible for various applications related to digit recognition like an ATM. The slow growth and a little to no adoption of neural networks in the early days is mainly due to the massive computational requirements involved with their processing which limited their study to theoretical concepts. Over the past decade, there has been an exponential growth in the research on deep neural networks (DNNs) with many new high accuracy DNNs being deployed for various applications. This has only been possible because of two factors. The first factor is the advancements in the processing power of semiconductor devices and technological breakthroughs in computer architecture. Nowadays, computers have significantly higher computing capability. This enables the processing of a neural network within a reasonable time frame, something that was not achievable in the early days. The second factor is the availability of a large amount of training datasets. As neural networks learn over time, providing huge amounts of training data enables better accuracy. For example, Facebook receives close to a billion user images per day, whereas YouTube has 300h of video uploaded every minute [6]. This enables the service providers to train their neural networks for targeted ad campaigns bringing in billions of dollars of ad revenue. Apart from their use in social media platforms, DNNs are impacting many other domains and expect to make a huge impact. One of the domains where DNNs have contributed significantly is speech processing. Nowadays, many applications have been developed that use DNNs to perform real-time speech recognition with unprecedented levels of accuracy [7–9]. Many technology companies are also using DNNs to perform language translation used in a wide variety of applications. Google, for example, uses Google's Neural Machine Translation system (GNMT) [10] which uses recurrent neural networks (RNNs), a type of

Accelerators for Convolutional Neural Networks, First Edition.
Arslan Munir, Joonho Kong, and Mahmood Azhar Qureshi.
© 2024 The Institute of Electrical and Electronics Engineers, Inc. Published 2024 by John Wiley & Sons, Inc.

DNN, for their language translation applications. Autonomous driving has been one of the biggest technological breakthroughs in the auto industry since the invention of the internal combustion engine. It is not a coincidence that the self-driving boom came at the same time when high accuracy DNNs became increasingly popular. Companies like Tesla and Waymo are using various types of self-driving technology including visual feeds and Lidar for their self-driving solutions. One thing which is common in all these solutions is the use of DNNs for visual perception of the road conditions which is the main back-end technology used in advanced driver assistance systems (ADAS). Another crucial area where DNNs have become increasingly useful is medicine. Nowadays, doctors can use artificial intelligence (AI)-assisted medical imagery to perform various surgeries. AI systems use DNNs in genomics to gather insights about genetic disorders like autism [13, 14]. DNNs are also useful in the detection of various types of cancers like skin and brain cancer [15, 16]. The advent of AI has also challenged many traditional security approaches that were previously deemed sufficient. The rollout of 5G technology has caused a massive surge of IoT-based deployments which traditional security approaches are not able to keep up with. Physical unclonability approaches [17–19] were introduced to protect this massive deployment of IoTs against security attacks with minimum cost overheads. These approaches, however, were also unsuccessful in preventing AI-assisted attacks using DNNs [22, 23]. Researchers have now been forced to upgrade the security threat models to incorporate AI-based attacks [24, 25]. Because of a massive increase in AI-assisted cyber-attacks on cloud and datacenters, corporations and governments have realized that the best way of defeating offensive AI attacks is by incorporating AI-based defensive strategies.

Overall, the use of DNNs in various applications has seen exponential growth over the past decade and this trend has been on the rise for the past many years. The massive increase in DNN deployments on the edge devices requires the development of efficient processing architectures to keep up with the computational requirements for successful DNN inference.

CNNs for vision AI applications have reached an unprecedented accuracy ever since the introduction of AlexNet [30] about a decade ago. Many of the previously proposed high-accuracy CNNs [30–32, 35] have tremendous amounts of computations owing to a large number of model parameters. These parameters and the associated massive number of computations generate exorbitant amounts of data in the form of partial sums (psums) and feature maps. This massive data, in addition to the model parameters, raise concerns in regards to both compute and memory bandwidth. In addition, it also raises concerns about energy consumption of a neural network accelerator (NNA), since on-chip memory is not sufficient to store the entire model, which, in some cases, can be in the order of hundreds of MBs. To support this massive model size of a CNN, off-chip dynamic random access memory (DRAM) memories are generally employed. It has been shown that the energy cost per fetch for 32b coefficients in an off-chip LPDDR2 DRAM is about 640 pJ, which is about 6400× the energy cost of a 32b integer ADD operation [36]. The power dissipation resulting from just the DRAM accesses would be well beyond the limits of an embedded mobile device employing the NNA.

Various techniques have been developed to address the compute and memory bandwidth issues of an NNA, running a CNN. *Mobilenets* [33, 34] were developed to reduce the total number of computations by splitting a regular convolution operation into separable convolutions (depthwise and pointwise), without incurring a loss in accuracy. Another widely used approach for decreasing the model size is the reduction in precision of both weights and activations using various quantization strategies [37–39]. This again does not result in a significant loss in accuracy and reduces the model size by a considerable amount. Hardware implementations like Envision [40], NeuroMAX [96], UNPU [41], and Stripes [42] show how reduced bit precision, and quantization, translates into increased throughput and savings in energy.

Modern CNNs owe their high accuracy to deep layers and the nonlinearity in their design. Typically, nonlinearity is added by incorporating activation functions, the most common being the rectified linear unit (ReLU) [6]. The ReLU converts all negative values in a feature map to zeros. Since the output of one layer is the input to the next layer, many of the computations, within a layer, involve multiplication with zeros. These feature maps containing zeros are referred to as *one-sided sparse feature maps*. The multiplications resulting from this one-sided sparsity wastes compute cycles and decreases the *effective* throughput and hardware utilization, thus, reducing the overall performance of the accelerator. It also results in high energy cost as the transfer of zeros to/from off-chip memory is a wasted memory access. In order to reduce the computational and memory access volume, previous works [43–45] have exploited this one-sided sparsity and displayed some performance improvements.

Compression of DNN models was introduced the first time in [46]. Han et al. [46] iteratively pruned the connections based on parameter threshold, and performed retraining to retain accuracy. This process resulted in *two-sided* sparsity, i.e., sparsity in both weights and activations, which led to approximately 9× model reduction for AlexNet, and 13× reduction for VGG-16. It also resulted in 4–9× *effective* compute reduction (depending on the model). These gains, in theory, are very promising, however, designing an accelerator that leverages the two-sided sparsity is quite challenging as explained in Chapter 11.

Considering the aforementioned issues, many previously proposed accelerators attempt to strike a balance between hardware complexity and performance improvements; however, the contemporary accelerators have many shortcomings as explained in Chapter 11.

To address the issues in contemporary sparse CNN accelerators, this chapter proposes and introduces *Phantom*, a flexible and high throughput neural computational core which promises high hardware utilization. The core works for both dense and sparse networks by dynamically mapping valid computations on the processing threads. The core also addresses the systematic load imbalance by using a two-level, dynamic, load balancing strategy. Unlike some of the previous works, the core can work on any input layer, be it CONV or fully connected (FC), and supports any type of convolution (regular or separable). *Phantom* is based on Sparse-PE presented in Chapter 11 and like Sparse-PE, *Phantom* utilizes binary mask representation to actively lookahead into sparse computations, and dynamically schedule its computational threads to maximize the thread utilization and throughput. Many concepts in *Phantom* overlap with Sparse-PE, and these concepts are presented in this chapter again for completeness. In summary, the main contributions of this chapter include

- A *multithreaded* neural computational core architecture, called **Phantom**, designed to maximize the hardware utilization and throughput of CNN models.
- *Phantom* exploits the sparsity in *both* weights, and activations, simultaneously, by incorporating simple, yet powerful circuits like *Lookahead Mask*, *Top-Down Selector*, and *Thread Mapper*. These circuits, when used in conjunction, map the *effective*, *nonzero* computations onto an array of multiplier threads within a PE. The core also has the capability to skip huge number of nonessential computations ($zero_w \times zero_a$, $zero_w \times non\text{-}zero_a$, $non\text{-}zero_w \times zero_a$), while simultaneously favoring essential computations ($non\text{-}zero_w \times non\text{-}zero_a$), without wasting compute cycles (subscripts "w" and "a" here refer to weights and activations, respectively). This drastically improves the core's hardware utilization, consequently improving the throughput.
- Addressing the systematic load imbalance by using a two-tiered, on-the-fly, load balancing strategy. Unlike some previous approaches, this balancing does not require offline processing or modification of the CNN model.
- Generating a two-dimensional (2D) mesh architecture of *Phantom* neural computational cores, which we refer to as **Phantom-2D** accelerator. Unlike some previous works that only support either CONV layers or FC layers, we show how *Phantom-2D* supports different CONV types (unit and nonunit stride) and FC layers, in addition to supporting both sparse and dense CNN models.
- Simulations show that the *Phantom-2D* accelerator has a performance gain of 12×, 4.1×, 1.98×, and 2.36×, over dense architectures, SCNN, SparTen, and Eyeriss v2, respectively, while retaining the energy efficiency of SparTen.

The remainder of the chapter is organized as follows: Section 12.1 presents relevant works in literature. Section 12.2 presents the proposed *Phantom* core and its inner workings. Section 12.3 presents the design of a two-dimensional accelerator comprising of *Phantom* cores. Experimental methodology, simulation results, comparisons, and implementation cost are given in Section 12.4. Lastly, Section 12.5 concludes this chapter.

12.1   Related Work

Many dense architectures have been proposed in the literature that optimize compute [39, 126, 127] and memory bandwidth [131, 132] for CNN inferences. Quantization of weights and activations using log [37, 38] and linear [39, 175] techniques further reduce the memory footprint. This does not result in a significant loss in accuracy and reduces the CNN model size by a considerable amount. Hardware implementations such as Envision [40], VWA [142], NeuroMAX [96], UNPU [41], and Stripes [42], show how reduced bit precision, efficient dataflow, and quantization, translates into increased throughput and savings in energy. Efficient data reuse-based accelerators [45, 184] maximize the data reuse within different layers to minimize the memory accesses, thereby, reducing energy consumption. Separable accelerators [138, 139] implement efficient hardware on programmable gate array (FPGA) for accelerating separable convolutions. These accelerators, however, cannot handle a vast majority of CNNs that employ regular convolutions and FC layers. Bit-serial accelerators [133, 134] use booth encoding to suppress the use of zero bits, and, thereby, reduce the total computations. These schemes, however, transfer zeros to and from memory which incurs SRAM area and energy. CirCNN [135] uses block circulant matrices for weights to improve the performance. It, however, utilizes complex hardware to perform the Fourier transform (FFT) operations, and also, does not capture full sparsity. In-memory accelerators [136, 137] use simple analog logic to implement matrix multiplications within memory. These accelerators, however, cannot exploit sparsity as it requires complex arithmetic logic unit (ALU) and buffering logic. Analog circuits also suffer heavily from noise and process variations which can drastically reduce the CNN accuracy.

Sparse architectures try to reduce the compute and data volume by exploiting the naturally occurring zeros in weights or activations (one-sided), or both weights and activations (two-sided). Cnvlutin [43] and Cambricon-X [44] exploit one-sided sparsity of either weights or input maps but not both. Cnvlutin, also, does not avoid transfer of zeros and only skips cycles for activations. Cambricon-X does not store activations in compressed format, while Cambricon-S [174] forces regularity by employing coarse grain pruning that affects accuracy. Even though it discards zeros during computation, it still retrieves and stores them. Tensaurus [176] accelerates dense and sparse tensor factorizations by introducing a new dataflow which they refer to as compressed interleaved sparse slice (CISS) dataflow. Tensaurus, however, is capable of supporting only one-sided sparsity. Some recent sparse GEMM (SpGEMM) accelerators [153, 154, 156, 158, 177, 178] target general sparse-matrix, sparse-matrix multiplications. Extensor [177] and Sigma [153] use output stationary (inner-product) dataflow for sparse matrix multiplications. Inner-product, however, is inefficient against highly sparse matrices because every element of the rows and columns must be traversed even though there are less effectual computations (nonzero × nonzero). This leads to a massive amount of wasted computations. SpArch [154] and OuterSPACE [178] use input stationary (or outer-product) dataflow to avoid the inefficiencies associated with the inner-product dataflow. Outer-product, however, gives poor output reuse as the partial outputs generated are more in quantity than the final outputs which can cause significant memory traffic. Finally, MatRaptor [156] introduces channel cyclic sparse row (C^2SR) dataflow for better reuse and memory efficiency. It is a modified version of the CSR format but requires complex encoding for output matrices. Finally, SCNN, SparTen, and Eyeriss v2, exploit the full two-sided sparsity, but, as explained previously, suffer from either inefficient micro-architecture, no support for FC layers and nonunit stride convolutions, complex PE design to incorporate compressed sparse column (CSC) compression format, or systematic load imbalance. *Phantom* addresses all of these issues while also providing higher performance and energy efficiency.

12.2 Phantom

This section describes the architecture and inner workings of the *Phantom* core. As mentioned earlier in the chapter, the *Phantom* core in itself provides two major contributions. First, it considers both activation and weight sparsity simultaneously and *looks ahead* into future computations to determine only the valid MAC operations ($non\text{-}zero_w \times non\text{-}zero_a$). Second, because of the multithreaded design of the PEs, the scheduling of data into each thread is handled dynamically in a nonlinear fashion, based on the sparsity of input and weight matrices. This ensures that only valid computations are mapped on to the multithreaded PEs and that the compute cycles are not wasted. This is opposed to the designs which schedule data into the PEs in a constant manner and gate the computations whenever zeros are read, thereby, wasting the compute cycles.

Figure 12.1 shows a 3×3 convolution example, where a 3×8 input is convolved with a 3×3 filter to produce a 1×6 output. The six individual convolution chunks which produce the output are also shown. The effective and ineffective

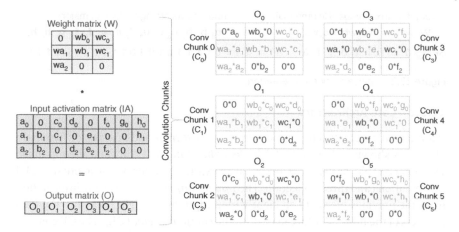

Figure 12.1 3 × 3 convolution example.

multiplications are shown in light gray and dark gray, respectively. It can be seen that, on average, 55% computations involve multiplication with zeros which result in wasted compute cycles. This causes a significant drop in the effective throughput, as many cycles are wasted in *zero* multiplications. The *Phantom* core addresses this issue and uses look-ahead masking to maximize the effective throughput by skipping ineffectual computations involving zeros.

12.2.1 Sparse Mask Representation

Unlike the recent approaches that use compressed sparse row (CSR) or CSC formats to represent non-zero data [43, 44, 53], we use a binary mask called *sparse mask* for both weight and activation data. Sparse mask provides an efficient and simplistic way for data representation and enables identification of zero and nonzero data without explicitly storing zeros. It also does not require storage of *count* and *data pointers* which are needed for CSC (and CSR) formats. Figure 12.2 shows the equivalent sparse mask representation and storage of the input and the weight matrix shown in Figure 12.1. For a particular matrix, two arrays are stored in the column major format. The data array contains the nonzero data, whereas the binary array contains the sparse mask. The ones in the sparse mask array represent the location of *stored* nonzero values, whereas zeros represent *unstored* zero data. To process a specific type of convolution, the sparse mask and the data array is broken into chunks and scheduled to the core. Although, the core can work on any type of CONV or FC layers, for ease of understanding, we will explain the working of *Phantom* core using the 3 × 3 unit stride convolution example, shown in Figure 12.1.

Weight matrix storage (Column major)   Input matrix storage (Column major)

W	wa$_1$	wa$_2$	wb$_0$	wb$_1$	wc$_0$	wc$_1$

SPM$_W$	0	1	1	1	1	0	1	1	0

IA	a$_0$	a$_1$	a$_2$	b$_1$	b$_2$	c$_0$	c$_1$	d$_0$	d$_2$	e$_1$	e$_2$	f$_0$	f$_2$	g$_0$	h$_0$	h$_1$

SPM$_{IA}$	1	1	1	0	1	1	1	1	0	1	0	1	0	1	1	1	0	1	1	0	0	1	1	0

Figure 12.2   Sparse mask representation.

12.2.2   Core Architecture

Phantom core accepts data in the sparse mask format and consists of five main blocks, as shown in Figure 12.3. The *lookahead mask* (LAM) and the *top-down selector* (TDS) blocks use the sparse mask to extract the information about the valid computations and thread selection. The *thread mapper* (TM) uses the information from the previous blocks to efficiently map input and weight data onto the data registers of the multiplier threads within the *compute engine* (CE). The CE consists of an array of *multithreaded* PEs and level 1 (L1) configurable adders. The *output buffer* (OB) block consists of an array of FIFO buffers and level 2 (L2) accumulators which generate the final output.

12.2.3   Lookahead Masking

Dot product between two vectors is the basic unit of computation in a convolution operation. Considering two-sided sparsity, there are four possible multiplication outcomes as a result of sparse vector-vector dot product.

(A) $zero_w \times zero_a$
(B) $zero_w \times non\text{-}zero_a$
(C) $non\text{-}zero_w \times zero_a$
(D) $non\text{-}zero_w \times non\text{-}zero_a$

The only valid multiplication is when a nonzero weight data is multiplied by a nonzero activation data. As the name implies, the lookahead mask (LAM) block *looks ahead* into *n* convolution chunks to determine the locations of valid multiplications. We refer to the value *n* as the *lookahead factor* (L_f).[1] To perform its

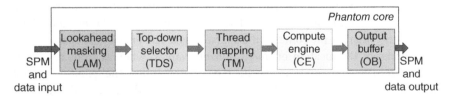

Figure 12.3   Phantom block diagram.

---

1 Notations *n* and L_f will be used interchangeably throughout the text.

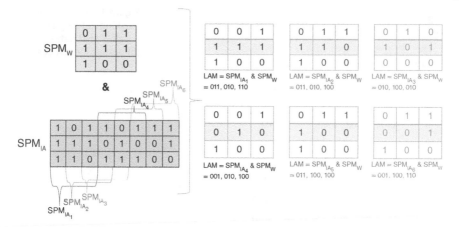

Figure 12.4 ANDing of sparse masks.

task, the LAM block performs an AND operation between the sparse masks of the weight matrix and the input chunks to generate output masks. Figure 12.4 shows the process of ANDing. Here, SPM_W and SPM_{IA} are the sparse masks of the weight and the input matrix of the example in Figure 12.1. Six output chunks are generated based on the AND operation.

To perform this ANDing, the LAM consists of a series of n AND gates, as shown in Figure 12.5a. Bitwise ANDing is performed between the weight and the activation sparse mask. For this example, we set the value of n to 3. This means that to generate six output masks in Figure 12.4, two cycles will be needed for the six AND operations.

Figure 12.5b shows the output of LAM for the test example. The $n = 3$ AND gates produce outputs (LAM_1, LAM_2, LAM_3) on every cycle edge. It takes two cycles to slide over the entire 3×8 activation matrix. The ones in the outputs of AND gates represent the location of a valid vector-vector dot product, whereas the zeros represent a product resulting in a zero. Overall, it can be seen that by using a sequence of n-AND gates, we can accurately determine the positions of *valid* computations in n convolution chunks.

12.2.4 Top-Down Selector

The top-down selector (TDS) receives the LAM outputs on every cycle edge and selects a subsequence of LAM outputs that can maximize the utilization of multiplier threads in the PEs within the CE. There are a total of p parallel selectors, with p equal to the total number of PEs in the CE. In this design, we consider $p = 3$, since there are a total of three PEs in the CE. We develop two selection algorithms for the TDS block namely, *in-order selection* and *out-of-order selection*.

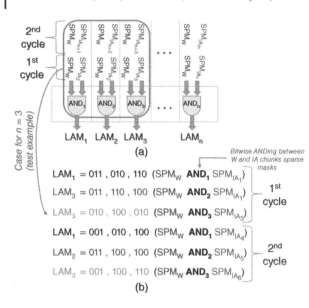

Figure 12.5 Lookahead masking: (a) Sequence of parallel AND gates and (b) output for test case.

12.2.4.1 In-Order Selection

Figure 12.6a shows the process of in-order selection. The three selectors work on the three *comma-separated* columns in parallel. The selection is performed iteratively in an *ordered* fashion on the entire column in a top-down manner. For column 1 in Figure 12.6a, the first selector loops through the first n elements in the current iteration, i.e., 011 (black), 011 (dark gray), and 010 (light gray). Here, n equals the *lookahead factor* (L_f), which is three in this design. The first 011 (in black) is assigned the highest priority and is selected. The selector counts the

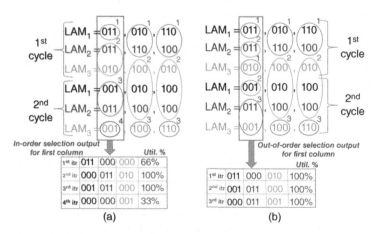

Figure 12.6 Top down selector (a) In-order selection and (b) out-of-order selection.

number of ones from this entry and stores the result. The selector then proceeds to the next entry, i.e., 011 (in dark gray), and counts the number of ones. If the combined sum of the number of ones of the current and the previous entry is greater than n, the current **and** the next entries, in the current iteration are not considered, and instead, replaced by zeros. Here, we see that 011 (in black) + 011 (in dark gray) = 4 > ($n = 3$). Therefore, only the first 011 (in black) is selected and the rest two entries are replaced by zeros in the first iteration. Here, every 1 in the selected output corresponds to a valid multiplication. Since, there are a total of three multiplier threads within a single PE, if the selected values contain a total of three 1s, then all the threads within a PE are utilized, giving a utilization of 100% (as shown in Figure 12.6a). The utilization decreases if the order in which the entries appear do not align with the priority of selection. The circles around the values and the numbers on top represent the iteration number during which the particular value was selected by the selector. In the second iteration, the selector goes on to the first unselected value (011 in dark gray) and follows the same selection process. It takes a total of four iterations (cycles) for the selector to select all the values in the first column, as shown in Figure 12.6a. We can also see that the second and the third columns require a total of three cycles for selection, but need to wait one additional cycle for the selection of the first column to complete. This can cause computational idling and underutilization of the PE multipliers.

12.2.4.2 Out-of-Order Selection

In-order selection is highly dependent on the order in which the inputs appear. This can lead to underutilization of the multiplier threads in the PE, as shown in Figure 12.6a. Figure 12.6b shows the out-of-order selection method, where after the selection of the first entry (011 in black), **all** next entries (011 in dark gray, 010 in light gray) in an iteration are considered for selection. Therefore, as shown in Figure 12.6b, in the first iteration, after the selection of 011(in black), the next value 011 (in dark gray) is not considered (011 + 011 = 4 > n), but the subsequent value 010 (in light gray) is considered because 011(in black) + 010 (in light gray) $\leq n$. This small, yet efficient change greatly improves the thread utilization and consequently the throughput, as shown in Figure 12.6b. Figure 12.7 shows the implementation of the out-of-order selection variant of the TDS for the first column in Figure 12.6b. A small block memory, having independent read and write ports, receives the LAM outputs on every cycle. P1 and P2 are the high and low priorities, respectively. The read address (rd_addr) of the memory increments every time a value is selected and the tag bits are set to 1 for those values. The tag bits serve the purpose of accumulation during the output buffering (explained in Section 12.2.7). The priority of selection is reversed on the next input to ensure that the values missed in the previous iteration are given the highest priority in the current iteration. map_{11}, map_{12}, and map_{13} are the final outputs, as shown in

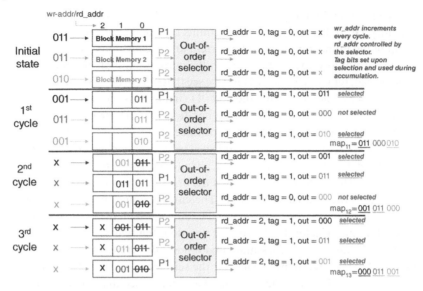

Figure 12.7 Out-of-order selection implementation.

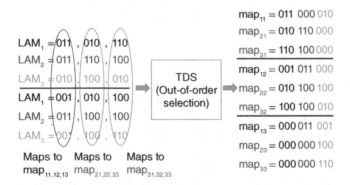

Figure 12.8 TDS out-of-order variant input-output.

Figure 12.8. The hardware overhead of the out-of-order selector is roughly 1.03×️ that of the in-order selector variant, but can increase the hardware utilization by as much as 60%. *Phantom*, therefore, employs the out-of-order selection variant of the TDS for higher thread utilization and efficient mapping.

12.2.5 Thread Mapper

The Thread Mapper (TM) takes the input from the TDS (map_{1x}, map_{2x}, and map_{3x}) and uses this information to map the length equalized sparse data (weight and activation) onto the internal registers of the multithreaded PEs. The length equalization is done by adding appropriate zeros at specific locations using the sparse masks. Figure 12.9 shows the map operation for the three PEs in this design. Out of the $2^9 = 512$ combinations, the mapper only needs to store those for which the total number of ones do not exceed the multiplier count of each PE (3 in this case). This drastically reduces the total combinations needed to be stored ($(\binom{9}{0} + \binom{9}{1} + \binom{9}{2} + \binom{9}{3} = 130$, a 74% reduction in the memory footprint). Each PE has a 50 bit internal register, out of which, 48 bits are the data bits, and 2 bits are the L1 adder control bits. The first 48 bits are divided into a set of 16 bits (8 bits for both activations and weights). The total memory requirement for storage of all three mappers is approximately 2.5 kB. One key observation from Figure 12.9 is that the mappers 2 and 3 map the data in a similar fashion as the mapper 1, but only use different location bits for weights and data. We, therefore, remove the two mappers (map_{2x} and map_{3x}), and only use one mapper (map_{1x}) sequentially three times, and adjusting the location bits afterwards. This only incurs an initial latency of two cycles but reduces the memory footprint by approximately 66% (2.5 to 0.83 kB). Appropriate delay registers are added in the PEs to account for the initial delay.

12.2.6 Compute Engine

The *Phantom* core uses a multithreaded CE block. In this particular design, the CE block consists of three multi-threaded PEs, with each PE containing three multiplier threads, as shown in Figure 12.10a. The mapper maps the data to the individual threads which perform independent computations. The outputs of the threads, local to a particular PE, are provided to the L1 adder. The L1 adder is provided by the configuration bits from the last 2 bits of the mapper (Figure 12.9). There are four cases for the configuration bits:

$C1: 00 \rightarrow$ *The individual outputs of the multiplier threads within the PE are not added and simply passed.*

$C2: 01 \rightarrow$ *The outputs of the first two multiplier threads ($th_{0,x}, th_{1,x}$) are added, whereas, the third one ($th_{2,x}$) is passed as is.*

$C3: 10 \rightarrow$ *the outputs of $th_{1,x}$ and $th_{2,x}$ are added and the output of $th_{0,x}$ is passed as is.*

$C4: 11 \rightarrow$ *the outputs of all the multiplier threads are added.*

Figure 12.10b shows the cycle by cycle scheduling of the multiplier threads with data (weights and activations) mapped using the logic in Figure 12.9. The mapping inputs (map_{11}, etc.) and L1 adder configuration outputs are also shown. It can be seen that all the multiplier threads are efficiently utilized even though the output is 55% sparse (counting number of zeros from the left side of Figure 12.8, 30/54). The hardware utilization during the first and second cycle is 100%, whereas, for

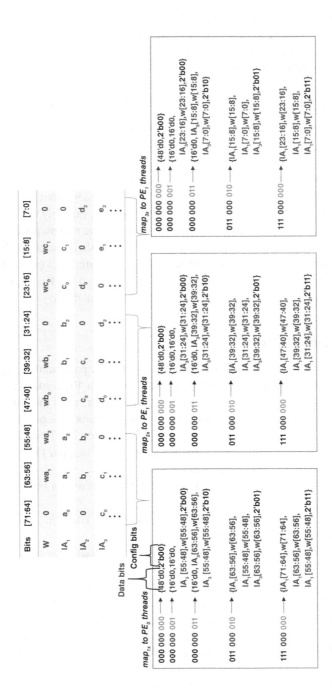

Figure 12.9 Thread mapping.

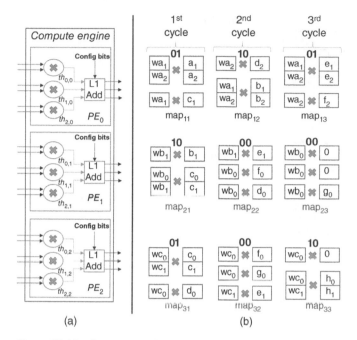

Figure 12.10 Compute engine (a) Multithreaded design and (b) scheduling for example in Figure 12.1.

the third cycle, it is 66%. The reason for low utilization in the last cycle is because the input is at the *boundary* and the LAM block does not have more data to *look ahead* into.

12.2.7 Output Buffer

The final block in the *Phantom* core is the output buffer (OB). OB is responsible for buffering the outputs of the CE, and accumulation of data using the L2 adder to generate the final outputs. The buffering is performed using a system of m first-in, first out (FIFO) buffers, where m is equal to the total number of multiplier threads in the CE (9). Figure 12.11 shows the OB block for the example in Figure 12.1. F1-F9 are the 9 fifos receiving data from the L1 adders in the CE. The *ones* (in light gray) and *zeros* (in dark gray) within the parenthesis represent the *tag* bits which were set by the TDS block, as shown in Figure 12.7. Accumulation is performed in two stages by the same colored fifos (F1 + F4 + F7), (F2 + F5 + F8), and (F3 + F6 + F9). The outputs are either *valid* or *partial*, based on the associated tags. If the tags of all the values being accumulated are equal to **1**, the output is considered *valid*, otherwise, it is considered *partial*. For the example

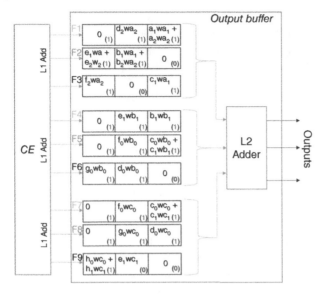

Figure 12.11 Output buffer for example in Figure 12.1.

Cycle 1

$(a_1 wa_1 + a_2 wa_2)\,(1) + (b_1 wb_1)(1) + (c_0 wc_0 + c_1 wc_1)(1) = O_0 \text{(valid)}$

$(0)\,(0) + (c_0 wb_0 + c_1 wb_1)(1) + (d_0 wc_0)(1) = O_1 \text{(partial)}$

$(c_1 wa_1)\,(1) + (0)(0) + (0)(0) = O_2 \text{(partial)}$

Cycle 2

$(d_2 wa_2)\,(1) + (e_1 wb_1)(1) + (f_0 wc_0)(1) = O_3 \text{(valid)}$

$(b_1 wa_1 + b_2 wa_2)\,(1) + O_1 \text{(partial)} = O_1 \text{(valid)}$

$(0)(0) + (f_0 wb_0)(1) + (g_0 wc_0)(1) = O_4 \text{(partial)}$

$O_2 \text{(partial)} + (d_0 wb_0)(1) + (e_1 wc_1)(1) = O_2 \text{(valid)}$

$(0)(0) + (0)(0) + (0)(0) = O_5 \text{(partial)}$

Cycle 3

$(0)(1) + (0)(1) + (0)(1) = \text{Outputs Exhausted}$

$(e_1 wa_1 + e_2 wa_2)(1) + O_4 \text{(partial)} = O_4 \text{(valid)}$

$(0)(1) + (0)(1) + (0)(1) = \text{Outputs Exhausted}$

$(f_2 wa_2)(1) + (g_0 wb_0)(1) + (h_0 wc_0 + h_1 wc_1)(1) + O_5 \text{(partial)} = O_5 \text{(valid)}$

$(0)(1) + (0)(1) + (0)(1) = \text{Outputs Exhausted}$

Figure 12.12 L2 accumulation for the example in Figure 12.1.

in Figure 12.1, the outputs in L2 adder are calculated as shown in Figure 12.12. The two stages of accumulation are also shown. In the first stage, the previously accumulated *partial* output is added to the new entry in the fifo to make the output *valid*. This is done by checking the tag bits in the *partial* output and adding the missing tag **1** in the new value to generate the *valid* output from *partial* output. In the second stage, new partial values are generated by replacing the used tag **1** value in the first stage by 0 and accumulating the rest of the tag **1** values. The process ends once the input is exhausted and all the tag **1** values have been accumulated to generate *valid* outputs.

12.2.8 Output Encoding

Figure 12.13 shows the process of output sparse mask generation. Unlike the weights, the output activation sparsity is dynamic and the sparse mask needs to be generated on-the-fly. From Figure 12.4, we can see that the presence of even a single *one* in the LAM outputs represent a nonzero output. To determine the output sparse mask, the same metadata can be used. The first step involves reduction of the individual LAM outputs to a single bit (LAM_{xr}), based on an *all-zero* check, as shown in Figure 12.13a. This generates the sparse mask for the outputs before ReLU. Note that the LAM values are taken from the test example (Figure 12.1). Figure 12.13b shows the second step after ReLU, where the negative outputs, and their corresponding sparse mask locations, are converted into zeros. This final sparse mask is stored as is, whereas the output is shifted first to omit zero data entries, and then stored.

This concludes the processing in a single *Phantom* core. In Section 12.3, we will introduce *Phantom-2D*, a two-dimensional accelerator having a system of *Phantom* cores for processing CNN layers during the inference process.

12.3 Phantom-2D

Section 12.2 describe the working of the various blocks in the *Phantom* core. The individual core works by computing a dot product between a weight matrix and

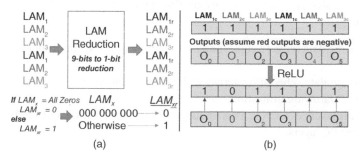

Figure 12.13 Output sparse mask generation.

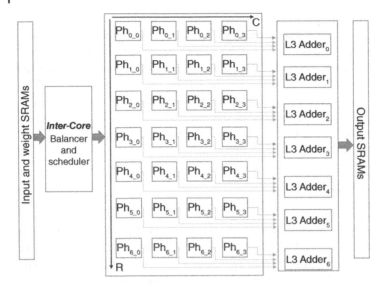

Figure 12.14 Phantom-2D architecture.

a subsection of the input feature map to compute a subsection of the output feature map. To compute the *full* output feature map, corresponding to a particular layer, we design a two-dimensional accelerator comprising of the *Phantom* cores, which we refer to as *Phantom-2D*, as shown in Figure 12.14. We envision that the *Phantom-2D* accelerator connects to a memory bus and accepts data and instructions from a CPU. The accelerator contains on-chip SRAMs (weight, input, and output), the *inter-Core* balancer and scheduler, the $R \times C$ compute matrix, comprising of *Phantom* cores, and the accumulator circuits.

12.3.1 $R \times C$ Compute Matrix

The compute unit consists of an $R \times C$ matrix of the *Phantom* cores and R adders for channel accumulation. The design choice for R and C, and the dataflow associated with the transfer of data across various *Phantom* cores, is based on the following design goals:

G1: To maximize the data reuse (weights and input) across multiple input subsections.

G2: To optimize the data scheduling across various *Phantom* cores to maximize the *theoretical* hardware utilization.

G3: To support **all** layers of a CNN. This includes support for a variety of CONV layers and the FC layers.

Looking deeper into the dimensions and configurations of various popular CNN models (VGGnet [31], Resnet [32], MobileNets [33, 34], Googlenet [35], etc.), we observe that the channel count for various CNN layers is almost always a multiple of 4. In the *Phantom-2D* architecture, the channels in a CNN layer are broken along the columns. Therefore, to ensure that the cores are engaged *most* of the time, and thus, satisfy G2, we set the C value equal to 4. Similar rationale applies for the choice of $R = 7$. The input subsections are broken along the vertical axis and distributed along the rows. Most of the popular CNNs have an input layer size (width or height) S, a multiple of 7, thus, having $R = 7$, ensures equal distribution of chunks of data among all the cores.

12.3.2 Load Balancing

The design choice for $R \times C$ matrix is highly dependent on the layer dimensions of various CNNs. It, however, has no relevance to the static and dynamic sparsity in weights and inputs, respectively. Efficient reuse of data is one of the key requirements to minimize the memory accesses, repeatedly, for the same data. This reuse, however, amplifies the computational imbalance among different PEs. If the same filter is held in the local memory of the PEs and the input subsections are swept across the PEs, the subsections with higher density would inevitably take more cycles to compute the output, compared to the PEs receiving the subsections with lower density. This varying sparsity of the input maps would create a *system-level* load imbalance among the PEs which would be exposed during the next filter broadcast. Holding the input maps and sweeping the filters would also have similar results, as would the buffering of data. In order to address this *system-level* load imbalance, we incorporate a two-level load balancing strategy in the *Phantom* architecture. The **Inter-Core** balancer (Figure 12.14), balances the computational load dynamically using the density of the weight matrix such that each phantom core works on the weight matrices with the same/similar density over the CNN layers (as described in Section 12.3.3.1 with an example). This balancing is only performed when the weight data is actively being reused (e.g., in regular and depthwise separable CONV). The second balancer, referred to as **Intra-Core** balancer, is local to each core, and performs columnwise balancing of the weight matrix. This balancer is always enabled, regardless of the layer, and significantly improves the individual multiplier thread scheduling performed by the TDS.

In Sections 12.3.3–12.3.6, we demonstrate, with examples, the designed dataflow for various CONV and FC layers. We choose the input sizes that fit well with the layer sizes of actual CNNs. We also show how the balancing is performed to prevent idling of the cores, which in turn, maximizes the throughput, all the while ensuring high data reuse.

12.3.3 Regular/Depthwise Convolution

Figure 12.15 shows a 3×3 depthwise separable convolution example, where 4, 3×3 filters are convolved with a $9 \times 5 \times 4$ input to generate a $7 \times 3 \times 4$ output. We choose these size parameters as an example because they fit well when considering the layer sizes of the actual CNNs. The figure also shows the scheduling and mapping of data on to the $R \times C$ matrix. The input is broken down into n chunks along the rows, where n is the number of rows of the output. These n chunks are then scheduled along the rows of the $R \times C$ matrix. Each *Phantom* core processes a 3×5 input chunk to generate a 1×3 output chunk. The filters F0 to F3 represent the channel wise filters, with each column of the $R \times C$ matrix processing a different channel. The reuse of filters (G1) along the rows is also shown. The nonunit stride convolutions follow the same dataflow. Because of the efficient dataflow and choice of the $R \times C$ dimensions, all *Phantom* cores are provided data for a particular processing chunk, thereby, achieving a 100% intercore utilization (G2).

12.3.3.1 Intercore Balancing

The intercore balancing is performed for the layers that support filter reuse because of the static nature of the weights. In the proposed dataflow, the layers that support filter reuse are the regular and the depthwise separable convolution layers. As shown in Figure 12.15, each $R \times C$ matrix column, at any given time, processes the same filter. The filters are scheduled in a *low latency, more dense* and *high latency, less dense* approach. Assuming that during the first iteration, the four filters (F0, F1, F2, F3) are broadcasted and the first column's processing latency is the lowest. In the next filter broadcast, the next set of filters will be broadcasted in such a way that the filter with the highest density and the associated input channel will be scheduled to the first column. In a similar fashion, as the columns proceed to completion, the next filters are scheduled based on the order of their completion. This ensures that the processing completes uniformly across all the columns so that the idle time for the individual *phantom* cores is minimized. Computation of density is trivial as it involves finding the total number of ones in the sparse mask of the filters, and thus, requires minimal resources.

12.3.4 Pointwise Convolution

Figure 12.16 shows a pointwise convolution example where a set of $1 \times 1 \times 36 \times 7$ sparse filters convolve with a $3 \times 3 \times 36$ sparse input to produce a $3 \times 3 \times 7$ output. These dimensional parameters are a good representative of the layer dimensions of actual CNNs. Figure 12.16 also shows the dataflow and the mapping of the various computations involved for this example. It can be seen that the 7 filters are scheduled along the 7 rows of the *Phantom* cores with each row processing equal

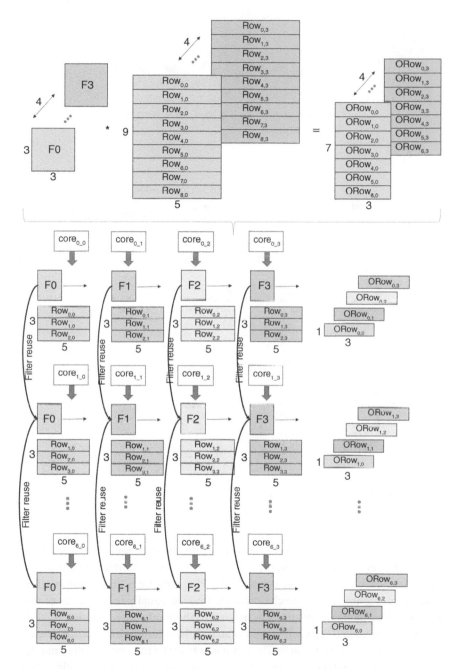

Figure 12.15 Regular/depthwise convolution.

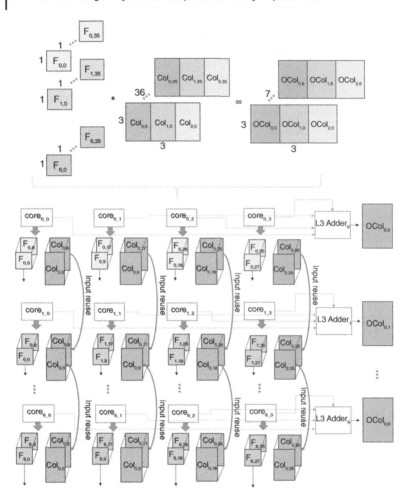

Figure 12.16 Pointwise convolution.

number of channels along the columns. The channels are equally divided based on the number of combined multiplier threads in each *Phantom* core. Since, in this design, each *Phantom* core consists of 3 PEs, with each PE containing three multipliers (Figure 12.10), the channels are divided equally into batches of nine and scheduled along the columns to maximize the hardware utilization (G2). To enhance data reuse (G1), each weight matrix is held locally in a particular core, while the input is swept across it. The input is scheduled in a *channel-first* manner, followed by rows, and then columns. Figure 12.16 only shows the generation of the first column of the output. After all the rows for a particular channel have been exhausted, the next column is evaluated in a similar fashion till all the columns have been swept through. The L3 adder circuit gathers all the partial outputs from the cores along the columns to generate the required outputs.

12.3.5 FC Layers

FC layers are an inherent part of modern CNN designs and, therefore, need to be accounted for in CNN accelerator designs (G3). AlexNet and VGG-16 both have FC layers with activation vectors that are 4K long and weight matrix that is 4K × 4K long. Similarly, Mobilenet has an FC layer with activation vector that is 1K long and weight matrix that is 1K × 1K long. The FC parameters comprise of a total of 24.3% of all the parameters in the Mobilenet. FC computations, therefore, are crucial and need to be accounted for in CNN accelerator designs (G3). Figure 12.17 shows an FC computation example where a length 36 sparse input vector (R_0-R_{35}) is element-wise convolved with a 36 × 49 sparse weight matrix to generate a length 49 output vector. Figure 12.17 also shows the dataflow and the computational mapping of the example onto the *Phantom* cores in the *Phantom-2D* architecture. Similar to the pointwise convolution, the input and the weight channels are broken into four batches of length nine and scheduled across the columns. The input vector, is held stationary (input stationary) across the rows and the individual weight vectors are swept over the input vector to generate the partial outputs. Similar accumulation is performed by the L3 adders to generate the final outputs.

12.3.6 Intracore Balancing

The *Intracore* balancer performs thread-level balancing inside every *Phantom* core. This is opposed to the *Intercore* balancer which performs balancing across all the *Phantom* cores in the *Phantom-2D* architecture. Recall that the TDS (Section 3.4) operates in a columnwise manner where each column of the LAM outputs are evaluated concurrently, as shown in Figure 12.6. Also, recall that the total number of ones selected by the TDS per column are less than or equal to the number of multiplier threads per PE (3 in this case). Because of the columnwise selection, the TDS latency is bounded by the column with the highest density. Figure 12.18a shows a test example to explain the intracore balancing and its significance. Figure 12.18b shows the core operation without any balancing. The first column of the weight matrix has the highest density. This is also reflected in the generated LAM values. This uneven distribution results in the first column taking the highest number of cycles, whereas, the second and the third column selection completing in only one cycle, as shown in Figure 12.18b. This stalls the core as the core must wait for the first column to complete all three cycles before processing

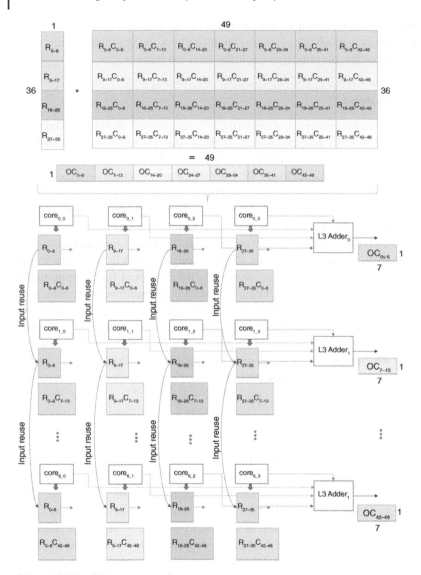

Figure 12.17 FC layer processing.

the next block which significantly decreases the thread utilization of the core (Valid Computations/(Cycles × PEs × ThreadsPerPE) = $9/(3 \times 3 \times 3) = 33\%$).

Figure 12.18c shows how the intracore balancer mitigates this issue by efficient distribution of the load, prior to the TDS operation, in a relatively simplistic manner. A right circular shift is performed on LAM_2 and LAM_3 values, as shown in Figure 12.18c. This modifies the load distribution among the three LAM columns.

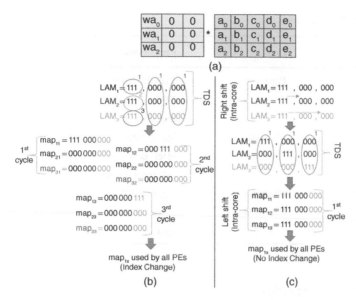

Figure 12.18 Intracore balancing (a) Test example, (b) without balancing, and (c) with balancing.

Operation of the TDS this time ensures the selection of all three columns in one cycle. A circular left shift is performed on the generated map inputs (map_{11} = 111 000 000, map_{12} = 000 111 000, map_{13} = 000 000 111) in the same manner as the circular right shift in the first step to ensure a valid mapping by the mapper. The updated map values, after shifting, are shown in Figure 12.18c. The updated map values are then used in the map_{1x} without adjustment in the location/index (Section 3.5) to accurately map data to the individual threads. The thread utilization of the core, in this case, increases drastically (Valid Computations/(Cycles × PEs × ThreadsPerPE) = 9/(1 × 3 × 3) = 100%). Finally, it should be noted that the evaluation of the example in Figure 12.18 is performed with L_f = 3. However, the same process follows for any value of L_f. We will further explore the combined effect of both, the intercore, and the intra-core balancing, on performance, in Section 5.

12.4 Experiments and Results

12.4.1 Evaluation Methodology

12.4.1.1 Cycle-Accurate Simulator

To accurately model the performance of an individual *Phantom* core and the *Phantom-2D* accelerator, as a whole, we design a software-based, cycle-level

Table 12.1 Operation parameters.

Operation	Level	Parameters
TDS	*Phantom*	TDS_inOrder
		TDS_outOrder
Balancing		unbalanced
	Phantom/	intra_core
	Phantom-2D	inter_core
		full(inter + intra)
Lookahead factor (L_f)	*Phantom*	$3 \leq L_f \leq 27$
CNN models	*Phantom-2D*	dense
		sparse

Table 12.2 Accelerator configuration.

Configuration parameter	Value
Compute matrix size	$28\,(7 \times 4)$
PEs per core	3
Multiplier threads per PE	3
Total multiplier threads	252

performance simulator. The simulator is parameterizable across various core and architecture level design parameters to capture their effect on the performance. Table 12.1 shows the modifiable design parameters. The operations are categorized as core level and architecture-level. Table 12.2 shows the arrangement and configuration of the *Phantom-2D* accelerator's compute matrix containing *Phantom* cores.

The simulator has a set of five built-in test scenarios which covers the sweeping of all the parameters shown in Table 12.1. The simulator also contains routines for SparTen, SCNN, and Eyeriss v2 for performing comparisons. During the processing of each layer, every *Phantom* core outputs seven values which includes the total cycles by a dense design, the cycles of TDS in-order and TDS out-of-order, coupled with two-level load balancing, and the average thread utilization for various *Phantom-2D* configurations. The total cycle count for SparTen, SCNN, and Eyeriss v2 is also outputted. The evaluation files in the simulator use the data provided by the individual routines and schedulers to generate the throughput and speedup results for dense and sparse accelerator designs.

12.4.1.2 Simulated Models

Although we test our design on many CNN models including Alexnet [30], VGG16 [31], MobileNets [33, 34], GoogleNet [35], and recently proposed EfficientNetV2 [46], we present the results for sparse versions of VGG16 and MobileNet for comparison purposes. We use the approach presented in [46] to prune these networks using the MATLAB's *Deep Learning Toolbox* and ensure that we achieve the same level of weight sparsity as previous approaches, for fair comparisons. The activation sparsity is highly dependent on the input and changes dynamically during the inference process. We, therefore, average out the input sparsity for a batch of 100 randomly selected inputs. After pruning of the network, we generate the sparse binary masks for every layer and generate a network containing only the sparse masks, since only this information is needed to efficiently represent the MAC operations needed per layer for the *Phantom-2D* accelerator. The sparse masks are fed into the simulator in the model dimensions (i.e., mapped to the dimension of each CNN layer in the model). The simulator's scheduler uses the dataflow for various layers, presented in Figures 12.15–12.17, to break down the dimensions and schedule the individual binary masks to different *Phantom* cores.

12.4.2 Results

We capture the simulator's results in an incremental approach, starting from the basic core-level configurations, and moving toward system-level configurations. All the comparisons are made with an equivalent dense architecture, having an equal number of MAC units, but without leveraging the sparse optimizations. At the end, we compare different versions of *Phantom-2D* accelerator against previously proposed two-sided sparse architectures.

12.4.2.1 TDS Variants Comparison

Figure 12.19a shows the performance comparison of the two TDS variants, namely, the in-order TDS (TDS-IO) and the out-of-order TDS (TDS-OO), evaluated on a sparse VGG16 net. We set the lookahead factor (L_f) for this test to six for both the variants. The performance of the dense architecture can be modeled by setting the L_f value equal to 1. This would ensure that no future computations are observed by the TDS, thus, replicating a dense accelerator. It can be seen that the first layer does not have any significant performance gains over a dense architecture because of very low sparsity. The performance gains increase drastically in subsequent layers with TDS-IO variant, on average, being 4.5×, and the TDS-OO variant, being

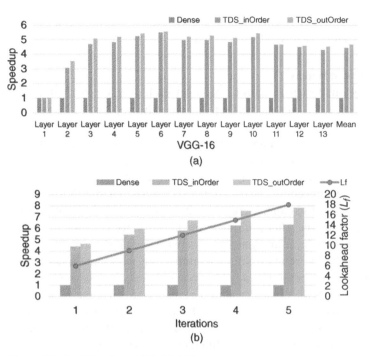

Figure 12.19 TDS-IO vs. TDS-OO (a) Per layer comparison with $L_f = 6$ and (b) comparisons with changing L_f.

4.8× faster, than the equivalent dense architecture. This represents a 1.07× performance improvement of TDS-OO over TDS-IO. The performance difference, however, improves substantially as L_f is increased, as shown in Figure 12.19b. We run the VGG16 net a total of five times, and average out the speedups, while sweeping L_f from 6 to 18, with a jump of three in every iteration. For $L_f = 18$, we observe a 6.35× and a 7.9× performance gain of TDS-IO and TDS-OO, respectively, over dense architecture, representing a 43% and a 68% increase, when switching from $L_f = 3$ to $L_f = 18$, respectively. TDS-OO, for $L_f = 18$, gives a 1.24× performance gain over TDS-IO, a jump of 16% from $L_f = 6$. These results are inline with our preliminary observations in Section 3.4. The improvement in the core's thread utilization from TDS-OO directly correlates to the increase in performance. For the next experiments, we will always use the TDS-OO variant.

12.4.2.2 Impact of Load Balancing
Figure 12.20 shows the impact of load balancing (*intercore* + *intracore*) on the performance for sparse VGG16 and MobileNet with $L_f = 6$. During the initial layers for both the CNNs, we observe a drastic improvement in performance (as much as 1.5× for VGG16 and 1.3× for MobileNet). On average, we observe a performance

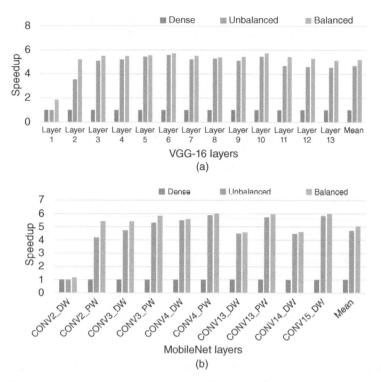

Figure 12.20 Balanced vs unbalanced at $L_f = 6$ for (a) Sparse VGG16 and (b) sparse MobileNet.

difference of 1.1× and 1.08× for VGG16 and MobileNet, respectively. From our experiments, we also observe that the performance difference due to *intracore* balancing increases drastically at high sparsity and greater value of L_f. This conclusion is inline with the example in Figure 12.18, where the increase in thread utilization from *intracore* balancing increases the speedup by 3×. The *intercore* balancing is dominant in later layers where there are a large number of channels. For reduction in simulation times, we only use approximately 25% of the channel filters for our simulations in the case of regular (and depthwise seperable) convolutions, which prevents us from exploiting the full power of the *intercore* balancing. Hence, Figures 12.20a,b do not show a significant improvement in layers with a large number of channels. Based on our experiments, we observe, on average, a 7% increase in speedup by having 15% more filters in our simulations.

12.4.2.3 Sensitivity to Sparsity and L_f

Our performance simulator has the capability to sweep the weight/activation sparsity from low 0.1/0.1 (10%) to high 1.0/1.0 (100%). This is shown in Figures 12.21

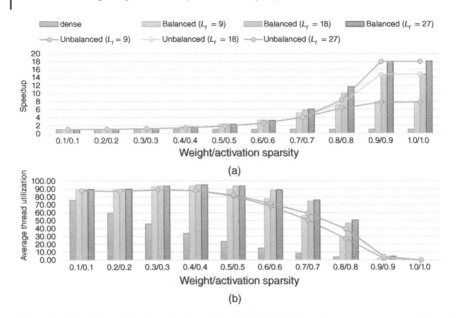

Figure 12.21 Sensitivity to sparsity and L_f for VGG16 (a) Speedup and (b) average thread utilization.

and 12.22. We also plot the average multiplier thread utilization at different levels of sparsity for VGG16 and MobileNet. For a dense architecture, we observe a higher thread utilization at low sparsity and lower thread utilization at a higher sparsity, as shown in Figures 12.21b and 12.22b. *Phantom-2D*, however, exhibits significantly higher thread utilization compared to a dense architecture, even at high levels of sparsity. For VGG16, *Phantom-2D* consistently keeps the thread utilization higher than 90% even at 60% sparsity for both weights and activations, whereas as expected, the utilization for the dense architecture decreases by 25 – 30% and decreases by almost 50% at higher sparsity levels. This thread utilization difference directly correlates to greater speedups at mid to high levels of sparsity, as shown in Figures 12.21a and 12.22a. At higher sparsity levels (0.8/0.8–1.0/1.0), we observe a massive speedup over dense architecture even when the thread utilization starts decreasing. This is because the *Phantom-2D* accelerator starts actively skipping all the *zero* computations without wasting compute cycles.

For convenience in comparing different versions of the *Phantom-2D* accelerators, we rename them as *Phantom-2D-CV* (conservative, with $L_f = 9$, balanced), *Phantom-2D-MD* (moderate, with $L_f = 18$, balanced), and *Phantom-2D-HP* (high-performance, with $L_f = 27$, balanced). At low sparsity, all three versions exhibit similar speedups and thread utilization. This difference increases at higher sparsity levels with *Phantom-2D-MD* and *Phantom-2D-HP* being 1.43× and 1.65×

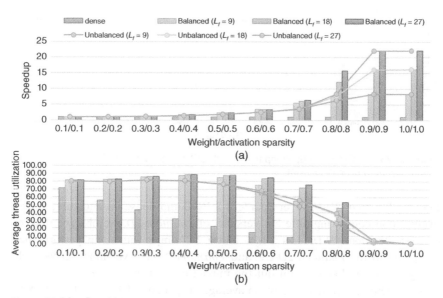

Figure 12.22 Sensitivity to sparsity and L_f for MobileNet (a) Speedup and (b) average thread utilization.

faster, respectively, than *Phantom-2D-CV*, at 80% sparsity. The unbalanced configurations display a similar trend among each other. Comparison between the *Phantom-2D-HP*, balanced and unbalanced configurations, show a 1.4× speedup of balanced over unbalanced at 80% sparsity. Analysis of hardware resources show that the *Phantom-2D-HP* requires only 1.05× more lookup table (LUT)s than *Phantom-2D-CV*. This is because the higher values of L_f only increase the LUT count of LAM and TDS blocks, whereas the Mapper, CE, and the OB blocks' LUT count remains the same.

12.4.2.4 Comparison Against Past Approaches

Figure 12.23 shows the speedup comparison of the different versions of the *Phantom-2D* accelerators over dense architecture, SCNN, and SparTen, for sparse VGG16 net. The average sparsity for the weights and activations is 77% and 68%, respectively. Note that both the SCNN, and SparTen, do not support FC layers, whereas *Phantom-2D* does. In addition, SCNN also does not support nonunit stride convolutions present in AlexNet and MobileNet. Therefore, for fair comparison, we omit the last three FC layers in our results and use sparse VGG16 which does not contain any nonunit stride convolution. We observe that the *Phantom-2D-CV* version, on average, performs 1.05×, 2.56×, and 6.4×, better than SparTen, SCNN, and dense architecture, respectively. The speedup increases to approximately 1.57×, 3.8×, and 9.9× for *Phantom-2D-MD*, and 1.98×, 4.1×, and

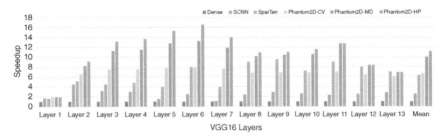

Figure 12.23 VGG16 speedup comparison with SCNN [163] and SparTen [152]. Source: Adapted from [152, 163].

11×, for *Phantom-2D-HP* over SparTen, SCNN, and dense architecture, respectively. Upon comparing different versions of *Phantom-2D*, we observe that, on average, *Phantom-2D-HP* has a 67% and a 14% improvement in performance, compared to the *Phantom-2D-CV* and *Phantom-2D-MD* versions, respectively. Lastly, we would like to point out the impact of FC layers on the *Phantom-2D* versions. Our experiments show, on average, a speedup of 13×, 11.4×, and 8.6× for *Phantom-2D-HP*, *Phantom-2D-MD*, and *Phantom-2D-CV*, respectively, over dense architecture after inclusion of FC14, FC15, and FC16 layers of the VGG16 net. This improvement corresponds to our efficient dataflow and scheduling for the FC layers.

Figure 12.24 shows the performance comparison of the *Phantom-2D* versions against Eyeriss v2 on sparse MobileNet. The average sparsity for the weights and activations is 73% and 64%, respectively. Authors of Eyeriss v2 performed their comparisons against their previous approach (Eyeriss [45]). Eyeriss v2 uses twice the number of MACs as Eyeriss, which doubles their final speedups. For fair comparison, we adjust the speedup values of Eyeriss v2 for comparison against a

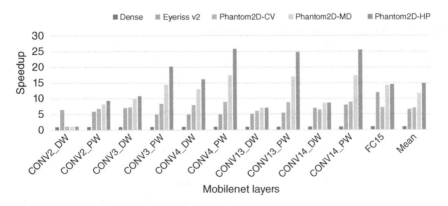

Figure 12.24 Speedup comparison with Eyeriss v2. Source: Adapted from [52].

dense accelerator having the same number of MACs and only use the layers used by Eyeriss v2. We observe that, on average, *Phantom-2D-CV* performs 1.04× better than Eyeriss v2, whereas the *MD* and *HP* versions, on average perform 1.71× and 2.86×, respectively, better than Eyeriss v2. Doing a layer-by-layer comparison, we observe that Eyeriss v2 performs better than *Phantom* in CONV2-DW (DW indicates depth-wise convolution) because of its efficient hierarchical mesh network-on-chip (NoC); however, *Phantom-2D-HP* catches up in deeper layers and almost always provides an improvement. Pointwise layers are especially faster in the case of *Phantom-2D-HP*, with the average speedup of 4.5× over Eyeriss v2, and 25× over a dense architecture. This is because of the efficient channelwise breakdown offered by our dataflow for these layers.

Comparing different versions of the *Phantom-2D* accelerators, *Phantom-2D-HP*, on average, offers 108.9% and 27.4% increase in speedup over *Phantom-2D-CV* and *Phantom-2D-MD*, respectively, for sparse MobileNet.

Comparing energy among different accelerators is quite challenging as it requires working register transfer level (RTL)s. The energy consumption of an accelerator is dominated by the DRAM accesses, therefore, by estimating the DRAM accesses, energy difference among the accelerators can be approximated. Since many of the recent works rely on the CSC format for nonzero data storage, we compare the accessed memory for the CSC format against the sparse mask format. Figure 12.25 shows the intermediate activations' memory access comparison for selected VGG 16 and MobileNet layers.[2] The activation sparsity for different layers is also shown. In the initial layers with low activation sparsity, the CSC format has approximately 4× and 3.7× higher DRAM memory accesses than the sparse mask for VGG16 and Mobilenet, respectively. In the deeper layers with moderate-to-high sparsity, the memory requirement for the CSC format is around 1.7× that of the sparse mask.

This shows that the sparse mask representation not only needs less encoding/decoding logic but is also efficient in terms of memory requirements when compared against the CSC format. This translates directly to higher energy, area, and compute savings for the accelerators employing the sparse mask format.

12.4.2.5 RTL Synthesis Results

We wrote the RTL Verilog for a single *Phantom* core with $L_f = 27$ (high performance) and synthesized it for the Xilinx Zynq 7100 SoC's programmable logic (PL), running at 150 MHz. The SoC's ARM-based processing system (PS) was used to transfer data to/from a desktop computer to DRAM. The PL acquires this data and stores it in its global buffers (input and weight SRAMs), shown in Figure 12.14.

---

2 The required memory for the stored nonzero data is not shown since it is the same for both the sparse mask and the CSC format. The accessed memory is shown for the binary sparse mask and the location vectors (column, index) of the CSC format.

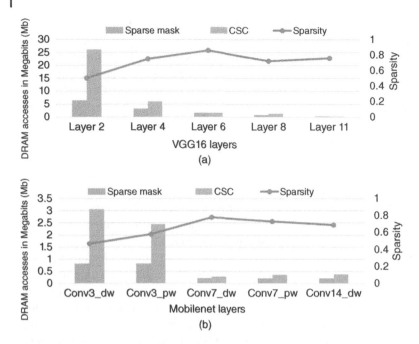

Figure 12.25 Sparse mask vs. CSC DRAM access for (a) VGG16 and (b) MobileNet.

The generated outputs and the sparse masks are stored in the output SRAMs and transferred to DRAM for the next layer. Table 12.3 shows the total resource utilization among various sub-blocks of the *Phantom* core. The main takeaway is that the novel components of the *Phantom* core (LAM, TDS, Mapper, and intracore balancer) only account for approximately 48% and 35% of the utilized LUT and the FF cost, respectively. The local SRAM utilization is dominated by the mapper and the output buffering block (approximately 78%). The design has a power consumption of 2.48 W with the PS dominating the consumption (55%). Eyeriss v2, implemented on a 65 nm application-specific integrated circuit (ASIC), utilizes 2695k gates which represents a 108% increase in area cost when compared to the original semisparse Eyeriss [45]. This drastic increase in area is the result of the complex encoding/decoding logic required by the CSC format in their design. SCNN has a 35% increase in area compared to their dense design, whereas SparTen does not report the resource utilization of their PEs.

12.5 Chapter Summary

Designing a CNN accelerator to leverage the two-sided sparsity is quite challenging owing to the varying layer shapes and sizes, associated with a sparse model.

Table 12.3 Resource utilization for a single *Phantom* core with $L_f = 27$.

Property	Available	Used	Utilization (%)
LUTs	277k	3.4k	1.23
FFs	554k	6k	1.1
On-chip SRAM	26.5Mb	2.1kB	0.01

In this chapter, we introduced *Phantom*: a novel *multithreaded*, flexible, neural computational core that exploits the two-sided sparsity to provide high gains in performance at a relatively low hardware complexity. Using a system of *Phantom* cores, we then designed the *Phantom-2D* accelerator, and presented a novel dataflow that efficiently used the capabilities of the *Phantom* cores. As opposed to many previous approaches, the *Phantom-2D* accelerator supports **all** layers of a CNN, including unit and non-unit stride convolutions, and FC layers. In addition, we discussed a two-level load balancing strategy that efficiently balanced the load across the architecture level (*inter-core*), and at the thread level (*intracore*) to minimize idling of the compute threads, thereby, further increasing the throughput. The chapter presented performance comparison of *Phantom-2D* against many previous state-of-the-art two-sided sparse CNN accelerators. The simulation results show that, on average, *Phantom-2D* accelerator performed 12×, 4.1×, 1.98×, and 2.36×, better than an equivalent dense CNN architecture, SCNN, SparTen, and Eyeriss v2, respectively, while retaining the energy efficiency of SparTen.

Part V

HW/SW Co-Design and Co-Scheduling for CNN Acceleration

13

State-of-the-Art in HW/SW Co-Design and Co-Scheduling for CNN Acceleration

This chapter provides an overview of hardware/software (HW/SW) co-design and co-scheduling for convolutional neural network (CNN) acceleration. This chapter can be broadly divided into two parts: HW/SW co-design and co-scheduling. For the first part, this chapter defines HW/SW co-design and provides background of HW/SW co-design. The chapter then presents a case study of cognitive Internet of things (IoT) as an example of HW/SW co-design. This chapter then describes recent advancements in the HW/SW co-design for resource-constrained systems. For the second part, this chapter provides background of HW/SW co-scheduling and then highlights recent advancements in HW/SW co-scheduling.

13.1 HW/SW Co-Design

The traditional computer system architecture is based on central processing unit (CPU) based design. The CPU has been widely deployed and is used to execute a wide spectrum of the applications. As transistor size approaches the size of a single atom, Moore's Law is not strictly applicable to the modern computer systems, and thus performance improvements attained by CPUs that have benefited from Moore's Law for decades have seen a slower increase over the years. Furthermore, memory wall and power wall make the continuous performance improvements from general-purpose computer systems even harder. Consequently, computing and architecture landscape has transitioned toward multicore and domain-specific architectures where multiple accelerators are available on-chip (i.e., system on-chip) or off-chip. These accelerators are utilized when executing specific workloads. The software of these domain-specific architectures is also often designed and optimized by considering the underlying hardware. This software design and optimization is very important for attaining

Accelerators for Convolutional Neural Networks, First Edition.
Arslan Munir, Joonho Kong, and Mahmood Azhar Qureshi.
© 2024 The Institute of Electrical and Electronics Engineers, Inc. Published 2024 by John Wiley & Sons, Inc.

high performance and energy efficiency in particular in embedded system domain where hardware resources are scarce. Software design and optimization considering the underlying hardware architecture can significantly improve performance and energy efficiency in domain-specific HW/SW systems because the architecture of the underlying hardware is different and can be best exploited by optimizing the software for that specific hardware. That is why, hardware and software are often co-designed for an application-specific workload or system, and this approach is referred to as hardware/software co-design.

HW/SW co-design concept emerged in 1990s. The notion of HW/SW co-design is essentially the concurrent design of hardware and software components of complex electronic systems [184]. HW/SW co-design aims to exploit the synergy between hardware and software in order to optimize and meet design constraints such as cost, performance, power, energy, and reliability of the final product. In HW/SW co-design concept, when the system is being designed, tasks/subtasks, functionalities/subfunctionalities, and different aspects or facets of the system are partitioned into hardware and software components depending on the design requirements. Software can provide flexibility and programmability whereas hardware can optimize aspects of a system that do not require change over the lifetime of a product. Modern HW/SW codesign techniques target SoC design that integrates general-purpose microprocessors/CPUs, digital signal processors (DSPs), programmable logic (FPGA), application-specific integrated system (ASIC) cores, memory blocks, peripherals, and interconnection buses on one chip. HW/SW co-design techniques aim to determine an optimal partitioning and assignment of tasks between software running on microprocessors or DSPs and hardware implemented on ASIC or FPGA for a given application [185].

For CNN acceleration, HW/SW co-design is imperative. When designing a computing system for CNNs, certain tasks in the CNNs can be offloaded to the hardware. For instance, since CPU is not suitable for data parallel workloads, the general matrix multiplication (GEMM) task can be offloaded to a dedicated hardware accelerator while other tasks can performed in software on CPU. In this way, task offloading afforded by HW/SW co-design can lead to a huge performance and energy efficiency benefit for CNN execution as compared to a system with only software-based execution on the CPU. On the software-side, the task scheduling by exploiting the task-level parallelism is also beneficial. In a HW/SW co-designed CNN acceleration system, when the dedicated hardware accelerator is performing some tasks/sub-tasks of CNN execution, other CNN tasks/sub-tasks can be executed in parallel in software running on the CPU. Figure 13.1 summarizes the comparison between the conventional CPU-based design and execution versus HW/SW co-design and execution.

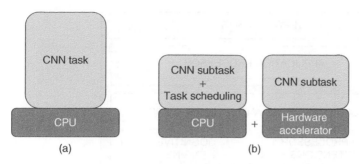

Figure 13.1 Comparison between (a) conventional software-based design and execution, and (b) HW/SW co-design and execution.

13.1.1 Case Study: Cognitive IoT

This section discusses cognitive IoT as a case study example of HW/SW co-design for CNN acceleration. Many of the IoT applications not only require the IoT devices to perform compute-intensive tasks but also to *learn, think,* and *understand* both physical and social worlds by themselves thus motivating the development of a new paradigm, named cognitive IoT [186]. Cognitive IoT outfits the current IoT with a "brain" for high-level intelligence. Cognitive IoT will be able to accomplish various application tasks including resource control (e.g., sensing resolution, actuation), inference, and decision-making with minimum human intervention/supervision thus saving human's time and effort and will also provide efficient resource usage. Hence, there is a need to develop a flexible, high-performance, energy-efficient, and cognitive IoT architecture to assist with various emerging IoT applications (e.g., agriculture, smart homes, smart cities, military).

Figure 13.2 depicts an example of cognitive IoT architecture. This architecture consists of a host processor which comprises of an application processor, co-processors, and accelerators. The host processor is connected to various low-power interface processors that collect data from sensors and control actuation elements.

The core component of a cognitive IoT architecture is *cognitive engine*, which provides cognition capabilities to the IoT device. The cognitive engine implements various deep learning accelerators, such as CNNs, recurrent neural networks (RNNs), and multilayer perceptrons (MLPs). The cognitive engine helps with various cognitive tasks in IoT devices, such as in situ analysis of the sensed data, local resource management, inference, decision-making, and response calculation for the IoT devices based on the analysis of the sensed data. Increasing cyber-physical

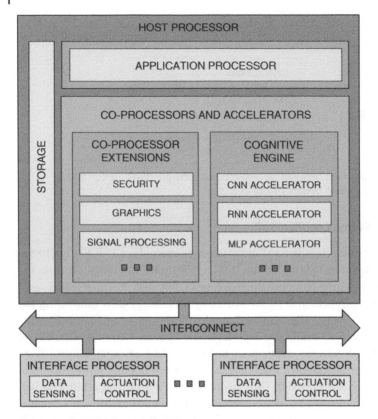

Figure 13.2 Cognitive IoT architecture.

and vision applications of IoT make CNNs an integral part of cognitive engine for imparting real-time object detections and/or classifications. To enable efficient on-device CNN inferences, hardware-based CNN inference engines are often used instead of general-purpose CPUs or graphics processing units (GPUs). With the hardware components, the software which actually controls the hardware also hugely contributes to the performance, energy efficiency, and cost of the systems. This section focuses on HW/SW co-design of CNN inference engine for cognitive IoT.

For cognitive IoT computing platforms, implementing the cognitive engine with ASICs would be desirable for better optimization; however, ASICs being hardwired provide no flexibility to adopt a new cognitive engine. Alternatively, field-programmable gate array system-on-chip (FPGA-SoC) that equips programmable logic, CPU, and other hard intellectual properties (IPs) provides an attractive platform because of its reconfigurability, flexibility, cost efficiency, and faster time-to-market. *Cost efficiency* is an important metric to consider for real-world adoption of on-device CNN inference architectures in IoT devices. We define cost efficiency metric as: an architecture (or implementation) is cost-efficient if it requires fewer resources under performance and energy efficiency constraints as compared to other architectures (implementations). Though there have been many studies and proposals on fast and efficient CNN inference for FPGA platforms (e.g., [146–148, 166], and [187]), cost efficiency of the implementations has been largely ignored, which may make those designs infeasible for low-power and resource-constrained cognitive IoT.

The designed hardware for cognitive IoT can also be supported by software. For example, software can perform scheduling of the underlying hardware resources for improving the hardware resource utilization. In addition, the operating system support can also be available to meet the real-time constraints when executing the IoT applications that have a hard deadline.

13.1.2 Recent Advancements in HW/SW Co-Design

Many recent CNN inference engines leverage HW/SW co design. Sugimoto et al. [187] have proposed a method to accelerate execution of the convolution layer with general matrix multiplication (GEMM) hardware, whereas implementing image-to-column (im2col) operations in software. In [147], Qiu et al. have proposed an acceleration technique via dynamic data quantization and convolver design, leading to an improved bandwidth and resource utilization in an embedded FPGA platform. Meloni et al. [146] have proposed a new methodology to utilize both hardware accelerator and embedded CPU in Zynq-based FPGA-SoC platform. Their methodology utilizes a 16-bit fixed-point convolution engine implemented in the programmable arrays and ARM CPU's NEON units for processing the convolution layers. The proposed software framework orchestrates the overall convolution layer processing. Zhong et al. [166] have proposed a unified framework for accelerating CNNs on heterogeneous embedded platforms. The proposed framework in [166] utilizes GEMM hardware with multithreading to efficiently hide latencies.

In [188], authors have proposed a HW/SW codesign approach for cost-efficient on-device CNN inference in resource-constrained cognitive IoT devices. The authors have utilized the CNN hardware accelerator introduced in Chapter 7 as the main hardware part. For the software part, the authors have proposed and implemented two important software-level support mechanisms: (i) efficient channel partition and input/weight allocation, and (ii) the pipelined execution of the front-end (e.g., input data transfer, im2col, and MAC) and the back-end part (e.g., bias addition and activation) of the execution. The efficient input channel partition, input/weight allocation, and the pipelined execution are essential parts to maximize the resource utilization in the system. Experimental results demonstrate the superiority of our FPGA-based implementation for Tiny-Darknet [145] CNN model with full-stack software including operating system (PetaLinux) and Darknet framework [143] in terms of response time and energy consumption as compared to the implementations using the CPU with NEON (SIMD, Single Instruction Multiple Data) architecture extension for the Arm Cortex processors) supports as well as the implementations that only offload the GEMM to the hardware accelerator.

13.2 HW/SW Co-Scheduling

Although many hardware accelerators and algorithmic advancements have been proposed for CNNs, efficient CNN inference in resource-constrained edge systems is still an arduous undertaking. Modern SoCs, which are generally used in many resource-constrained edge systems, employ many different hardware IPs to support a wide range of tasks. Recently, CNN accelerators are also being incorporated as hardware IP in modern edge devices and servers. For CNN inference in such environments, the main CPU triggers the CNN accelerator with direct memory access (DMA)-based data transfer. The CNN accelerators in most cases can execute CNN inferences faster than the CPU or other hardware IPs. However, in most of the contemporary CNN acceleration systems, the CPU or hardware IPs other than the CNN accelerator remain idle during the CNN inference. These idle hardware resources could otherwise be utilized for accelerating the CNN inferences alongside the CNN accelerator. For example, a typical CPU in embedded platforms can perform matrix–vector operations. With SIMD supports, these matrix–vector operations can be made much faster. Consequently, idle hardware resources in CPU can be utilized to execute a certain portion of CNN inference tasks to make the CNN inference faster than using only the CNN accelerator. *The process of scheduling tasks on both hardware and software (CPU) is referred to as HW/SW co-scheduling.* In regards to CNN acceleration, the concept of scheduling and executing CNN inference tasks/subtasks on both the CNN hardware accelerator as well as the CPU to share the workload of the CNN acceleration for improving performance is referred to as HW/SW co-scheduling for CNN acceleration.

For efficient utilization of hardware resources in an intelligent SoC-based platform, an important design decision is how to distribute the CNN inference tasks in a load-balanced manner. The "ideal load balancing" for CNN inference means the distribution of CNN tasks in a manner that maximizes the utilization of multiple hardware resources. Such distribution of CNN tasks also increases the possibility of idle time minimization of SoC hardware resources when executing the parallel tasks in multiple different hardware resources. An important metric to consider for load balancing of CNN inferences is *relative performance ratio*. Relative performance ratio (RPR) is the ratio of the performance between various hardware resources. For two resources (or components or subsystems) A and B, the RPR is defined as the performance of A relative to B, that is, RPR $= \frac{Perf_A}{Perf_B}$, where $Perf_A$ and $Perf_B$ denote the performances of A and B, respectively. Load imbalance can result in idle time for various hardware resources, which lead to underutilization of the hardware resources. Thus, in order to minimize load imbalance in SoC platforms (i.e., to minimize idle time in hardware resources), a careful consideration of task distribution is required at a fine granularity by considering the relative performance ratio.

13.2.1 Recent Advancements in HW/SW Co-Scheduling

Recent efforts have focused on co-scheduling of CNN workloads with various hardware IPs in SoC platforms. In [166], a framework to utilize heterogeneous hardware resources in SoCs when executing CNN inferences is proposed. The framework utilizes CPU (with SIMD engine) and accelerator to expedite multiple CONV layer executions for different image frames. In [189], a technique to utilize CPU, GPU, and hardware accelerator for CNN acceleration by partitioning a batch of images is proposed. By exploiting the roofline model, the technique partitions a batch of images and then distributes these partitioned images to CPU, GPU, and FPGA accelerator for efficient CNN acceleration. In [190], a task assignment technique is proposed for multi-CNN acceleration, which utilizes multiple deep learning processing units (DPUs) for CNN inference, while CPU is responsible for task initialization. Similarly, [146] proposes a technique to utilize both an FPGA-based accelerator and a CPU for CNN inferences. The technique [146] offloads the convolution operation to the FPGA accelerator, while the other parts of CNN (such as fully connected layer or shortcut connection, etc.) are executed in the CPU. Though the technique proposed in [146] can improve the throughput of CNN inference by exploiting both the CPU and the FPGA-based accelerator, it is very hard to fully utilize both the hardware accelerator and the CPU because granularity for task distribution is still large (e.g., layer granularity). Further, due to coarse granularity, there is a high probability for having idle period in hardware resources, thus incurring throughput loss. In [191], a single layer acceleration technique is proposed by utilizing both CPU and GPU. The technique in [191] distributes the output channels with a fixed ratio (e.g., 0.25, 0.5, and 0.75). In [109], a technique to accelerate memory streaming workloads (memory-to-memory data transfer with or without simple arithmetic operations such as memory COPY, ADD, SCALE, and TRIAD [192]) via cooperation between a CPU and an FPGA-based accelerator is proposed. Though the technique in [109] can accelerate 1×1 convolution operations, it has limitations on accelerating $N \times N$ convolution operations where $N > 1$.

The previously proposed approaches targeting heterogeneous hardware utilization for CNN inferences use multiple available resources (CPU and FPGAs in [166], CPU, GPU, and FPGAs in [189], and CPU and multiple DPUs in [190]); however, the previously proposed approaches can only be employed when simultaneously executing multiple CNN inferences, thus limiting their applicability. In addition, the coarse-grained task partitioning employed in previously proposed approaches may not work well in resource-constrained edge devices because it is very rare to execute a large batch of images together in edge devices.

In Chapter 15, we introduce a recently proposed HW/SW co-scheduling technique [125] in detail. The work presented in [125] can be applied to a single CONV layer acceleration, which has wider applicability as compared to the HW/SW co-scheduling techniques proposed in [189], [166], and [190]. In addition, the HW/SW co-scheduling technique presented in [125] employs a finer-grained approach that distributes output channels in a single CONV layer to the accelerator and the CPU, which is more suitable for resource-constrained edge devices. Furthermore, the technique proposed in [125] is based on task distribution with a finer granularity (i.e., CNN output channels in a CONV layer), and thus has a higher probability of keeping the accelerator and the CPU busy. Lastly, the accurate latency estimation in [125] guides the load-balanced task distribution to the accelerator and CPU, thereby minimizing idle time in the hardware resources when executing the CONV layer operations.

13.3 Chapter Summary

This chapter defined HW/SW co-design and HW/SW co-scheduling. Furthermore, this chapter provided a background of HW/SW co-design followed by a case study of cognitive IoT as an example of HW/SW co-design. The chapter then discussed some recent advancements in HW/SW co-design. The chapter then provided a background of HW/SW co-scheduling followed by a reviewof recent advances in HW/SW co-scheduling. In Chapter 14, this book introduces a HW/SW co-design technique for CNN acceleration in resource-constrained edge devices. Chapter 15 discusses a HW/SW co-scheduling technique for CNN acceleration in resource-constrained edge devices.

14

Hardware/Software Co-Design for CNN Acceleration

In Chapter 7, this book has already explained the iMAC hardware accelerator. This chapter focuses on the software partition/portion of the iMAC. This chapter introduces two important software-level support mechanisms: (i) efficient channel partition and input/weight allocation, and (ii) the pipelined execution of the front-end (e.g., input data transfer, image-to-column (im2col), and multiply-accumulate (MAC)) and the back-end part (e.g., bias addition and activation) of the execution. The efficient input channel partition, input/weight allocation, and the pipelined execution are essential parts to maximize the resource utilization in the system.

14.1 Background of iMAC Accelerator

This chapter mainly explains the software supports for the iMAC accelerator. In order to help the readers understand better this chapter, we briefly discuss how the tasks are offloaded in the iMAC accelerator.

HW/SW partitioning of the iMAC accelerator architecture is shown in Figure 14.1. As we explained in Chapter 7, the iMAC accelerator incorporates the im2col and general matrix multiplication (GEMM) operations in the hardware accelerator to reduce the data transfer between the main memory and the accelerator on-chip memory. As shown in four processing element (PE) architecture of the iMAC accelerator in Figure 14.2, the iMAC accelerator has multiple MAC arrays to perform the parallel MAC operations for GEMM. In Section 14.2, we explain the software partition/portion of the iMAC accelerator with a detailed channel partition algorithm for convolutional neural network (CNN)s.

Accelerators for Convolutional Neural Networks, First Edition.
Arslan Munir, Joonho Kong, and Mahmood Azhar Qureshi.
© 2024 The Institute of Electrical and Electronics Engineers, Inc. Published 2024 by John Wiley & Sons, Inc.

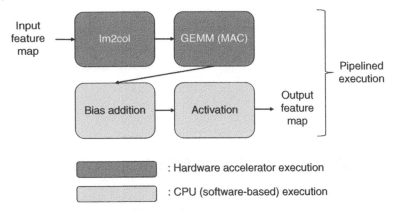

Figure 14.1 HW/SW partitioning for iMAC accelerator.

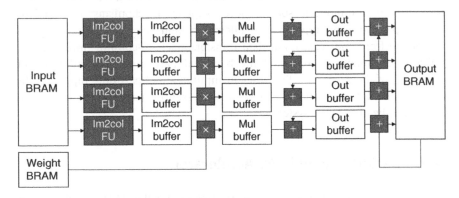

Figure 14.2 4PE iMAC accelerator architecture. FU stands for the functional unit.

14.2 Software Partition for iMAC Accelerator

Sections 14.2.1 and 14.2.2 discuss the software partitioning of the HW/SW co-designed iMAC accelerator, which includes channel partition and software-based pipelined execution.

14.2.1 Channel Partition and Input/Weight Allocation to Hardware Accelerator

Provisioning the hardware resources for in situ execution of the entire convolution layer could not be a desirable solution for resource-constrained Internet of things (IoT) or edge systems. Since the presented design is geared toward resource-constrained systems, we only have limited on-chip memories and PEs which are not enough to implement a whole convolution layer. Since our iMAC hardware can only execute a part of the convolution layer (i.e., only a part of the entire input channels in a convolution layer) at once, efficient partition and allocation of input channels to the iMAC hardware accelerator are very crucial.

In the presented design, the hardware accelerator (iMAC) operates by a unit(s) of an input channel. Thus, we try to put the input feature map and weight data for as many input channels as possible to the input and weight block random access memory (BRAM)s, respectively, to minimize the number of data transfer. Figure 14.3 shows a pseudocode of the presented channel partition method controlled by software. One outer-loop iteration generates results for one output channel (lines 2–19). Thus, if we would like to generate more than one output channel, we need to execute the outer loop by *NumOutputChannel* times (i.e., equal to the number of the total output channels in a certain convolution layer). For each inner-loop iteration (lines 3–14), we generate partial results for one

---

Pseudocode for Software-Level Supports

```
1  out = 0;
2  for (i=1; i<=NumOutputChannel; i ++)
3    for (j =1; j <=NumPartition; j ++)
4      DMA_Transfer_to_iMAC (jth_Weight);
5      while (!DMA_done);
6      DMA_done = 0;
7      DMA_Transfer_to_iMAC (jth_InputFeatureMAP);
8      if (out)
9        Bias_Addition_and_Activation ((i−1)th_OutputChannel);
10       out = 0;
11     end if
12     while ((!Check_iMAC_done()) || (!DMA_done));
13     DMA_done = 0;
14   end for
15   DMA_Transfer_to_Memory (ith_OutputChannel);
16   out = 1;
17   while (!DMA_done);
18   DMA_done = 0;
19 end for
20 Bias_Addition_and_Activation ((i−1)th_OutputChannel);
```

Figure 14.3 Pseudocode of the software-level supports for the iMAC accelerator. The "DMA_done" is a flag variable that autonomously set as "1" as soon as the direct memory access (DMA) transfer is finished. The "Check_iMAC_done()" is a function that returns whether or not the iMAC accelerator is finished (it returns "1" if finished, "0" if not).

output channel. The inner-loop iterations are executed by *NumPartition* times where *NumPartition* is equal to [(the total number of input channels/the number of maximum input channels that the iMAC hardware can accommodate)]. How many input channels can be accommodated is bound to input and weight BRAM size. For a hypothetical example, we have $50,176 \times 4B$ input BRAMs with $288 \times 4B$ weight BRAMs. We also have $112 \times 112 \times 12$ input feature maps (an element size=4B: one floating-point variable) with 32 $3 \times 3 \times 12$ weights (filters). The input and weight BRAM can accommodate input feature maps for up to 4 input channels ($50,176*4B = 4*112*112*4B$) and 12 layers of filters ($288 * 4B \geq 12 \times 3 \times 3 \times 4B$), respectively. In this example, the number of input channels we can accommodate is bound to the input BRAM size ($12>4$). Thus, *NumOutputChannel* and *NumPartition* values will be set as "32" (same as the number of the filters) and "3" ($=12$ input channels / 4 channels at maximum with available BRAMs), respectively.

14.2.2 Exploiting Parallelism Within Convolution Layer Operations

By exploiting the parallelism that exists in different operations in the convolution layer, the presented design implements a pipelined execution of the operations. As shown in Figure 14.3, in lines 7–11, as soon as the direct memory access (DMA) transfer is triggered for input feature maps (during the DMA transfer, the CPU can perform another task), the bias addition and activation for the previous output channel are performed (lines 8–11). Since the iMAC hardware is implemented to autonomously perform the im2col and MAC operations as soon as finishing the DMA transfer for input feature maps, the CPU waits for finishing the DMA transfer for input feature map and im2col and MAC operations in the while loop (line 12). In lines 15–18, DMA transfer for the results of output channel i is performed and the CPU waits for finishing the DMA transfer. After the termination of the outer-loop iterations, the bias addition and activation operations for the last output channel ($i - 1$ because we already incremented i by 1 before we terminate the outer loop) are carried out in the CPU in line 20.

For comparison, Figure 14.4 shows the timing diagrams without pipelined execution (a) and with pipelined execution (b) for three output channels (OCs). Without pipelining (Figure 14.4 a), the bias addition and activation are performed when the iMAC hardware computation and DMA transfers for outputs are entirely finished. Thus, iMAC accelerator and CPU are not used in parallel and either of hardware resources is idle, causing a throughput loss. In the presented design, as shown in Figure 14.4b, we exploit the data independence between the output channels. It means we can overlap the executions of the bias addition and activation for the previous output channel $N - 1$ with the iMAC execution for the current output channel N. Please note that the bias addition and activation for

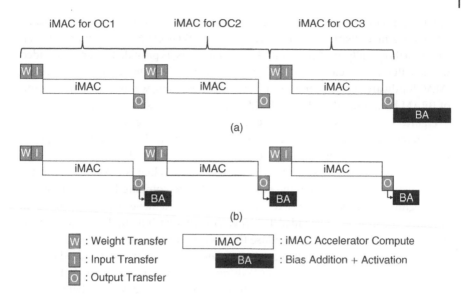

Figure 14.4 Comparison between (a) nonpipelined and (b) pipelined execution.

the last output channel of a convolution layer cannot be overlapped as shown in Figure 14.4b. This part also corresponds to the line 20 in the pseudocode shown in Figure 14.3.

In this design, we do not apply double buffering. The rationale behind this design decision is cost (resource) efficiency. To support double buffering with the same PE utilization, we need twice more BRAMs, which are not desirable for resource-constrained system. In the presented implementation, the computation time dominates the data transfer time, which also means a performance gain from double buffering would be marginal. Instead of applying the double buffering, we exploit parallelism in the convolution layer operations by overlapping the im2col+GEMM and bias addition/activation, leading to cost- and resource-efficient design.

14.3 Experimental Evaluations

We show the experimental results with four different designs: *CPU*, *GEMM*, *iMAC_NPL*, and *iMAC_PL*. *CPU* only uses CPU without an additional hardware accelerator. *GEMM* only offload GEMM to the dedicated field-programmable gate array (FPGA)-based logic. *iMAC_NPL* offloads im2col and MAC to the dedicated FPGA hardware (iMAC accelerator), while the pipelining described in Section 14.2.2 is not applied. *iMAC_PL* offloads im2col and MAC to the iMAC accelerator with the pipelining supports in the software. We also show the results when the single instruction multiple data (SIMD) (ARM NEON) support, which can be orthogonally applied to four different designs, is provided and not provided in the CPU. In the cases of *iMAC_PL* and *iMAC_NPL*, the identical 8PE-based iMAC hardware accelerator is used. For fair comparison, we use the same amount of BRAM blocks in *GEMM* (with 95 MHz FPGA clock) as that in *iMAC_PL*.

Figure 14.5 shows the response time and energy results for eight cases (4 different designs * 2 (w/ NEON and w/o NEON)). In the case of response time, our *iMAC_PL* significantly reduces response time of the CNN inference regardless of the NEON support is available or not. When the NEON support is not available, the speedup of the *iMAC_PL* is 1.97× compared to *CPU*. It means the cognitive engine (i.e., iMAC accelerator) can achieve a huge speedup in resource-constrained embedded/IoT environments with a small hardware overhead. In the case of *GEMM*, response time is rather increased compared to *CPU*. This is because of the huge increase in the amount of data transfer caused by data replication (i.e., unrolling the input) during im2col. Compared to *iMAC_NPL*, *iMAC_PL* shows 1.12× speedup which is attributed to the overlap between the computation times for data transfer/accelerator and bias addition/activation. The relative performance impact of pipelining could be further improved as we put more PEs and/or increase the clock frequency of the iMAC so that we can reduce the execution time of the im2col and MAC operations. When the NEON support is available, performance of *CPU* is increased by 52.9% compared to *CPU* without NEON. However, *iMAC_PL* with NEON still shows better performance by 29.2% compared to *CPU* with NEON. It implies the presented acceleration technique can achieve better response time regardless of NEON supports in the CPU. In the

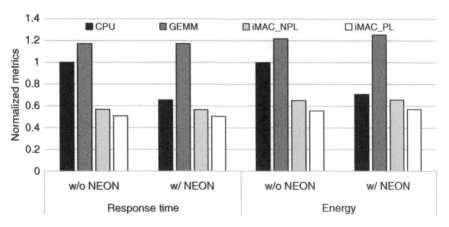

Figure 14.5 Response time and energy comparison. The results are normalized to the results of *CPU* w/o NEON.

case of platform-level energy, the *iMAC_PL* shows the highest energy reductions among *GEMM*, *iMAC_NPL*, and *iMAC_PL* compared to *CPU*. The *iMAC_PL* shows energy reductions by 44.3% and 19.4% compared to the *CPU* without and with NEON supports, respectively.

14.4 Chapter Summary

This chapter discussed a HW/SW co-designed CNN accelerator for resource-constrained systems. Hardware partitioning of the discussed iMAC accelerator had been elaborated in Chapter 7, so this chapter focused on the software partition of the design. This chapter discussed software-level supports to efficiently partition and allocate the input channels to the iMAC hardware accelerator and exploit the parallelism inside the convolution layer operations. Experimental results revealed that the iMAC implementation attained 1.3× ~ 2.0× speedup and energy reduction of 19.4% ~44.3% as compared to using only the CPU. Experimental results verified that the presented HW/SW co-design achieves a good trade-off between response time, energy, and cost for CNN inference in intelligent systems under tight resource budgets.

15

CPU-Accelerator Co-Scheduling for CNN Acceleration

This chapter introduces a technique to utilize idle hardware resources for convolution (CONV) layer acceleration, which generally constitutes the largest portion of convolutional neural network (CNN) inference latency. The introduced technique exploits the central processing unit (CPU) for sharing load of CNN inference tasks along with the CNN hardware accelerator. The main reasons of utilizing CPUs for sharing CNN inference load with the hardware accelerator in the introduced technique are (i) CPUs are hardware IPs employed in most of the resource-constrained edge systems, and (ii) CPUs can execute matrix-vector (or matrix-matrix) operations with reasonable efficiency [166], which makes CPUs attractive components for sharing CNN tasks with the CNN accelerator. In order to distribute CNN inference tasks between the hardware accelerator and the CPU, the parallelism in generating multiple CNN output channels (which can be generated independently) in a single CONV layer is exploited. To help minimize the idle time in both the accelerator and the CPU, this chapter also introduces a linear regression-based latency model for CONV layer execution. By referring to the estimated latency from the presented model, the introduced co-scheduling technique distributes the CNN output channels between the accelerator and the CPU to maximize the utilization of the both (i.e., to minimize the idle time in both the accelerator and the CPU).

There have been previous works that achieve more than 10× reduction of the computation [94] or more than 40× weight size reduction [46, 62] with a negligible accuracy loss; however, those works focus on improving the CNN models [62] or changing data format (quantization) and value (pruning) of the weights [46, 94]. On the contrary, the introduced acceleration technique utilizes CPU and the CNN accelerator co-scheduling and can be employed orthogonally with the existing CNN acceleration techniques that utilize quantization and pruning. Furthermore, the introduced technique is applicable to any CNN model because this technique focuses on utilizing both the CPU and the CNN accelerator when executing a

Accelerators for Convolutional Neural Networks, First Edition.
Arslan Munir, Joonho Kong, and Mahmood Azhar Qureshi.
© 2024 The Institute of Electrical and Electronics Engineers, Inc. Published 2024 by John Wiley & Sons, Inc.

CNN inference with a given CNN model (i.e., this technique is not limited to any particular CNN model). Thus, the introduced technique can be much more broadly applied for CNN inference acceleration at the edge as compared to other CNN acceleration techniques.

The main contributions related to HW/SW co-scheduling covered in this chapter are

- A CNN output channel distribution technique with CPU-accelerator co-scheduling, which utilizes both the CNN accelerator and the CPU
- A simple, yet accurate convolution layer latency model for the CNN accelerator and the CPU
- Implementation of the introduced co-scheduling technique in a CNN framework [143] while verifying it in various field programmable gate array system-on-chip (FPGA-SoC) based platforms as a proof-of-concept
- The experimental results reveal that the introduced co-scheduling technique improves the performance of convolution layer operations by 1.18x to 2.00x while at the same time reducing the energy consumption by 14.9%–49.7% as compared to the accelerator-only execution.

15.1 Background and Preliminaries

In this section, we cover the generic topics for CNNs and the baseline system architecture used in this chapter. For baseline system architecture, we also explain how the underlying systems and accelerators are organized and how they exploits parallelism in the CNN.

15.1.1 Convolutional Neural Networks

CNNs are generally composed of multiple different types of layers. Though some CNN architectures contain specialized layers (e.g., Inception layer in [35]), most of the modern CNN architectures are composed of CONV layers, pooling layers, and fully connected layers. Among those layers, it is known that the CONV layer takes the largest portion of the execution time in a CNN inference. Thus, in this chapter, we mainly focus on accelerating the CONV layers.

A deep look into the CONV layer (Figure 15.1) divulges that input feature maps (IFMs) and weights (filters) mainly constitute an input for the CONV layer. Bias values (*gamma* and *beta* for batch normalization) are sometimes included in the inputs for CONV layers though they are omitted in Figure 15.1. With the IFMs (IH × IW × IC) and weights (N × N × IC × OC), the convolution operations are performed. After the convolution, depending on the CNN models, the batch

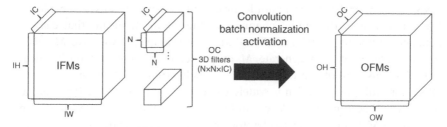

Figure 15.1 Typical convolutional layer operations. IH, IW, IC, OH, OW, and OC stand for input height, input width, input channel, output height, output width, and output channel, respectively.

normalization can be performed to the output from the convolution operations. Lastly, the activation is performed, typically by rectified linear units (ReLUs), which generate the output feature maps (OFMs) of dimension OH× OW × OC.

15.1.2 Baseline System Architecture

In this work, we assume a resource-constrained edge system with a CNN accelerator (such as Coral platform [115] which has a CPU with edge tensor processing unit). As shown in Figure 15.2, the baseline SoC is similar to a typical embedded system which includes CPU and memory controller. In the baseline system, we also use the CNN accelerator to expedite the CNN inference in the system. Though there can be various types of CNN accelerator, we assume that the

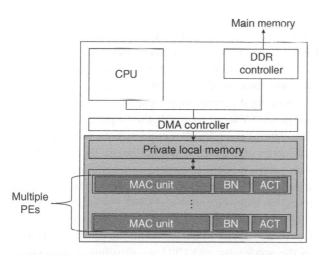

Figure 15.2 Baseline system architecture. The light gray-shaded area corresponds to the CNN accelerator while the dark gray-shaded area corresponds to the processing elements in the accelerator.

CNN accelerator leverages multiple processing elements (PEs) by exploiting the parallelism in the output channels of the OFMs. It means that each PE generates different 2D (OH × OW) OFMs. For example, if we have M PEs in the accelerator, we can generate M output channels simultaneously. Please note that this type of accelerator design which exploits output channel parallelism for multiple PE design is widely used [193–195]. Inside the PE, there are multiply-and-accumulation (MAC) units, batch normalization (BN) units, and activation (ACT) units. The accelerator on-chip memory, which is also referred to as private local memory (PLM) is used as a local buffer in which we store IFMs, weights, and OFMs (or intermediate results). Similar to typical embedded systems, we use direct memory access (DMA) for data transfer between the CPU's main memory and the accelerator's PLM.

15.2 CNN Acceleration with CPU-Accelerator Co-Scheduling

This section provides an overview of the introduced CNN acceleration with CPU-accelerator co-scheduling technique. This section further presents the convolution layer latency model for the CNN accelerator and the CPU that is utilized by the introduced CPU-accelerator co-scheduling technique for CNN acceleration.

15.2.1 Overview

To fully utilize both the CNN accelerator and the CPU in resource-constrained edge devices, this work aims at distributing the CNN CONV layer tasks to the CNN accelerator and the CPU in a load-balanced manner by carefully considering the performance ratio between the CPU and the accelerator. Since there is no dependency when generating different output channels (i.e., they can be executed in parallel) in a single CONV layer, we divide the output channels to distribute the tasks into the accelerator and CPU. Consequently, we perform CONV layer operations in the accelerator and the CPU with different 3D filter tensors. Figure 15.3 demonstrates an overview of the presented co-scheduling technique. To fully utilize the accelerator and CPU, we need to estimate the relative difference of the achievable performance in the accelerator and CPU. For accurate estimation, we use a latency model of the CONV layer operations for the accelerator and CPU, which is described in Section 15.2.2 in details. With the estimated relative attainable performance of the accelerator and CPU, we distribute output channels (i.e., 3D filter tensors) to the accelerator and CPU. The information on the output channel distribution is stored in the CNN framework (Figure 15.3), which

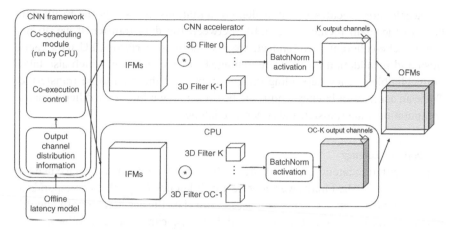

Figure 15.3 An overview of the presented CPU-accelerator co-scheduling.

will be referenced at runtime. In the example shown in Figure 15.3, we assign "K" 3D filter tensors (which will be used for generating "K" output channels) to the CNN accelerator while we assign "$OC - K$" filter tensors to the CPU. At run time, the co-execution control module, which is executed on the CPU in the presented co-scheduling technique, launches the accelerator, and CPU co-execution for given output channels. The CONV layer operation includes convolution, batch normalization (BatchNorm), and activation. After we generate "K" and "$OC - K$" 2D OFMs in the accelerator and the CPU, respectively, we aggregate those OFMs to compose the full 3D OFM tensor.

15.2.2 Linear Regression-Based Latency Model

For latency estimation, we use a linear regression-based methodology. In general linear regression, we use a following form of the equation:

$$Y = \alpha X + \beta \tag{15.1}$$

where X and Y are explanatory and dependent variables, respectively. With the pairs of X and Y values, we determine α and β values through the linear regression training (line fitting). Based on the above form of the equation, we extend it to estimate accelerator and CPU latencies when processing a single CONV layer.

15.2.2.1 Accelerator Latency Model

In this chapter, we present a linear regression-based latency model for CONV layer executions in the CNN accelerators introduced in Section 15.1.2. For typical task offloading to the hardware IPs in embedded systems, we firstly need to send the data from the main memory to the accelerator's PLM via DMA. After that, the accelerator executes the offloaded computations and sends the result data back to the main memory via DMA. Between the data transfer, if we do not use a cache-coherent interconnect, we also need to perform CPU data cache flush and invalidation for software managed cache coherence, which also takes nonnegligible latency depending on the amount of the data to be transferred. Thus, an accelerator latency requires to be broken down into three different parts: computation, data transfer, and coherence latency.

Computation Latency

For computation latency, it mainly depends on how many operations we need to generate the OFMs. Firstly, we generate a unit latency L_{uACC} that corresponds to the computation latency in the 1PE accelerator (i.e., the accelerator with one PE) when generating one OFM element. Deriving L_{uACC} can be done as follows:

$$L_{uACC} = \alpha_{comp} \times Size_{FT} + \beta_{comp} \tag{15.2}$$

where $Size_{FT}$ indicates the number of elements in one 3D filter tensor. For example, if one 3D filter tensor size is 3×3×3, the $Size_{FT}$ is 27. The α_{comp} and β_{comp} are determined by the linear regression analysis. We can extend it to derive the accelerator computation latency (L_{comp}) when generating N_F OFMs (i.e., N_F output channels) as follows:

$$L_{comp} = L_{uACC} \times Size_{OFM} \times \left\lceil \frac{N_F}{N_{PE}} \right\rceil \tag{15.3}$$

where $Size_{OFM}$, N_F, and N_{PE} correspond to the number of the elements in one 2D OFM, the total number of output channels in a certain CONV layer, and the number of PEs in the accelerator, respectively. The $\left\lceil \frac{N_F}{N_{PE}} \right\rceil$ equals to how many times the accelerator execution must be triggered. For example, if we run a CONV layer with $N_F = 28$ in the accelerator with $N_{PE} = 10$, the number of times the accelerator's PE execution will be triggered is equal to 3 ($= \lceil 28/10 \rceil$). Accordingly, we calculate the latency of the accelerator when generating the total number of the output channels (i.e., N_F output channels) in a certain CONV layer because we need to calculate the relative performance ratio between the accelerator and CPU. In other words, we should derive the latency of the accelerator and CPU when we execute the CONV layer with the identical input data size.

Transfer Latency

The transfer latency is also linearly proportional to the size of data to be transferred. Thus, the transfer latency can be estimated by the following equation:

$$L_{tran} = \alpha_{tran} \times Size_{Data} + \beta_{tran} \tag{15.4}$$

where $Size_{Data}$ indicates a total size of the data (in the number of the elements) to be transferred. The α_{tran} and β_{tran} are also determined by the linear regression analysis. The $Size_{Data}$ can be calculated as follows:

$$Size_{Data} = Size_{IFMs} + Size_{gamma} + Size_{beta}$$
$$+ Size_{FT} \times N_F + Size_{OFM} \times N_F. \tag{15.5}$$

For input data transfer, we need to count $Size_{IFMs}$, $Size_{gamma}$, and $Size_{beta}$ which correspond to the number of elements of (multiple) input feature maps, *gamma* values, and *beta* values for batch normalization. Depending on the CONV layer configurations, $Size_{gamma}$ and/or $Size_{beta}$ can be neglected. We also need to count the total number of the elements in N_F 3D filter tensors, which can be derived by multiplying $Size_{FT}$ by N_F. For output transfer, we count the data size (in the number of elements) of the OFMs generated by the accelerator, which is calculated by $Size_{OFM} \times N_F$.

Coherence Latency

The coherence latency model is composed of two parts: cache flush and cache invalidation. The cache flush is required before we trigger DMA read (send input data to the accelerator PLM) while the cache invalidation is required before we trigger DMA write (send output data from the PLM to the main memory). For cache flush latency (L_{fl}), we use the following equation:

$$L_{fl} = \alpha_{fl} \times (Size_{IFMs} + Size_{gamma} + Size_{beta}$$
$$+ Size_{FT} \times N_F) + \beta_{fl} \tag{15.6}$$

where α_{fl} and β_{fl} correspond to the coefficient values for cache flush. Cache invalidation latency (L_{inv}) can also be estimated by using the following equation:

$$L_{inv} = \alpha_{inv} \times Size_{OFM} \times N_F + \beta_{inv} \tag{15.7}$$

where α_{inv} and β_{inv} correspond to the coefficient values for cache invalidation. By adding L_{fl} and L_{inv}, we can estimate the total latency required for cache coherence as shown in the following equation:

$$L_{cohr} = L_{fl} + L_{inv}. \tag{15.8}$$

Latency Aggregation

The total latency taken by the accelerator can be derived by adding the computation, transfer, and coherence latency as follows:

$$L_{ACC} = L_{comp} + L_{tran} + L_{cohr}. \tag{15.9}$$

In the baseline system, the data transfer, computation, and coherence operations are not overlapped. However, the presented latency model can also be extended to other systems where an overlap exists between data transfer, computation, and coherence operations. For example, when we use cache-coherent interconnects, we can just remove L_{cohr} because the explicit cache flush and invalidation are not required in the system with cache-coherent interconnects. When using double buffering where the transfer latency and computation latency can be overlapped, we can replace $L_{comp} + L_{tran}$ with $MAX(L_{comp}, L_{tran})$.

15.2.2.2 CPU Latency Model

We also present a linear regression-based latency model for CONV layer executions in the CPU. Different from the accelerator latency model, CPUs use cache memories for data transfer between the CPU core and main memory. Since it is not explicitly controlled by software programmer, accurately estimating the data transfer time in the CPU would be more challenging than that in the accelerator. Hence, we use a unified latency model, which means we do not distinguish the data transfer and computation latency. By leveraging the linear regression-based latency model, we figure out the CPU latency depending on the number of the OFM elements generated by the CPU along with the CPU unit latency (L_{uCPU}: a CPU latency for generating one OFM element). This is because the computation and data transfer (implicitly via caches) latencies will be linearly proportional to the number of the generated OFM elements. The CPU unit latency can be derived as follows:

$$L_{uCPU} = \alpha_{CPU} \times Size_{FT} + \beta_{CPU} \tag{15.10}$$

where the $Size_{FT}$ equals to the size (in the number of elements) of the one 3D filter tensor. The coefficients α_{CPU} and β_{CPU}, which will inherently incorporate the effect of both computation and data transfer on CPU unit latency, are also determined by the linear regression. With the CPU unit latency model, we can extend it to estimate the total CONV layer latency in the CPU (L_{CPU}) as follows:

$$L_{CPU} = L_{uCPU} \times Size_{OFM} \times N_F \tag{15.11}$$

where $Size_{OFM} \times N_F$ corresponds to the number of the total OFM elements in a certain CONV layer.

15.2.3 Channel Distribution

With the estimated latency from the presented model, we distribute the output channels in order to fully utilize the accelerator and CPU in the system. To accomplish it, we need to distribute the output channels so that the execution time of the accelerator and the CPU is (almost) equivalent. Thus, we use the following equations for the output channel distribution for the accelerator:

$$N_{FA} = \left\lceil \left(\frac{L_{CPU}}{L_{ACC} + L_{CPU}} \right) \times N_F \right\rceil \tag{15.12}$$

where N_{FA} means the number of the output channels which will be processed in the accelerator. For example, assuming that the accelerator performance is three times better than the CPU (i.e., $L_{ACC}:L_{CPU}=1:3$), the accelerator should process three times more tasks than the CPU in order to fully remove the idle time in both the CPU and the accelerator. Obviously, the rest of the filter tensors must be processed in the CPU, which means:

$$N_{FC} = N_F - N_{FA} \tag{15.13}$$

where N_{FC} corresponds to the number of the output channels which will be processed in the CPU. As we mentioned in Section 15.2.1, determining the N_{FA} and N_{FC} is performed offline, which means the distribution decision for a given embedded system and CNN model is performed at the design time. Once we determine the output channel distribution, this information is stored in the CNN framework (Figure 15.3). At runtime, when processing a certain CONV layer, the CNN framework can distribute the tasks (output channels) to the accelerator and CPU by the distribution information stored in the framework.

15.2.4 Prototype Implementation

We have implemented the presented co-scheduling technique in Darknet framework [143], which is used as the baseline CNN framework, and have verified the presented co-scheduling technique using four off-the-shelf FPGA-SoC platforms: Ultra96 [196], Zed [144], ZCU104 [197], and ZCU106 [160]. These platforms deploy various types of the CPUs, which are summarized in Table 15.1. For the implementation, we use interrupt-based mechanism to simultaneously execute the CONV layer operations on the accelerator and the CPU, which is similar to that introduced in [109]. In the presented prototype implementation, though we do not employ double buffering, the presented latency model and co-scheduling can also be extended to support double buffering as we explained in Section 15.2.2.1. Since the prototype is mainly for verification and proof of the implementation, we run the modified framework in each platform without running an operating system (OS). Please note that this environment is similar to resource-constrained embedded edge devices where the firmware orchestrates the system without running OS. The precision for CNN models used in this work is 32-bit floating-point; however, the presented technique can also be applied to other precisions such as 16-bit fixed-point and 8-bit integer without modifying the latency model and channel distribution mechanism.

Figure 15.4 shows the timing diagram of the presented co-scheduling technique based on the interrupt mechanism. The main framework runs on the CPU, and initialization is performed before the co-execution in the CPU and the accelerator. The initialization (①) includes information fetching required for the presented

Table 15.1 CPU specifications for four FPGA-SoC platforms.

Platform	Ultra96	Zed	ZCU104, ZCU106
CPU architecture	Quad-core Cortex-A53	Dual-core Cortex-A9	Quad-core Cortex-A53
Clock Frequency	Up to 1200 MHz	Up to 667 MHz	Up to 1334 MHz
Per core L1 Cache	32 KB I-Cache, 32 KB D-Cache	32KB I-Cache, 32 KB D-Cache	32 KB I-Cache, 32 KB D-Cache
L2 Cache	Shared 1 MB	Shared 512 KB	Shared 1 MB

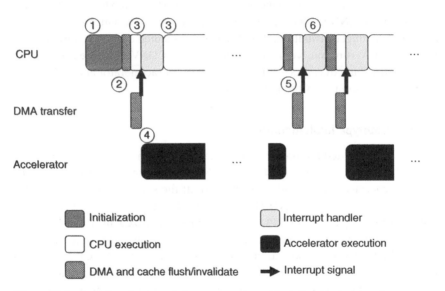

Figure 15.4 A timing diagram of the presented co-scheduling implementation.

co-scheduling technique (e.g., N_{FA} and N_{FC}). When a CONV layer execution begins, the CPU launches data transfer which includes cache flush in the CPU and DMA transfer (②). During the DMA transfer, the CPU begins to generate the N_{FC} OFMs (③). As soon as the DMA transfer finishes, the accelerator begins to generate N_{FA} OFMs (④). When the accelerator finishes the execution, a cache invalidation in the CPU and DMA write operation (⑤) begins in order to send the generated OFMs from the accelerator's PLM to the main memory to make the data visible to the CPU. During the DMA write operations, the CPU can continue executing the CONV layer operations for generating the N_{FC} OFMs because the DMA transfer and CPU execution can be performed in parallel. When the accelerator needs to be triggered by multiple times during a single CONV layer

Table 15.2 Obtained α and β values through linear regression analysis.

	Ultra96	Zed	ZCU104	ZCU106
α_{tran}	0.01	0.009999	0.009998	0.009999
β_{tran}	2.697551	2.162106	2.458088	2.472711
α_{comp}	0.099999	0.150077	0.090014	0.090021
β_{comp}	0.237558	0.309062	0.218302	0.218306
α_{fl}	0.008811	0.009323	0.006082	0.006101
β_{fl}	0.514771	6.101897	0.491329	0.314022
α_{inv}	0.008812	0.003748	0.006084	0.006091
β_{inv}	1.663402	0.986305	1.036251	0.900236
α_{CPU}	0.049176	0.072254	0.049155	0.049176
β_{CPU}	0.116896	0.164479	0.113563	0.113043

execution because of the larger number of OFMs than the accelerator's PEs can handle concurrently, these steps can be iterated (⑥) until the accelerator and CPU generates N_{FA} and N_{FC} OFMs, respectively.

For prototype implementation, we acquire α and β values via linear regression analysis. For training the linear regression model (i.e., acquiring α and β values), we use synthetically generated arbitrary 32 data points each for regression training of transfer time, flush and invalidation (coherence) time, and computation time. Please note that the range of the arbitrarily generated data points sufficiently covers the range of the data points used in real CNN models, resulting in accurate latency estimation. We demonstrate the coefficient values and plots obtained from the presented linear regression analysis in Table 15.2 and Figures 15.5–15.8,

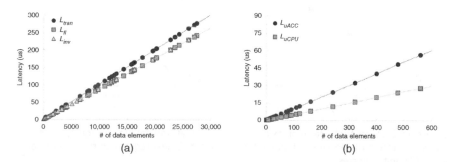

(a)   (b)

Figure 15.5 Plots for linear regressions in Ultra96 platform. (a) Linear regression for transfer, cache flush, and invalidation latencies and (b) Linear regression for accelerator and CPU unit latencies.

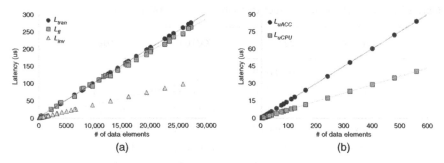

Figure 15.6 Plots for linear regressions in Zed platform. (a) Linear regression for transfer, cache flush, and invalidation latencies and (b) Linear regression for accelerator and CPU unit latencies.

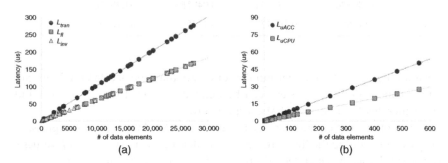

Figure 15.7 Plots for linear regressions in ZCU104 platform. (a) Linear regression for transfer, cache flush, and invalidation latencies and (b) Linear regression for accelerator and CPU unit latencies.

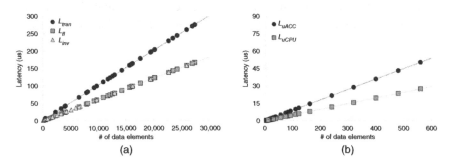

Figure 15.8 Plots for linear regressions in ZCU106 platform. (a) Linear regression for transfer, cache flush, and invalidation latencies and (b) Linear regression for accelerator and CPU unit latencies.

respectively. We use Microsoft Excel for linear regression analysis. As shown in Figures 15.5–15.8, the computation time and transfer time are well fitted to the linear function (as a form of $Y = \alpha X + \beta$). We can notice that the plots in Figures 15.7 and 15.8 seem to be almost identical. This is because ZCU104 and ZCU106 have almost identical specifications except for the connectivity parts.

15.3 Experimental Results

In this section, we present the experimental results for the presented co-scheduling technique related to various metrics, such as latency model accuracy (measured via mean absolute percentage error (MAPE)), performance, and energy consumption. We evaluate these metrics for the implemented prototypes in Ultra96, Zed, ZCU104, and ZCU106. For CPU clock frequencies, we use the following clock frequencies for each platform: Ultra96, ZCU104, and ZCU106 at 1.2 GHz and Zed at 667 MHz. We also perform the linear regression analysis with these CPU clock frequencies. To evaluate the presented technique across the wide spectrum of accelerators, we implement three different accelerator versions for each platform while varying the number of PEs: 2PE, 4PE, and 8PE, where xPE denotes an accelerator with the "x" number of PEs. Since the target is resource-constrained edge devices, we do not consider the CNN accelerator design with massive number of PEs (e.g., over 100 PEs).

For workloads, we use 14 different CONV layers as shown in Table 15.3. Six layers (Layer 0, 1, 2, 3, 5, and 6) are from SqueezeNet [62] while five layers (Layer 4, 7, 8, 9, and 10) are from MobileNet-v2 [34]. The rest of the three layers (Layer 11, 12, and 13) are synthetically generated for the evaluation. Please note that the results shown in this section are the averaged results of the 14 CONV layer executions (i.e., we measure the results of each CONV layer separately and average them out).

15.3.1 Latency Model Accuracy

We show the MAPE results of the presented latency model. With the obtained α and β values in the presented latency model, we measured the error rate between the measured and estimated (from the presented model) latency of the accelerator and CPU. As summarized in Table 15.4, the MAPE of the presented latency model is 0.11–1.06%, which means the presented latency model estimates the accelerator and CPU latency of the CONV layer execution very accurately. It also implies that with the accurate latency estimation, we can distribute output channels to the accelerator and the CPU so that both the hardware resources can be fully utilized, minimizing the idle time and improving performance.

Table 15.3 Convolutional layer configurations for the benchmarks.

	$Size_{IFMs}$	$Size_{OFM} \times N_F$	$Size_{FT} \times N_F$	Network
Layer 0	$57 \times 57 \times 16$	$57 \times 57 \times 64$	$1 \times 1 \times 16 \times 64$	SN
Layer 1	$57 \times 57 \times 16$	$57 \times 57 \times 64$	$3 \times 3 \times 16 \times 64$	SN
Layer 2	$29 \times 29 \times 32$	$29 \times 29 \times 128$	$1 \times 1 \times 32 \times 128$	SN
Layer 3	$29 \times 29 \times 32$	$29 \times 29 \times 128$	$3 \times 3 \times 32 \times 128$	SN
Layer 4	$28 \times 28 \times 32$	$28 \times 28 \times 192$	$1 \times 1 \times 32 \times 192$	MN
Layer 5	$15 \times 15 \times 64$	$15 \times 15 \times 256$	$3 \times 3 \times 64 \times 256$	SN
Layer 6	$15 \times 15 \times 48$	$15 \times 15 \times 192$	$3 \times 3 \times 48 \times 192$	SN
Layer 7	$14 \times 14 \times 96$	$14 \times 14 \times 576$	$1 \times 1 \times 96 \times 576$	MN
Layer 8	$7 \times 7 \times 576$	$7 \times 7 \times 160$	$1 \times 1 \times 576 \times 160$	MN
Layer 9	$7 \times 7 \times 320$	$7 \times 7 \times 1280$	$1 \times 1 \times 320 \times 1280$	MN
Layer 10	$7 \times 7 \times 160$	$7 \times 7 \times 960$	$1 \times 1 \times 160 \times 960$	MN
Layer 11	$7 \times 7 \times 160$	$7 \times 7 \times 160$	$3 \times 3 \times 160 \times 160$	SG
Layer 12	$7 \times 7 \times 160$	$7 \times 7 \times 960$	$3 \times 3 \times 160 \times 960$	SG
Layer 13	$7 \times 7 \times 160$	$7 \times 7 \times 1280$	$3 \times 3 \times 160 \times 1280$	SG

In the fifth column, SN, MN, and SG indicate SqueezeNet, MobileNet-V2, and Synthetically Generated, respectively.

Table 15.4 MAPE results of the presented latency model.

		Ultra96	Zed	ZCU104	ZCU106
L_{ACC} PE2	1×1 CONV	1.01%	0.82%	1.06%	1.06%
	3×3 CONV	0.14%	0.18%	0.13%	0.13%
L_{ACC} PE4	1×1 CONV	0.74%	0.26%	0.63%	0.63%
	3×3 CONV	0.16%	0.17%	0.12%	0.11%
L_{ACC} PE8	1×1 CONV	0.47%	0.98%	0.87%	0.87%
	3×3 CONV	0.26%	0.26%	0.19%	0.19%
L_{CPU}	1×1 CONV	0.65%	0.40%	0.48%	0.47%
	3×3 CONV	0.76%	0.67%	0.68%	0.68%

PE2, PE4, and PE8 corresponds to the MAPEs of the accelerator latency model.

15.3.2 Performance

We evaluate the performance of the presented co-scheduling technique through experimental results. Figure 15.9 shows the performance results across three different configurations: *CPU_ONLY* (only CPU execution), *ACC_ONLY* (only accelerator execution), and *CPU+ACC* (co-scheduling). Experimental results indicate that when we use 2PE accelerator version, relative performance of the accelerator compared to *CPU_ONLY* is $0.97 \times -1.09\times$. This limited performance improvement for 2PE case is due to small number of PEs in the accelerator. The presented co-scheduling (*CPU+ACC*) results in better performance by $1.93 \times -2.05\times$ and $1.89 \times -2.00\times$ than *CPU_ONLY* and *ACC_ONLY*, respectively. By utilizing both accelerator and CPU, the presented co-scheduling technique leads to better performance than *CPU_ONLY* and *ACC_ONLY*.

Experimental results indicate that in the case of 4PE accelerator version, relative performance of the accelerator compared to the CPU is better than the case of 2PE accelerator. Thus, *CPU+ACC* leads to better performance as compared to the *CPU_ONLY* by $2.84 \times -3.07\times$. As compared to *ACC_ONLY*, *CPU+ACC* shows better performance by $1.43 \times -1.48\times$. Though the relative performance improvement of the *CPU+ACC* is less than that in the case of 2PE accelerator version, the *CPU+ACC* still results in better performance due to the concurrent execution of the CONV layer in the accelerator and CPU.

In the case of 8PE accelerator version, the *CPU+ACC* shows better performance than *CPU_ONLY* and *ACC_ONLY* by $4.58 \times -4.98\times$ and $1.18 \times -1.21\times$, respectively. As demonstrated in the evaluation results, due to the accurate latency model, the presented technique minimizes the idle time in either accelerator or CPU, leading to better performance as compared to *CPU_ONLY* and *ACC_ONLY*.

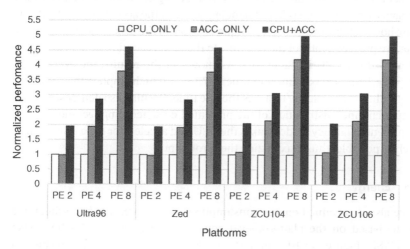

Figure 15.9 Performance results of *ACC_ONLY* and *CPU+ACC* normalized to *CPU_ONLY*.

Table 15.5 Results for a ratio (%) of the idle time to the total execution time.

	Ultra96			Zed			ZCU104			ZCU106		
	PE2	PE4	PE8	PE2	PE4	PE8	PE2	PE4	PE8	PE2	PE4	PE8
Layer 0	2.22	**3.04**	**6.85**	2.81	2.79	**7.16**	0.14	1.63	**6.00**	0.13	1.64	**5.97**
Layer 1	**0.35**	**3.19**	**1.94**	**1.02**	**3.98**	**3.06**	**0.85**	**0.31**	**0.39**	**0.84**	**0.33**	**0.39**
Layer 2	**0.63**	0.06	1.83	**0.41**	**0.83**	**6.55**	1.34	**0.91**	**3.84**	1.33	**0.92**	**3.86**
Layer 3	**0.73**	**0.77**	**1.14**	**0.60**	**0.38**	**2.15**	**1.02**	**0.37**	**1.59**	**1.02**	**0.38**	**1.59**
Layer 4	**1.11**	**1.06**	1.93	**1.50**	**2.50**	0.81	**0.61**	**1.86**	**2.88**	**0.61**	**1.86**	**2.90**
Layer 5	0.07	0.43	1.71	**0.31**	0.03	0.47	0.33	0.74	1.49	0.33	0.75	1.49
Layer 6	0.66	1.51	1.91	0.25	0.65	0.70	0.74	0.81	0.94	0.74	0.79	0.98
Layer 7	**2.91**	4.92	2.08	4.18	3.43	0.70	4.14	**2.29**	4.89	4.10	**2.29**	4.91
Layer 8	1.17	**1.51**	**2.89**	**0.17**	**0.60**	1.79	**0.56**	**2.41**	**1.51**	**0.57**	**2.40**	**1.52**
Layer 9	**0.73**	0.15	0.07	**1.85**	**0.56**	0.18	0.45	1.29	**1.04**	0.45	1.29	**1.03**
Layer 10	0.08	1.16	**1.41**	**0.86**	0.91	**0.67**	**0.82**	2.36	**1.32**	**0.82**	2.35	**1.34**
Layer 11	1.36	2.52	4.82	**0.90**	**1.12**	6.59	**1.95**	**1.97**	**3.28**	1.94	**1.95**	**3.29**
Layer 12	**0.82**	**1.22**	**1.56**	**0.23**	**0.71**	1.77	**1.01**	**1.55**	**1.40**	**1.00**	**1.54**	**1.40**
Layer 13	**0.85**	**1.09**	2.29	**0.44**	**0.88**	1.28	**0.61**	1.10	1.67	0.60	1.09	1.66

The **bold** cells represent the CPU idle time (i.e., the case in which the CPU finishes faster than the accelerator) while the underlined cells denote the accelerator idle time (i.e., the case in which the accelerator finishes faster than the CPU).

The main reason why the presented co-scheduling techniques obtains a huge performance improvement is load balancing between the accelerator and CPU. To measure how well the presented technique distributes the tasks in a load-balanced manner, we present a ratio of the idle time to the total execution time in either the accelerator or the CPU in Table 15.5. As shown in the results, the average idle time is only 1.61% (maximum idle time is 7.16%), which implies the presented technique almost completely removes the idle time. Results also demonstrate that the output channel distribution of the presented co-scheduling technique based on the presented latency model makes the CPU and accelerator to be fully utilized as much as possible, thus maximizing the throughput.

15.3.3 Energy

We have also determined energy consumption for the presented co-scheduling technique based on the platform-level power measured by HPM-300A power meter [198]. Figure 15.10 summarizes the normalized energy results of

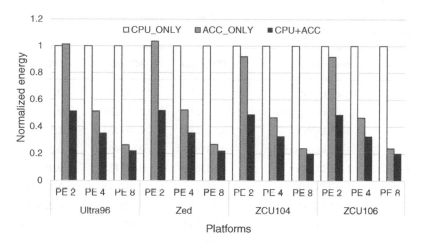

Figure 15.10 Energy results of *ACC_ONLY* and *CPU+ACC* normalized to *CPU_ONLY*.

CPU_ONLY, *ACC_ONLY*, and *CPU+ACC*. Due to the reduced execution time, the presented co-scheduling approach *CPU+ACC* shows energy reduction across different accelerators with varying number of PEs by 48.0–79.8% and 14.9–49.7% as compared to *CPU_ONLY* and *ACC_ONLY*, respectively. Results indicate that the power consumption of the *CPU+ACC* increases as compared to *CPU_ONLY* and *ACC_ONLY* because the *CPU+ACC* makes the CPU and the accelerator to stay in the active state most of the time during the CONV layer operations. In fact, *CPU+ACC* shows higher power consumption than *CPU_ONLY* and *ACC_ONLY* by up to 1.8% and 1.3%, respectively, when we use 8PE accelerator version. However, the reduced execution time overwhelms the increased power consumption, resulting in huge energy reductions.

15.3.4   Case Study: Tiny Darknet CNN Inferences

In this subsection, we show CNN inference latency results for all the layers in the Tiny Darknet model [145]. As in Sections 15.3.2 and 15.3.3, we compare the results of *CPU_ONLY*, *ACC_ONLY*, and *CPU+ACC* when executing a CNN inference with the Tiny Darknet model. For a comprehensive analysis, we breakdown the latencies of each layer in Tiny Darknet across *CPU_ONLY*, *ACC_ONLY*, and *CPU+ACC* as shown in Table 15.6. Since the target platform is a resource-constrained edge, we use 2PE CNN accelerator in the *ACC_ONLY* and *CPU+ACC*. We use pretrained weight in Darknet framework and ImageNet dataset [121] for the input. The results verify that the presented *CPU+ACC* leads to a latency reduction of CNN inference (i.e., performance improvement) by 49.6% and 44.8% as compared to *CPU_ONLY* and *ACC_ONLY*. Since the presented

Table 15.6 Per-layer latency results (in seconds) for CNN inferences with Tiny Darknet model across *CPU_ONLY*, *ACC_ONLY*, and *CPU+ACC*.

CNN Layer #	Description	CPU_ONLY	ACC_ONLY	CPU+ACC
Layer 0	3 × 3 CONV	1.283221	1.057395	0.736854
Layer 1	2 × 2 max pooling	0.073256	0.073281	0.073755
Layer 2	3 × 3 CONV	3.039238	2.644233	1.526805
Layer 3	2 × 2 max pooling	0.035911	0.035959	0.036173
Layer 4	1 × 1 CONV	0.083625	0.078752	0.051595
Layer 5	3 × 3 CONV	2.895266	2.642671	1.419424
Layer 6	1 × 1 CONV	0.317731	0.328591	0.225072
Layer 7	3 × 3 CONV	2.894089	2.642836	1.419433
Layer 8	2 × 2 max pooling	0.035706	0.035747	0.035734
Layer 9	1 × 1 CONV	0.158447	0.148602	0.085157
Layer 10	3 × 3 CONV	2.841999	2.623150	1.401368
Layer 11	1 × 1 CONV	0.313930	0.294245	0.167850
Layer 12	3 × 3 CONV	2.841940	2.623151	1.401373
Layer 13	2 × 2 max pooling	0.017782	0.017908	0.017954
Layer 14	1 × 1 CONV	0.157549	0.147017	0.078937
Layer 15	3 × 3 CONV	2.830288	2.617322	1.373944
Layer 16	1 × 1 CONV	0.313590	0.292231	0.156487
Layer 17	3 × 3 CONV	2.830093	2.617305	1.373931
Layer 18	1 × 1 CONV	0.627162	0.583194	0.311537
Layer 19	1 × 1 CONV	1.239286	1.153453	0.609620
Layer 20	14 × 14 avg pooling	0.008565	0.008591	0.008588
Layer 21	Softmax	0.000197	0.000197	0.000197
	Total	24.838871	22.665831	12.511788

Source: Adapted from [145].

acceleration technique only accelerates the CONV layer, the latency of max pooling (Layers 1, 3, 8, and 13), average pooling (Layer 20), and softmax (Layer 21) layers in *CPU+ACC* is similar to the latency in the case of the *CPU_ONLY* and *ACC_ONLY* (i.e., the layers except for the CONV layers are performed in the CPU). However, since 16 layers in the Tiny Darknet model are CONV layers that accounts for 73% of the total layers, the presented *CPU+ACC* results in a huge CNN inference performance improvement of 1.81 × −1.99× as compared to the *CPU_ONLY* and *ACC_ONLY*. Please note that the latency of the *ACC_ONLY* in Layer 6 is a little higher than the *CPU_ONLY*, which is not consistent with the other CONV layers (i.e., for the CONV layers except for Layer 6, the latency of the *ACC_ONLY* is lower than that of the *CPU_ONLY*). This is because we trigger the accelerator twice in Layer 6 due to the limited on-chip memory size (i.e., block random access memory (BRAM) size), resulting in much longer data transfer latency.

15.4 Chapter Summary

Recent trend of artificial intelligence (AI) at the edge has resulted in assimilation of AI hardware accelerators in edge devices and edge servers for efficient AI inference. CNN acceleration at the edge has, in particular, gained tremendous attention as CNN acceleration at the edge can help enable many novel applications such as autonomous vehicles, surveillance, and robots. In typical resource-constrained edge systems, while hardware accelerators are running, CPUs remain idle. However, the CPU can also contribute to the CONV layer execution along with the accelerator, which can further improve performance and energy efficiency.

This chapter discussed the introduced CPU-accelerator co-scheduling technique to accelerate a single CONV layer operation during the CNN inference at the edge. By exploiting the independence among the operations for generating different CNN output feature maps, the presented co-scheduling technique distributes the output channels to the accelerator and CPU, which leads to further performance improvements as compared to the accelerator-only execution. For load balancing between the accelerator and CPU, we also presented a linear regression-based latency model which could estimate the CONV layer execution time on the CPU and the accelerator. Based on the latency estimation from the presented model, we can distribute the output channels in a load-balanced manner so that the accelerator and the CPU can be fully utilized. The presented technique helps in minimizing the idle time in the accelerator and the CPU, resulting in performance improvements. We have implemented the presented technique in four different FPGA-SoC platforms as a proof-of-concept. Experimental results indicated that the presented co-scheduling technique improved system performance by 1.18x to 2.00x as compared to the accelerator-only execution across a wide spectrum of the accelerator platforms. Moreover, the presented technique also reduced platform-level energy consumption by 14.9–49.7% as compared to the accelerator-only execution. In addition, as demonstrated in the case study, a full layer CNN inference for Tiny Darknet CNN model with the presented co-scheduling technique showed 1.81x to 1.99x better performance as compared to that without the presented technique.

16

Conclusions

Convolutional neural networks (CNNs) have revolutionized the field of artificial intelligence (AI) and computer vision because of their ability to automatically extract features from images and videos and make predictions about the content of images/videos with accuracy equal to or even surpassing humans in many tasks. To attain this high inference accuracy, size, and computational requirements of the CNN models have drastically increased over the years, which make the deployment of CNN models in resource-constrained devices a challenging endeavor. Furthermore, this exorbitant size and computational requirements make these highly accurate CNN models infeasible for real-time applications on edge devices. Thus, embedding CNN inference into various real-world applications on edge devices necessitate the design of high-performance, area, and energy-efficient CNN accelerator architectures. This book targeted the design of accelerators for CNNs and discussed different techniques and approaches for designing CNN accelerators.

Chapter 1 discussed the history and applications of deep neural networks (DNNs) with an emphasis on CNNs. The chapter also elaborated the compute and energy bottlenecks associated with high accuracy CNN inference on the edge device.

Chapter 2 discussed the composition and layers of different CNN models. The chapter also discussed various parameters and hyperparameters for CNNs. The chapter further described some of the prominent high-accuracy CNN models, such as AlexNet, VGGNet, and GoogleNet. The chapter further elucidated some well-known datasets, such as MNIST, CIFAR, and ImageNet, which are often used for training many of the contemporary CNNs. Furthermore, the chapter discussed some of the architectural and algorithmic techniques for efficient processing of high-accuracy CNN models.

Chapter 3 elaborated compressive coding methods for CNNs. The compressive coding for CNNs was classified into two categories, namely, lossy and lossless compression. For lossy compression, the chapter introduced quantization and pruning,

Accelerators for Convolutional Neural Networks, First Edition.
Arslan Munir, Joonho Kong, and Mahmood Azhar Qureshi.
© 2024 The Institute of Electrical and Electronics Engineers, Inc. Published 2024 by John Wiley & Sons, Inc.

whereas for lossless compression, the chapter discussed entropy-based coding and some other coding techniques that can be employed for sparse matrices or tensors. The chapter further provided a review of contemporary compressive coding methods for CNNs.

Chapter 4 presented a novel input feature map (IFM) compression method. The presented scheme exploited the activation sparsity in CNN models, which is attributed to the rectified linear unit (ReLU) activation function. The presented IFM data compression method, which is performed on the software side, removed the transfer of zero-valued elements in IFMs. The presented lossless compression method resulted in data transfer reduction between the memory and the accelerator. Experimental results indicated that the presented compression technique reduced the data size and latency for IFM data transfer by 34.0–85.2% and 4.4–75.7%, respectively, as compared to the case without the data compression.

Chapter 5 introduced an arithmetic coding-based 5-bit weight compression method. In addition, we have also introduced a decoding hardware for fast, yet efficient runtime weight decoding (decompression). When employing our technique to the pruned 5-bit quantized weights, our technique resulted in 57.5×–112.2× better compression ratio as compared to the uncompressed 32-bit floating-point (FP) weights. Due to the reduced weight data size, our technique also led to memory data transfer energy reduction by 89.2% (by up to 99.1% for pruned weights), on average, as compared to the uncompressed 32-bit FP weight data.

Chapter 6 provided an overview of dense CNN accelerators, which accept IFMs and weights as dense matrices, thus changing the convolution operations to dense matrix multiplication. The chapter also discussed the two widely used architectures to implement the dense CNN accelerators, viz., systolic arrays and multiply-accumulate (MAC) arrays. The chapter further provided a brief review of the contemporary advances in dense CNN accelerators.

Chapter 7 introduced an iMAC CNN accelerator for resource-constrained systems. The iMAC accelerator offloaded finer-grained operations required for convolution layers to the accelerator hardware instead of offloading the entire convolution layer operations. The chapter further presented the implementation results focusing on the hardware utilization for the iMAC accelerator prototyped on the ZED platform, which was equipped with Zynq-7020 system-on-chip, with full-stack software including operating system (petaLinux).

Chapter 8 presented NeuroMAX – a dense accelerator which incorporated multi-threaded processing element (PE) cores. NeuroMAX introduced an efficient 2D weight broadcast dataflow scheme which exploited the multilevel parallelism of the processing engine and enabled hardware utilization close to a 100%. The chapter discussed the hardware design and dataflow of NeuroMAX to elaborate dense CNN accelerators. Experimental results indicated that NeuroMAX provided a throughput increase of 77.4% and a latency decrease of 47% with a 28% decrease in the PE count against recently proposed dense accelerator designs for modern CNNs. Experimental results further showed that NeuroMAX provided at least a 27% and a 29% decrease in power consumption and lookup table (LUT) count, respectively, against prior field-programmable gate array (FPGA)-based CNN accelerators.

Chapter 9 provided an overview of sparse CNN accelerators. The chapter discussed the reason for sparsity in CNN models and the importance of exploiting this sparsity in CNN accelerators. The chapter further discussed the advances in contemporary sparse CNN accelerators.

Chapter 10 introduced a sparse CNN accelerator that exploited sparsity in IFMs to enhance performance, reduce energy consumption, and curtail data transfer between the accelerator and the off-chip main memory. The presented accelerator first compressed the IFMs and then performed convolution layer operations with the compressed IFM engendering performance improvement and energy reduction. Evaluation results from the prototype accelerator demonstrated that the accelerator improved performance by 1.1×–22.6× depending on the degree of the sparsity and filter size as compared to the central processing unit (CPU)-based convolution layer execution. In terms of energy, the presented accelerator led to 47.7–97.4% energy reduction as compared to the CPU-based execution. Furthermore, the accelerator attained 1.9× (on average) better cost efficiency with less or comparable power consumption as compared to several state-of-the-art CNN accelerator designs.

Chapter 11 presented Sparse-PE, a multithreaded, general purpose, dot product core for sparse CNNs. The core was designed to exploit *two-sided* sparsity, that is, sparsity in both the weights and activations, to maximize the throughput and hardware utilization. Unlike contemporary approaches for sparse accelerators that use the compressed sparse column (CSC) format and the associated complex PE design, the Sparse-PE core used the sparse binary mask format and had a relatively low complexity. The chapter also presented novel, low-cost circuits, including selection, computation, and accumulation, which, when used in conjunction, allowed the core to skip huge number of computations involving *zero* data and only favored computations involving *nonzero* data to maximize the throughput. Experimental results showed that the Sparse-PE core could effectively keep the hardware utilization above 85% at sparsity as high as 60%, for both the input activations and weights. The chapter also compared the performance of Sparse-PE core-based accelerator against previous state-of-the-art dense and two-sided sparse CNN accelerators. Sparse-PE offered, on average, 12×, 4.2×, 2.38×, and 1.98×, speedup over NeuroMAX (dense), SCNN (sparse), Eyeriss v2 (sparse), and SparTen (sparse), respectively.

Chapter 12 introduced Phantom – a novel multithreaded, flexible, neural computational core that exploited the two-sided sparsity to provide high gains in performance at a relatively low hardware complexity. Phantom extended Sparse-PE design introduced in Chapter 11. The chapter discussed the design of Phantom-2D accelerator that used a 2D array of Phantom cores and also presented a novel dataflow that efficiently used the capabilities of the Phantom cores. As opposed to many previous approaches, the Phantom-2D accelerator could support *all* layers of a CNN, including unit and nonunit stride convolutions, and fully connected (FC) layers. In addition, the chapter discussed a two-level load balancing strategy that efficiently balanced the load across the architecture level (*intercore*), and at the thread level (*intracore*) to minimize idling of the compute threads, thereby, further increasing the throughput. Experimental results showed that, on average, Phantom-2D accelerator performed 12×, 4.1×, 1.98×, and 2.36×, better than an equivalent dense CNN architecture, SCNN, SparTen, and Eyeriss v2, respectively, while retaining the energy efficiency of SparTen.

Chapter 13 provided an overview of hardware/software (HW/SW) co-design and co-scheduling. The chapter first discussed the recent advancements in the HW/SW co-design for resource-constrained systems. The chapter also discussed a cognitive Internet of things architecture as an example of HW/SW co-design. Afterwards, the chapter discussed the recent advancements in HW/SW co-scheduling.

Chapter 14 discussed the HW/SW co-design aspects of the iMAC accelerator discussed in Chapter 7. The chapter focused on software-level supports to efficiently partition and allocate the input channels to the iMAC accelerator and to exploit the parallelism inside the convolution layer operations. Experimental results revealed that the implementation attained $1.3\times \sim 2.0\times$ speedup and energy reduction of 19.4~44.3% as compared to using only the CPU. Experimental results verified that the HW/SW co-design in the iMAC accelerator achieved a balanced trade-off between response time, energy, and cost for CNN inference in resource-constrained systems.

Finally, Chapter 15 presented a CPU-accelerator co-scheduling technique to accelerate a single convolution (CONV) layer operation during the CNN inference at the edge. By exploiting the independence among the operations for generating different CNN output feature maps, the co-scheduling technique distributed the output channels to the accelerator and CPU, which led to further performance improvements as compared to the accelerator-only execution. For load balancing between the accelerator and the CPU, the chapter discussed a linear regression-based latency model which could estimate the CONV layer execution time on the CPU and the accelerator, based on which the output channels could be distributed in a load-balanced manner so that the accelerator and the CPU could be fully utilized. Experimental results showed that the presented CPU-accelerator co-scheduling technique improved system performance by 1.18×–2.00× as compared to the accelerator-only execution across a wide spectrum of the accelerator platforms. Moreover, the presented technique also reduced the platform-level energy consumption by 14.9–49.7% as compared to the accelerator-only execution.

Although this book covered a variety of approaches for CNN acceleration, new techniques for CNN acceleration are continuously being developed. Modern CNN accelerators deliberate on the following design factors:

- **Mixed Precision Support:** CNNs accelerators strive for a balanced tradeoff between the model accuracy, computation complexity, and the amount of data transfer. To reduce computation complexity and the amount of data transfer, low-precision weights, and feature maps are widely used. Accordingly, the modern CNN accelerator designs contrive to support mixed precision (i.e., combined use of different numerical precisions such as 8-bit integer, 16-bit, and 32-bit floating types, etc.) in a single CNN accelerator for better computation efficiency.

- **Memory/Storage Architecture:** As the weight and feature map sizes are continuously growing, efficient utilization of storage and memory bandwidth is becoming increasingly important for attaining better performance. Thus, modern CNN accelerators are incorporating 3D-stacked memories to provide high bandwidth memory. Furthermore, near-memory or in-memory processing for CNNs is being considered in modern CNN accelerator designs for reducing the amount of the data transfer between memory and the accelerator.

- **Data Characteristics:** As explained in this book, sparsity considerations and support are prevalent in many contemporary CNN accelerators. Skipping the ineffectual operations that result in zero value can greatly enhance the performance and energy efficiency of a CNN accelerator.

Finally, some futuristic approaches in CNN accelerator design are the following:

- **Exploiting New Technologies:** Exploiting new technologies, such as new memory cell or logic, will be a promising research direction for future CNN accelerators. With new memory cells, such as resistive random-access memory (ReRAM), we can easily implement compute-in-memory concept in the CNN accelerator [199] by exploiting the cell characteristics. In addition, with new logic, such as single-flux quantum (SFQ) logic [200], we can obtain much better performance as compared to the conventional logic-based CNN accelerators. According to [200], the SFQ-based neural processing unit (NPU) shows 23× better performance as compared to the state-of-the-art NPUs.

- **Security and Privacy Consideration:** CNNs may include processing of security or privacy-sensitive data. With the conventional encryption methods, encrypted data should be decrypted before performing the CNN operation, which means that the privacy of users may not be preserved. The homomorphic encryption, which enables operations over encrypted data, can be a good candidate for security- and privacy-preserving CNNs.

References

1 Chen, C., Seff, A., Kornhauser, A., and Xiao, J. (2015) DeepDriving: Learning Affordance for Direct Perception in Autonomous Driving, in *2015 IEEE International Conference on Computer Vision (ICCV)*, pp. 2722–2730, doi:10.1109/ICCV.2015.312.

2 Russakovsky, O., Deng, J., Su, H., Krause, J., Satheesh, S., Ma, S., Huang, Z., Karpathy, A., Khosla, A., Bernstein, M., Berg, A.C., and Fei Fei, L. (2015) ImageNet Large Scale Visual Recognition Challenge 115 (3), doi:10.1007/s11263-015-0816-y.

3 Deng, L., Li, J., Huang, J.T., Yao, K., Yu, D., Seide, F., Seltzer, M., Zweig, G., He, X., Williams, J., Gong, Y., and Acero, A. (2013) Recent Advances in Deep Learning for Speech Research at Microsoft, in *Proceedings of the IEEE International Conference on Acoustics, Speech, and Signal Processing (ICASSP)*, pp. 8604–8608, doi:10.1109/ICASSP.2013.6639345.

4 Tan, M. and Le, Q.V. (2021) EfficientNetV2: Smaller Models and Faster Training. CoRR, **abs/2104.00298**. URL https://arxiv.org/abs/2104.00298.

5 Le Cun, Y., Jackel, L., Boser, B., Denker, J., Graf, H., Guyon, I., Henderson, D., Howard, R., and Hubbard, W. (1989) Handwritten Digit Recognition: Applications of Neural Network Chips and Automatic Learning. *IEEE Communications Magazine*, 27 (11), 41–46, doi:10.1109/35.41400.

6 Sze, V., Chen, Y., Yang, T., and Emer, J.S. (2017) Efficient Processing of Deep Neural Networks: A Tutorial and Survey. *Proceedings of the IEEE*, 105 (12), 2295–2329.

7 Hinton, G., Deng, L., Yu, D., Dahl, G.E., Mohamed, A.r., Jaitly, N., Senior, A., Vanhoucke, V., Nguyen, P., Sainath, T.N., and Kingsbury, B. (2012) Deep Neural Networks for Acoustic Modeling in Speech Recognition: The Shared Views of Four Research Groups. *IEEE Signal Processing Magazine*, 29 (6), 82–97, doi:10.1109/MSP.2012.2205597.

Accelerators for Convolutional Neural Networks, First Edition.
Arslan Munir, Joonho Kong, and Mahmood Azhar Qureshi.
© 2024 The Institute of Electrical and Electronics Engineers, Inc. Published 2024 by John Wiley & Sons, Inc.

8 Collobert, R., Weston, J., Bottou, L., Karlen, M., Kavukcuoglu, K., and Kuksa, P. (2011) Natural Language Processing (Almost) from Scratch. *Journal of Machine Learning Research*, 12, 2493–2537.

9 van den Oord, A., Dieleman, S., Zen, H., Simonyan, K., Vinyals, O., Graves, A., Kalchbrenner, N., Senior, A.W., and Kavukcuoglu, K. (2016) WaveNet: A Generative Model for Raw Audio. *CoRR*, **abs/1609.03499**. URL http://arxiv.org/abs/1609.03499.

10 Wu, Y., Schuster, M., Chen, Z., Le, Q.V., Norouzi, M., Macherey, W., Krikun, M., Cao, Y., Gao, Q., Macherey, K., Klingner, J., Shah, A., Johnson, M., Liu, X., Kaiser, L., Gouws, S., Kato, Y., Kudo, T., Kazawa, H., Stevens, K., Kurian, G., Patil, N., Wang, W., Young, C., Smith, J., Riesa, J., Rudnick, A., Vinyals, O., Corrado, G., Hughes, M., and Dean, J. (2016) Google's Neural Machine Translation System: Bridging the Gap between Human and Machine Translation. *CoRR*, **abs/1609.08144**. URL http://arxiv.org/abs/1609.08144.

11 Tesla AI (2022) Artificial Intelligence & Autopilot. URL https://www.tesla.com/AI.

12 Waymo (2022) Waymo Driver. URL https://waymo.com/waymo-driver/.

13 Bi, X.a., Liu, Y., Jiang, Q., Shu, Q., Sun, Q., and Dai, J. (2018) The Diagnosis of Autism Spectrum Disorder Based on the Random Neural Network Cluster. *Frontiers in Human Neuroscience*, 12, 257, doi:10.3389/fnhum.2018.00257. URL https://www.frontiersin.org/article/10.3389/fnhum.2018.00257.

14 Guo, X., Dominick, K.C., Minai, A., Li, H., Erickson, C.A., and Lu, L. (2017) Diagnosing Autism Spectrum Disorder from Brain Resting-State Functional Connectivity Patterns Using a Deep Neural Network with a Novel Feature Selection Method. *Frontiers in Neuroscience*, 11, doi:10.3389/fnins.2017.00460.

15 Baştürk, A., Yüksei, M.E., Badem, H., and Çalışkan, A. (2017) Deep Neural Network Based Diagnosis System for Melanoma Skin Cancer, in *2017 25th Signal Processing and Communications Applications Conference (SIU)*, pp. 1–4, doi:10.1109/SIU.2017.7960563.

16 Siar, M. and Teshnehlab, M. (2019) Brain Tumor Detection Using Deep Neural Network and Machine Learning Algorithm, in *2019 9th International Conference on Computer and Knowledge Engineering (ICCKE)*, pp. 363–368, doi:10.1109/ICCKE48569.2019.8964846.

17 Qureshi, M.A. and Munir, A. (2020) PUF-IPA: A PUF-Based Identity Preserving Protocol for Internet of Things Authentication, in *2020 IEEE 17th Annual Consumer Communications Networking Conference (CCNC)*, pp. 1–7, doi:10.1109/CCNC46108.2020.9045264.

18 Qureshi, M.A. and Munir, A. (2019) PUF-RLA: A PUF-Based Reliable and Lightweight Authentication Protocol Employing Binary String Shuffling, in *2019 IEEE 37th International Conference on Computer Design (ICCD)*, pp. 576–584, doi:10.1109/ICCD46524.2019.00084.

19 Qureshi, M.A. and Munir, A. (2022) PUF-RAKE: A PUF-Based Robust and Lightweight Authentication and Key Establishment Protocol. *IEEE Transactions on Dependable and Secure Computing*, 19 (4), 2457–2475, doi:10.1109/TDSC.2021.3059454.

20 Kong, J. and Koushanfar, F. (2014) Processor-Based Strong Physical Unclonable Functions With Aging-Based Response Tuning. *IEEE Transactions on Emerging Topics in Computing*, 2 (1), 16–29, doi:10.1109/TETC.2013.2289385.

21 Kong, J., Koushanfar, F., Pendyala, P.K., Sadeghi, A.R., and Wachsmann, C. (2014) PUFatt: Embedded Platform Attestation Based on Novel Processor-Based PUFs, in *2014 51st ACM/EDAC/IEEE Design Automation Conference (DAC)*, pp. 1–6, doi:10.1145/2593069.2593192.

22 Santikellur, P., Bhattacharyay, A., and Chakraborty, R.S. (2019) Deep Learning based Model Building Attacks on Arbiter PUF Compositions. *IACR Cryptol. ePrint Arch.*, **2019**, 566.

23 Mursi, K.T., Thapaliya, B., Zhuang, Y., Aseeri, A.O., and Alkatheiri, M.S. (2020) A Fast Deep Learning Method for Security Vulnerability Study of XOR PUFs. *Electronics*, 9 (10), doi:10.3390/electronics9101715.

24 Mirsky, Y., Demontis, A., Kotak, J., Shankar, R., Gelei, D., Yang, L., Zhang, X., Lee, W., Elovici, Y., and Biggio, B. (2021) The Threat of Offensive AI to Organizations. *CoRR*, **abs/2106.15764**. URL https://arxiv.org/abs/2106.15764.

25 Miao, Y., Chen, C., Pan, L., Han, Q., Zhang, J., and Xiang, Y. (2021) Machine Learning Based Cyber Attacks Targeting on Controlled Information: A Survey. *CoRR*, **abs/2102.07969**. URL https://arxiv.org/abs/2102.07969.

26 Alavizadeh, H., Jang-Jaccard, J., Alpcan, T., and Çamtepe, S.A. (2021) A Markov Game Model for AI-Based Cyber Security Attack Mitigation. *CoRR*, **abs/2107.09258**. URL https://arxiv.org/abs/2107.09258.

27 Rao, D. and Mane, S. (2021) Zero-Shot Learning Approach to Adaptive Cybersecurity Using Explainable AI. *CoRR*, **abs/2106.14647**. URL https://arxiv.org/abs/2106.14647.

28 Silver, D., Huang, A., Maddison, C., Guez, A., Sifre, L., Driessche, G., Schrittwieser, J., Antonoglou, I., Panneershelvam, V., Lanctot, M., Dieleman, S., Grewe, D., Nham, J., Kalchbrenner, N., Sutskever, I., Lillicrap, T., Leach, M., Kavukcuoglu, K., Graepel, T., and Hassabis, D. (2016) Mastering the Game of Go with Deep Neural Networks and Tree Search. *Nature*, 529, 484–489, doi:10.1038/nature16961.

29 Levine, S., Finn, C., Darrell, T., and Abbeel, P. (2015) End-to-End Training of Deep Visuomotor Policies. *CoRR*, **abs/1504.00702**. URL http://arxiv.org/abs/1504.00702.

30 Krizhevsky, A., Sutskever, I., and Hinton, G.E. (2012) ImageNet Classification with Deep Convolutional Neural Networks, in *Proceedings of the 25th*

International Conference on Neural Information Processing Systems - Volume 1, Curran Associates Inc., Red Hook, NY, USA, NIPS '12, pp. 1097–1105.

31 Simonyan, K. and Zisserman, A. (2015) Very Deep Convolutional Networks for Large-Scale Image Recognition, in *3rd International Conference on Learning Representations (ICLR)*.

32 He, K., Zhang, X., Ren, S., and Sun, J. (2015) Deep Residual Learning for Image Recognition. *CoRR*, **abs/1512.03385**. URL http://arxiv.org/abs/1512 .03385.

33 Howard, A.G., Zhu, M., Chen, B., Kalenichenko, D., Wang, W., Weyand, T., Andreetto, M., and Adam, H. (2017) MobileNets: Efficient Convolutional Neural Networks for Mobile Vision Applications. *CoRR*, **abs/1704.04861**. URL http://arxiv.org/abs/1704.04861.

34 Sandler, M., Howard, A.G., Zhu, M., Zhmoginov, A., and Chen, L. (2018) Inverted Residuals and Linear Bottlenecks: Mobile Networks for Classification, Detection and Segmentation. *CoRR*, **abs/1801.04381**. URL http://arxiv .org/abs/1801.04381.

35 Szegedy, C., Liu, W., Jia, Y., Sermanet, P., Reed, S., Anguelov, D., Erhan, D., Vanhoucke, V., and Rabinovich, A. (2015) Going Deeper with Convolutions, in *Computer Vision and Pattern Recognition (CVPR)*. URL http://arxiv.org/abs/ 1409.4842.

36 Horowitz, M. (2014) 1.1 Computing's Energy Problem (and what we can do about it), in *2014 IEEE International Solid-State Circuits Conference Digest of Technical Papers (ISSCC)*, vol. 57, pp. 10–14, doi:10.1109/ISSCC.2014.6757323.

37 Miyashita, D., Lee, E.H., and Murmann, B. (2016) Convolutional Neural Networks using Logarithmic Data Representation. *CoRR*, **abs/1603.01025**. URL http://arxiv.org/abs/1603.01025.

38 Vogel, S., Liang, M., Guntoro, A., Stechele, W., and Ascheid, G. (2018) Efficient Hardware Acceleration of CNNs Using Logarithmic Data Representation with Arbitrary Log-Base, in *Proceedings of the International Conference on Computer-Aided Design*, Association for Computing Machinery, New York, NY, USA, ICCAD '18, doi:10.1145/3240765.3240803.

39 Lin, D.D., Talathi, S.S., and Annapureddy, V.S. (2015) Fixed Point Quantization of Deep Convolutional Networks. *CoRR*, **abs/1511.06393**. URL http:// arxiv.org/abs/1511.06393.

40 Moons, B., Uytterhoeven, R., Dehaene, W., and Verhelst, M. (2017) 14.5 Envision: A 0.26-to-10TOPS/W Subword-Parallel Dynamic-Voltage-Accuracy-Frequency-Scalable Convolutional Neural Network Processor in 28nm FDSOI, in *2017 IEEE International Solid-State Circuits Conference (ISSCC)*, IEEE, pp. 246–247.

41 Lee, J., Kim, C., Kang, S., Shin, D., Kim, S., and Yoo, H.J. (2018) UNPU: An Energy-Efficient Deep Neural Network Accelerator with Fully Variable Weight Bit Precision. *IEEE Journal of Solid-State Circuits*, 54 (1), 173–185.

42 Judd, P., Albericio, J., Hetherington, T., Aamodt, T.M., and Moshovos, A. (2016) Stripes: Bit-Serial Deep Neural Network Computing, in *The 49th Annual IEEE/ACM International Symposium on Microarchitecture*, IEEE Press, MICRO-49.

43 Albericio, J., Judd, P., Hetherington, T., Aamodt, T., Jerger, N.E., and Moshovos, A. (2016) Cnvlutin: Ineffectual-Neuron-Free Deep Neural Network Computing, in *2016 ACM/IEEE 43rd Annual International Symposium on Computer Architecture (ISCA)*, pp. 1–13, doi:10.1109/ISCA.2016.11.

44 Zhang, S., Du, Z., Zhang, L., Lan, H., Liu, S., Li, L., Guo, Q., Chen, T., and Chen, Y. (2016) Cambricon-X: An Accelerator for Sparse Neural Networks, in *2016 49th Annual IEEE/ACM International Symposium on Microarchitecture (MICRO)*, pp. 1–12, doi:10.1109/MICRO.2016.7783723.

45 Chen, Y., Krishna, T., Emer, J.S., and Sze, V. (2017) Eyeriss: An Energy-Efficient Reconfigurable Accelerator for Deep Convolutional Neural Networks. *IEEE Journal of Solid-State Circuits*, 52 (1), 127–138.

46 Han, S., Mao, H., and Dally, W.J. (2016) Deep Compression: Compressing Deep Neural Network with Pruning, Trained Quantization and Huffman Coding, in *4th International Conference on Learning Representations (ICLR) 2016*.

47 Pasandi, M.M., Hajabdollahi, M., Karimi, N., and Samavi, S. (2020) Modeling of Pruning Techniques for Deep Neural Networks Simplification. *CoRR*, **abs/2001.04062**. URL https://arxiv.org/abs/2001.04062.

48 Ma, X., Lin, S., Ye, S., He, Z., Zhang, L., Yuan, G., Tan, S.H., Li, Z., Fan, D., Qian, X., Lin, X., Ma, K., and Wang, Y. (2020) Non-Structured DNN Weight Pruning – Is It Beneficial in Any Platform? *CoRR*, **abs/1907.02124**. URL http://arxiv.org/abs/1907.02124.

49 Liu, N., Ma, X., Xu, Z., Wang, Y., Tang, J., and Ye, J. (2019) AutoCompress: An Automatic DNN Structured Pruning Framework for Ultra-High Compression Rates. *CoRR*, **abs/1907.03141**. URL http://arxiv.org/abs/1907.03141.

50 Min, C., Wang, A., Chen, Y., Xu, W., and Chen, X. (2018) 2PFPCE: Two-Phase Filter Pruning Based on Conditional Entropy. *CoRR*, **abs/1809.02220**. URL http://arxiv.org/abs/1809.02220.

51 Wen, W., Wu, C., Wang, Y., Chen, Y., and Li, H. (2016) Learning Structured Sparsity in Deep Neural Networks. *CoRR*, **abs/1608.03665**. URL http://arxiv.org/abs/1608.03665.

52 Chen, Y., Emer, J.S., and Sze, V. (2018) Eyeriss v2: A Flexible and High-Performance Accelerator for Emerging Deep Neural Networks. *CoRR*, **abs/1807.07928**. URL http://arxiv.org/abs/1807.07928.

53 Han, S., Liu, X., Mao, H., Pu, J., Pedram, A., Horowitz, M.A., and Dally, W.J. (2016) EIE: Efficient Inference Engine on Compressed Deep Neural Network, in *2016 ACM/IEEE 43rd Annual International Symposium on Computer Architecture (ISCA)*, pp. 243–254, doi:10.1109/ISCA.2016.30.

54 Samajdar, A., Zhu, Y., Whatmough, P.N., Mattina, M., and Krishna, T. (2018) SCALE-Sim: Systolic CNN Accelerator. *CoRR*, **abs/1811.02883**. URL http://arxiv.org/abs/1811.02883.

55 Gunturu, S., Munir, A., Ullah, H., Welch, S., and Flippo, D. (2022) A Spatial AI-Based Agricultural Robotic Platform for Wheat Detection and Collision Avoidance. *AI*, 3 (3), 719–738, doi:10.3390/ai3030042.

56 Nirthika, R., Manivannan, S., Ramanan, A., and Wang, R. (2022) Pooling in Convolutional Neural Networks for Medical Image Analysis: A Survey and an Empirical Study. *Springer Neural Computing and Applications*, 34, 5321–5347.

57 Nyuytiymbiy, K. (2020) Parameters and Hyperparameters in Machine Learning and Deep Learning. URL https://towardsdatascience.com/parameters-and-hyper parameters-aa609601a9ac.

58 Radhakrishnan, P. (2017) What are Hyperparameters? and How to Tune the Hyperparameters in a Deep Neural Network? URL https://towardsdatascience .com/what-are-hyperparameters-and-how-to-tune-the-hyperparameters-in-a-deep-neural-network-d0604917584a.

59 Yathish, V. (2022) Loss Functions and Their Use In Neural Networks. URL https://towardsdatascience.com/loss-functions-and-their-use-in-neural-networks-a470e703f1e9#:~:text=A%20loss%20function%20is%20a, the%20predicted%20and%20target%20outputs.

60 Szeliski, R. (2022) *Computer Vision: Algorithms and Applications*, 2nd edn, Springer.

61 Karim, R. (2018) 10 Stochastic Gradient Descent Optimisation Algorithms + Cheatsheet. URL https://towardsdatascience.com/10-gradient-descent-optimisation-algorithms-86989510b5e9.

62 Iandola, F.N., Moskewicz, M.W., Ashraf, K., Han, S., Dally, W.J., and Keutzer, K. (2016) SqueezeNet: AlexNet-Level Accuracy with 50x Fewer Parameters and <1MB Model Size.

63 Courbariaux, M., Bengio, Y., and David, J. (2015) BinaryConnect: Training Deep Neural Networks with Binary Weights During Propagations. *CoRR*, **abs/1511.00363**. URL http://arxiv.org/abs/1511.00363

64 Courbariaux, M., Hubara, I., Soudry, D., El-Yaniv, R., and Bengio, Y. (2016) Binarized Neural Networks: Training Deep Neural Networks with Weights and Activations Constrained to +1 or −1. *CoRR*, **abs/1602.02830**. URL http://arxiv.org/abs/1602.02830.

65 Rastegari, M., Ordonez, V., Redmon, J., and Farhadi, A. (2016) XNOR-Net: ImageNet Classification Using Binary Convolutional Neural Networks. *CoRR*, **abs/1603.05279**. URL http://arxiv.org/abs/1603.05279.

66 Tan, M. and Le, Q.V. (2019) EfficientNet: Rethinking Model Scaling for Convolutional Neural Networks. *CoRR*, **abs/1905.11946**. URL http://arxiv.org/abs/1905.11946.

67 Tensorflow-MNIST (2022) MNIST. URL https://www.tensorflow.org/datasets/catalog/mnist.

68 TensorFlow (2022) Tensorflow-CIFAR. URL https://www.tensorflow.org/datasets/catalog/cifar10.

69 Yuan, L., Chen, D., Chen, Y., Codella, N., Dai, X., Gao, J., Hu, H., Huang, X., Li, B., Li, C., Liu, C., Liu, M., Liu, Z., Lu, Y., Shi, Y., Wang, L., Wang, J., Xiao, B., Xiao, Z., Yang, J., Zeng, M., Zhou, L., and Zhang, P. (2021) Florence: A New Foundation Model for Computer Vision. *CoRR Arxiv*, **abs/2111.11432**. URL https://arxiv.org/abs/2111.11432.

70 Munir, A., Blasch, E., Kwon, J., Kong, J., and Aved, A. (2021) Artificial Intelligence and Data Fusion at the Edge. *IEEE Aerospace and Electronic Systems Magazine*, 36 (7), 62–78.

71 Munir, A., Kwon, J., Lee, J.H., Kong, J., Blasch, E., Aved, A., and Muhammad, K. (2021) FogSurv: A Fog-Assisted Architecture for Urban Surveillance Using Artificial Intelligence and Data Fusion. *IEEE Access*, 9, 111938–111959.

72 Poudel, B., Giri, N.K., and Munir, A. (2017) Design and Comparative Evaluation of GPGPU- and FPGA-Based MPSoC ECU Architectures for Secure, Dependable, and Real-Time Automotive CPS, in *Proceedings of IEEE International Conference on Application-Specific Systems, Architectures and Processors (ASAP)*, Seattle, Washington, USA.

73 Poudel, B. and Munir, A. (2021) Design and Evaluation of a Reconfigurable ECU Architecture for Secure and Dependable Automotive CPS. *IEEE Transactions on Dependable and Secure Computing (TDSC)*, 18 (1), 235–252.

74 Khan, A., Umar, A.I., Munir, A., Shirazi, S.H., Khan, M.A., and Adnan, M. (2021) A QoS-Aware Machine Learning-Based Framework for AMI Applications in Smart Grids. *Energies*, 14 (23), doi:10.3390/en14238171.

75 Archana, R., Vaishnavi, C., Priyanka, D.S., Gunaki, S., Swamy, S.R., and Honnavalli, P.B. (2022) Remote Health Monitoring using IoT and Edge Computing, in *2022 International Conference on IoT and Blockchain Technology (ICIBT)*, Ranchi, India, pp. 1–6, doi:10.1109/ICIBT52874.2022.9807710.

76 Hafeez, T., Xu, L., and Mcardle, G. (2021) Edge Intelligence for Data Handling and Predictive Maintenance in IIOT. *IEEE Access*, 9, 49355–49371, doi:10.1109/ACCESS.2021.3069137.

77 Qualcomm (2022) Snapdragon Neural Processing Engine SDK. URL https://developer.qualcomm.com/sites/default/files/docs/snpe/.

78 Jouppi, N.P., Yoon, D.H., Ashcraft, M., Gottscho, M., Jablin, T.B., Kurian, G., Laudon, J., Li, S., Ma, P., Ma, X., Norrie, T., Patil, N., Prasad, S., Young, C., Zhou, Z., and Patterson, D. (2021) Ten Lessons From Three Generations Shaped Google's TPUv4i: Industrial Product, in *2021 ACM/IEEE 48th Annual International Symposium on Computer Architecture (ISCA)*, pp. 1–14, doi:10.1109/ISCA52012.2021.00010.

79 Xilinx (2022) Zynq DPU Product Guide. URL https://www.xilinx.com/content/dam/xilinx/support/documentation/ip_documentation/dpu/v3_3/pg338-dpu.pdf.

80 Samsung (2022) Exynos 2100. URL https://www.samsung.com/semiconductor/minisite/exynos/products/mobileprocessor/exynos-2100/.

81 Ko, J.H., Mudassar, B., Na, T., and Mukhopadhyay, S. (2017) Design of an Energy-Efficient Accelerator for Training of Convolutional Neural Networks Using Frequency-Domain Computation, in *2017 54th ACM/EDAC/IEEE Design Automation Conference (DAC)*, pp. 1–6, doi:10.1145/3061639.3062228.

82 Mathieu, M., Henaff, M., and LeCun, Y. (2014) Fast Training of Convolutional Networks through FFTs, in *2nd International Conference on Learning Representations, ICLR 2014, Banff, AB, Canada, April 14–16, 2014, Conference Track Proceedings* (eds Y. Bengio and Y. LeCun). URL http://arxiv.org/abs/1312.5851.

83 Cong, J. and Xiao, B. (2014) Minimizing Computation in Convolutional Neural Networks, in *Artificial Neural Networks and Machine Learning – ICANN 2014* (eds S. Wermter, C. Weber, W. Duch, T. Honkela, P. Koprinkova-Hristova, S. Magg, G. Palm, and A.E.P. Villa), Springer International Publishing, Cham, pp. 281–290.

84 Strassen, V. (1969) Gaussian Elimination is not Optimal. *Numerische Mathematik*, 13, 354–356. URL http://eudml.org/doc/131927.

85 Lavin, A. (2015) Fast Algorithms for Convolutional Neural Networks. *CoRR*, **abs/1509.09308**. URL http://arxiv.org/abs/1509.09308.

86 Winograd, S. (1980) Arithmetic Complexity of Computations, Society for Industrial and Applied Mathematics, doi:10.1137/1.9781611970364. URL https://epubs.siam.org.

87 Sankaradass, M., Jakkula, V., Cadambi, S., Chakradhar, S.T., Durdanovic, I., Cosatto, E., and Graf, H.P. (2009) A Massively Parallel Coprocessor for Convolutional Neural Networks, in *2009 20th IEEE International Conference on Application-Specific Systems, Architectures and Processors*, pp. 53–60.

88 Chakradhar, S., Sankaradas, M., Jakkula, V., and Cadambi, S. (2010) A Dynamically Configurable Coprocessor for Convolutional Neural

Networks. *SIGARCH Computer Architecture News*, 38 (3), 247–257, doi:10.1145/1816038.1815993.

89 Chen, T., Du, Z., Sun, N., Wang, J., Wu, C., Chen, Y., and Temam, O. (2014) DianNao: A Small-Footprint High-Throughput Accelerator for Ubiquitous Machine-Learning, in *Proceedings of the 19th International Conference on Architectural Support for Programming Languages and Operating Systems*, Association for Computing Machinery, New York, NY, USA, ASPLOS '14, pp. 269–284, doi:10.1145/2541940.2541967.

90 Chen, Y., Luo, T., Liu, S., Zhang, S., He, L., Wang, J., Li, L., Chen, T., Xu, Z., Sun, N., and Temam, O. (2014) DaDianNao: A Machine-Learning Super-computer, in *2014 47th Annual IEEE/ACM International Symposium on Microarchitecture*, pp. 609–622, doi:10.1109/MICRO.2014.58.

91 Kim, D., Kung, J., Chai, S., Yalamanchili, S., and Mukhopadhyay, S. (2016) Neurocube: A Programmable Digital Neuromorphic Architecture with High-Density 3D Memory. *SIGARCH Comput. Archit. News*, 44 (3), 380–392, doi:10.1145/3007787.3001178.

92 Gao, M., Pu, J., Yang, X., Horowitz, M., and Kozyrakis, C. (2017) TETRIS: Scalable and Efficient Neural Network Acceleration with 3D Memory. *SIGARCH Computer Architecture News*, 45 (1), 751–764, doi:10.1145/3093337.3037702.

93 Zhang, J., Wang, Z., and Verma, N. (2016) A Machine-Learning Classifier Implemented in a Standard 6T SRAM Array. *2016 IEEE Symposium on VLSI Circuits (VLSI-Circuits)*, pp. 1–2.

94 Han, S., Pool, J., Tran, J., and Dally, W.J. (2015) Learning both Weights and Connections for Efficient Neural Network, in *Advances in Neural Information Processing Systems 28: Annual Conference on Neural Information Processing Systems 2015*, pp. 1135–1143.

95 Zhou, A., Yao, A., Guo, Y., Xu, L., and Chen, Y. (2017) Incremental Network Quantization: Towards Lossless CNNs with Low-Precision Weights, in *International Conference on Learning Representations, ICLR2017*.

96 Qureshi, M.A. and Munir, A. (2020) NeuroMAX: A High Throughput, Multi-Threaded, Log-Based Accelerator for Convolutional Neural Networks, in *2020 IEEE/ACM International Conference On Computer Aided Design (ICCAD)*, pp. 1–9.

97 Choi, Y., El-Khamy, M., and Lee, J. (2016) Towards the Limit of Network Quantization. **arXiv:1612.01543**. URL http://arxiv.org/abs/1612.01543.

98 Shahbahrami, A., Bahrampour, R., Rostami, M.S., and Mobarhan, M.A. (2011) Evaluation of Huffman and Arithmetic Algorithms for Multimedia Compression Standards. *CoRR*, **abs/1109.0216**. URL http://arxiv.org/abs/1109.0216.

99 Lee, J.H., Kong, J., and Munir, A. (2021) Arithmetic Coding-Based 5-Bit Weight Encoding and Hardware Decoder for CNN Inference in Edge Devices. *IEEE Access*, 9, 166736–166749, doi:10.1109/ACCESS.2021.3136888.

100 Saad, Y. (2003) *Iterative Methods for Sparse Linear Systems*, Society for Industrial and Applied Mathematics, 2nd edn., doi:10.1137/1.9780898718003. URL https://epubs.siam.org/doi/abs/10.1137/1.9780898718003.

101 Barrett, R., Berry, M., Chan, T.F., Demmel, J., Donato, J., Dongarra, J., Eijkhout, V., Pozo, R., Romine, C., and van der Vorst, H. (1994) *Templates for the Solution of Linear Systems: Building Blocks for Iterative Methods*, Society for Industrial and Applied Mathematics, doi:10.1137/1.9781611971538. URL https://epubs.siam.org/doi/abs/10.1137/1.9781611971538.

102 Lee, J.H., Park, B., Kong, J., and Munir, A. (2022) Row-Wise Product-Based Sparse Matrix Multiplication Hardware Accelerator With Optimal Load Balancing. *IEEE Access*, 10, 64547–64559, doi:10.1109/ACCESS.2022.3184116.

103 Ko, J.H., Kim, D., Na, T., Kung, J., and Mukhopadhyay, S. (2017) Adaptive Weight Compression for Memory-Efficient Neural Networks, in *Design, Automation, Test in Europe Conference Exhibition (DATE), 2017*, pp. 199–204.

104 Ge, S., Luo, Z., Zhao, S., Jin, X., and Zhang, X.Y. (2017) Compressing Deep Neural Networks for Efficient Visual Inference, in *2017 IEEE International Conference on Multimedia and Expo (ICME)*, pp. 667–672.

105 Reagan, B., Gupta, U., Adolf, B., Mitzenmacher, M., Rush, A., Wei, G.Y., and Brooks, D. (2018) Weightless: Lossy Weight Encoding for Deep Neural Network Compression, in *the 35th International Conference on Machine Learning*, pp. 4324–4333.

106 Choi, Y., El-Khamy, M., and Lee, J. (2020) Universal Deep Neural Network Compression. *IEEE Journal of Selected Topics in Signal Processing*, 14 (4), 715–726.

107 Young, S., Wang, Z., Taubman, D., and Girod, B. (2021) Transform Quantization for CNN Compression. *IEEE Transactions on Pattern Analysis and Machine Intelligence*, 44 (9), 5700–5714.

108 Kwon, J., Kong, J., and Munir, A. (2022) Sparse Convolutional Neural Network Acceleration with Lossless Input Feature Map Compression for Resource-Constrained Systems. *IET Computers & Digital Techniques*, 16 (1), 29–43, doi:10.1049/cdt2.12038.

109 Lee, K., Kong, J., Kim, Y.G., and Chung, S.W. (2019) Memory Streaming Acceleration for Embedded Systems with CPU-Accelerator Cooperative Data Processing. *Microprocessors and Microsystems - Embedded Hardware Design*, 71, 102897.

110 Darwish, S.M. and Noori, Z.H. (2019) Secure Image Compression Approach Based on Fusion of 3D Chaotic Maps and Arithmetic Coding. *IET Signal Processing*, 13, 286–295(9).

111 Guo, Z., Fu, J., Feng, R., and Chen, Z. (2021) Accelerate Neural Image Compression with Channel-Adaptive Arithmetic Coding, in *2021 IEEE International Symposium on Circuits and Systems (ISCAS)*, pp. 1–5.

112 Fong, C.F.B., Mu, J., and Zhang, W. (2019) A Cost-Effective CNN Accelerator Design with Configurable PU on FPGA, in *2019 IEEE Computer Society Annual Symposium on VLSI (ISVLSI)*, pp. 31–36.

113 Sit, M., Kazami, R., and Amano, H. (2017) FPGA-Based Accelerator for Losslessly Quantized Convolutional Neural Networks, in *2017 International Conference on Field Programmable Technology (ICFPT)*, pp. 295–298.

114 Struharik, R., Vukobratovic, B., Erdeljan, A., and Rakanovic, D. (2018) CoNNA – Compressed CNN Hardware Accelerator, in *2018 21st Euromicro Conference on Digital System Design (DSD)*, pp. 365–372.

115 Google (2022) Google Coral Dev Board. URL https://coral.ai/products/dev-board/.

116 Yuan, G., Ma, X., Ding, C., Lin, S., Zhang, T., Jalali, Z.S., Zhao, Y., Jiang, L., Soundarajan, S., and Wang, Y. (2019) An Ultra-Efficient Memristor-Based DNN Framework with Structured Weight Pruning and Quantization Using ADMM, in *2019 IEEE/ACM International Symposium on Low Power Electronics and Design (ISLPED)*.

117 Lin, M., Chen, Q., and Yan, S. (2014) Network in Network, in *2nd International Conference on Learning Representations, (ICLR)*.

118 Jia, Y., Shelhamer, E., Donahue, J., Karayev, S., Long, J., Girshick, R.B., Guadarrama, S., and Darrell, T. (2014) Caffe: Convolutional Architecture for Fast Feature Embedding. *CoRR*, **abs/1408.5093**. URL http://arxiv.org/abs/1408.5093.

119 Zhang, T., Ye, S., Zhang, K., Tang, J., Wen, W., Fardad, M., and Wang, Y. (2018) A Systematic DNN Weight Pruning Framework using Alternating Direction Method of Multipliers. *arXiv preprint arXiv:1804.03294*.

120 Zhang, T., Zhang, K., Ye, S., Li, J., Tang, J., Wen, W., Fardad, M., and Wang, Y. (2018) ADAM-ADMM: A Unified, Systematic Framework of Structured Weight Pruning for DNNs. *arXiv preprint arXiv:1807.11091*.

121 Deng, J., Dong, W., Socher, R., Li, L.J., Li, K., and Fei-Fei, L. (2009) ImageNet: A Large-Scale Hierarchical Image Database, in *2009 IEEE Conference on Computer Vision and Pattern Recognition (CVPR)*, pp. 248–255.

122 Stathis, D., Sudarshan, C., Yang, Y., Jung, M., Jafri, S.M.A.H., Weis, C., Hemani, A., Lansner, A., and Wehn, N. (2019) eBrainII: A 3 kW Real-time Custom 3D DRAM Integrated ASIC Implementation of a Biologically Plausible Model of a Human Scale Cortex. *CoRR*, **abs/1911.00889**. URL http://arxiv.org/abs/1911.00889.

123 Lee, S., Cho, H., Son, Y.H., Ro, Y., Kim, N.S., and Ahn, J.H. (2018) Leveraging Power-Performance Relationship of Energy-Efficient Modern DRAM Devices. *IEEE Access*, 6, 31387–31398.

124 Harris, B. and Altiparmak, N. (2020) Ultra-Low Latency SSDs' Impact on Overall Energy Efficiency, in *12th USENIX Workshop on Hot Topics in Storage and File Systems (HotStorage 20)*.

125 Kim, Y., Kong, J., and Munir, A. (2020) CPU-Accelerator Co-Scheduling for CNN Acceleration at the Edge. *IEEE Access*, 8, 211422–211433, doi:10.1109/ACCESS.2020.3039278.

126 Gokhale, V., Zaidy, A., Chang, A.X.M., and Culurciello, E. (2017) Snowflake: An Efficient Hardware Accelerator for Convolutional Neural Networks, in *2017 IEEE International Symposium on Circuits and Systems (ISCAS)*, pp. 1–4, doi:10.1109/ISCAS.2017.8050809.

127 Jouppi, N.P., Young, C., Patil, N., Patterson, D.A., Agrawal, G., Bajwa, R., Bates, S., Bhatia, S., Boden, N., Borchers, A., Boyle, R., Cantin, P., Chao, C., Clark, C., Coriell, J., Daley, M., Dau, M., Dean, J., Gelb, B., Ghaemmaghami, T.V., Gottipati, R., Gulland, W., Hagmann, R., Ho, C.R., Hogberg, D., Hu, J., Hundt, R., Hurt, D., Ibarz, J., Jaffey, A., Jaworski, A., Kaplan, A., Khaitan, H., Koch, A., Kumar, N., Lacy, S., Laudon, J., Law, J., Le, D., Leary, C., Liu, Z., Lucke, K., Lundin, A., MacKean, G., Maggiore, A., Mahony, M., Miller, K., Nagarajan, R., Narayanaswami, R., Ni, R., Nix, K., Norrie, T., Omernick, M., Penukonda, N., Phelps, A., Ross, J., Salek, A., Samadiani, E., Severn, C., Sizikov, G., Snelham, M., Souter, J., Steinberg, D., Swing, A., Tan, M., Thorson, G., Tian, B., Toma, H., Tuttle, E., Vasudevan, V., Walter, R., Wang, W., Wilcox, E., and Yoon, D.H. (2017) In-Datacenter Performance Analysis of a Tensor Processing Unit. *CoRR*, **abs/1704.04760**. URL http://arxiv.org/abs/1704.04760.

128 Guo, K., Zeng, S., Yu, J., Wang, Y., and Yang, H. (2019) [DL] A Survey of FPGA-Based Neural Network Inference Accelerators. *ACM Transactions on Reconfigurable Technology and Systems*, 12 (1), 1–26, doi:10.1145/3289185.

129 Lee, J., He, J., and Wang, K. (2020) FPGA-Based Neural Network Accelerators for Millimeter-Wave Radio-Over-Fiber Systems. *Optics Express*, 28 (9), 13384–13400, doi:10.1364/OE.391050. URL http://www.osapublishing.org/oe/abstract.cfm?URI=oe-28-9-13384.

130 Wang, T., Wang, C., Zhou, X., and Chen, H. (2019) An Overview of FPGA Based Deep Learning Accelerators: Challenges and Opportunities, in *2019 IEEE 21st International Conference on High Performance Computing and Communications; IEEE 17th International Conference on Smart City; IEEE 5th International Conference on Data Science and Systems (HPCC/SmartCity/DSS)*, pp. 1674–1681, doi:10.1109/HPCC/SmartCity/DSS.2019.00229.

131 Du, Z., Fasthuber, R., Chen, T., Ienne, P., Li, L., Luo, T., Feng, X., Chen, Y., and Temam, O. (2015) ShiDianNao: Shifting Vision Processing Closer to the Sensor, in *2015 ACM/IEEE 42nd Annual International Symposium on Computer Architecture (ISCA)*, pp. 92–104, doi:10.1145/2749469.2750389.

132 Liu, D., Chen, T., Liu, S., Zhou, J., Zhou, S., Teman, O., Feng, X., Zhou, X., and Chen, Y. (2015) PuDianNao: A Polyvalent Machine Learning Accelerator. *SIGPLAN Notices*, 50 (4), 369–381, doi:10.1145/2775054.2694358

133 Sharify, S., Lascorz, A.D., Mahmoud, M., Nikolic, M., Siu, K., Stuart, D.M., Poulos, Z., and Moshovos, A. (2019) Laconic Deep Learning Inference Acceleration, in *Proceedings of the 46th International Symposium on Computer Architecture*, Association for Computing Machinery, New York, NY, USA, ISCA '19, pp. 304–317, doi:10.1145/3307650.3322255.

134 Delmas, A., Judd, P., Stuart, D.M., Poulos, Z., Mahmoud, M., Sharify, S., Nikolic, M., and Moshovos, A. (2018) Bit-Tactical: Exploiting Ineffectual Computations in Convolutional Neural Networks: Which, Why, and How. *CoRR*, **abs/1803.03688**. URL http://arxiv.org/abs/1803.03688.

135 Ding, C., Liao, S., Wang, Y., Li, Z., Liu, N., Zhuo, Y., Wang, C., Qian, X., Bai, Y., Yuan, G., Ma, X., Zhang, Y., Tang, J., Qiu, Q., Lin, X., and Yuan, B. (2017) CirCNN: Accelerating and Compressing Deep Neural Networks Using Block-Circulant Weight Matrices, in *2017 50th Annual IEEE/ACM International Symposium on Microarchitecture (MICRO)*, pp. 395–408.

136 Ankit, A., Hajj, I.E., Chalamalasetti, S.R., Ndu, G., Foltin, M., Williams, R.S., Faraboschi, P., Hwu, W., Strachan, J.P., Roy, K., and Milojicic, D.S. (2019) PUMA: A Programmable Ultra-Efficient Memristor-Based Accelerator for Machine Learning Inference. *CoRR*, **abs/1901.10351**. URL http://arxiv.org/abs/1901.10351.

137 Shafiee, A., Nag, A., Muralimanohar, N., Balasubramonian, R., Strachan, J.P., Hu, M., Williams, R.S., and Srikumar, V. (2016) ISAAC: A Convolutional Neural Network Accelerator with In-Situ Analog Arithmetic in Crossbars, in *2016 ACM/IEEE 43rd Annual International Symposium on Computer Architecture (ISCA)*, pp. 14–26, doi:10.1109/ISCA.2016.12.

138 Liu, B., Zou, D., Feng, L., Feng, S., Fu, P., and Li, J. (2019) An FPGA-Based CNN Accelerator Integrating Depthwise Separable Convolution. *MDPI Electronics*, 8 (3), 1–18.

139 Bai, L., Zhao, Y., and Huang, X. (2018) A CNN Accelerator on FPGA Using Depthwise Separable Convolution. *IEEE Transactions on Circuits and Systems II: Express Briefs*, 65 (10), 1415–1419.

140 Huan, Y., Xu, J., Zheng, L., Tenhunen, H., and Zou, Z. (2018) A 3D Tiled Low Power Accelerator for Convolutional Neural Network, in *2018 IEEE International Symposium on Circuits and Systems (ISCAS)*, pp. 1–5.

141 Jo, J., Kim, S., and Park, I. (2018) Energy-Efficient Convolution Architecture Based on Rescheduled Dataflow. *IEEE Transactions on Circuits and Systems I: Regular Papers*, 65 (12), 4196–4207.

142 Chang, K. and Chang, T. (2020) VWA: Hardware Efficient Vectorwise Accelerator for Convolutional Neural Network. *IEEE Transactions on Circuits and Systems I: Regular Papers*, 67 (1), 145–154.

143 Redmon, J. (2022) Darknet: Open Source Neural Networks in C. URL `https://pjreddie`.com/darknet/tiny-darknet/.

144 AVnet (2022) Zedboard. URL http://www.zedboard.org/.

145 Redmon, J. (2022) Tiny Darknet. URL https://pjreddie.com/darknet/tiny-darknet/.

146 Meloni, P., Capotondi, A., Deriu, G., Brian, M., Conti, F., Rossi, D., Raffo, L., and Benini, L. (2017) NEURAghe: Exploiting CPU-FPGA Synergies for Efficient and Flexible CNN Inference Acceleration on Zynq SoCs. *CoRR*, **abs/1712.00994**. URL http://arxiv.org/abs/1712.00994.

147 Qiu, J., Wang, J., Yao, S., Guo, K., Li, B., Zhou, E., Yu, J., Tang, T., Xu, N., Song, S., Wang, Y., and Yang, H. (2016) Going Deeper with Embedded FPGA Platform for Convolutional Neural Network, in *Proceedings of the 2016 ACM/SIGDA International Symposium on Field-Programmable Gate Arrays*, pp. 26–35.

148 Zhang, C., Li, P., Sun, G., Guan, Y., Xiao, B., and Cong, J. (2015) Optimizing FPGA-Based Accelerator Design for Deep Convolutional Neural Networks, in *Proceedings of the 2015 ACM/SIGDA International Symposium on Field-Programmable Gate Arrays*, pp. 161–170.

149 Lin, Y. and Chang, T.S. (2018) Data and Hardware Efficient Design for Convolutional Neural Network. *IEEE Transactions on Circuits and Systems I: Regular Papers*, 65 (5), 1642–1651.

150 NVIDIA (2022) V100. URL https://www.nvidia.com/en-us/data-center/v100/.

151 Gondimalla, A., Chesnut, N., Thottethodi, M., and Vijaykumar, T.N. (2019) SparTen: A Sparse Tensor Accelerator for Convolutional Neural Networks, in *Proceedings of the 52nd Annual IEEE/ACM International Symposium on Microarchitecture*, Association for Computing Machinery, New York, NY, USA, MICRO '52, pp. 151–165, doi:10.1145/3352460.3358291.

152 Qin, E., Samajdar, A., Kwon, H., Nadella, V., Srinivasan, S., Das, D., Kaul, B., and Krishna, T. (2020) SIGMA: A Sparse and Irregular GEMM Accelerator with Flexible Interconnects for DNN Training, in *2020 IEEE International Symposium on High Performance Computer Architecture (HPCA)*, pp. 58–70, doi:10.1109/HPCA47549.2020.00015.

153 Zhang, Z., Wang, H., Han, S., and Dally, W.J. (2020) SpArch: Efficient Architecture for Sparse Matrix Multiplication, in *2020 IEEE International*

Symposium on High Performance Computer Architecture (HPCA), pp. 261–274, doi:10.1109/HPCA47549.2020.00030.

154 Hojabr, R., Sedaghati, A., Sharifian, A., Khonsari, A., and Shriraman, A. (2021) SPAGHETTI: Streaming Accelerators for Highly Sparse GEMM on FPGAs, in *2021 IEEE International Symposium on High-Performance Computer Architecture (HPCA)*, pp. 84–96.

155 Srivastava, N., Jin, H., Liu, J., Albonesi, D., and Zhang, Z. (2020) MatRaptor: A Sparse-Sparse Matrix Multiplication Accelerator Based on Row-Wise Product, in *2020 53rd Annual IEEE/ACM International Symposium on Microarchitecture (MICRO)*, pp. 766–780, doi:10.1109/MICRO50266.2020.00068.

156 Zhang, G., Attaluri, N., Emer, J.S., and Sanchez, D. (2021) Gamma: Leveraging Gustavson's Algorithm to Accelerate Sparse Matrix Multiplication, in *Proceedings of the 26th ACM International Conference on Architectural Support for Programming Languages and Operating Systems*, pp. 687–701.

157 Qureshi, M.A. and Munir, A. (2021) Sparse-PE: A Performance-Efficient Processing Engine Core for Sparse Convolutional Neural Networks. *IEEE Access*, 9, 151458–151475, doi:10.1109/ACCESS.2021.3126708.

158 Qureshi, M.A. and Munir, A. (2021) Phantom: A High-Performance Computational Core for Sparse Convolutional Neural Networks. *CoRR*, **abs/2111.05002**. URL https://arxiv.org/abs/2111.05002.

159 Gao, Z., Wang, L., and Wu, G. (2019) LIP: Local Importance-Based Pooling, in *2019 IEEE/CVF International Conference on Computer Vision (ICCV)*, pp. 3354–3363, doi:10.1109/ICCV.2019.00345.

160 Xilinx (2022) Xilinx Zynq UltraScale+ MPSoC ZCU106 Evaluation Kit. URL http://www.xilinx.com/products/boards-and-kits/zcu106.html# documentation.

161 ARM (2022) ARM Cortex-A53 MpCore Processor Technical Reference Manual. URL http://infocenter.arm.com/help/topic/com.arm.doc.ddi0500d/ DDI0500D_cortex_a53_r0p2_trm.pdf.

162 Parashar, A., Rhu, M., Mukkara, A., Puglielli, A., Venkatesan, R., Khailany, B., Emer, J., Keckler, S.W., and Dally, W.J. (2017) SCNN: An Accelerator for Compressed-Sparse Convolutional Neural Networks, in *2017 ACM/IEEE 44th Annual International Symposium on Computer Architecture (ISCA)*, pp. 27–40, doi:10.1145/3079856.3080254.

163 Kim, D., Ahn, J., and Yoo, S. (2017) A Novel Zero Weight/Activation-Aware Hardware Architecture of Convolutional Neural Network, in *Proceedings of the Conference on Design, Automation & Test in Europe*, pp. 1466–1471.

164 Raspberry Pi Foundation (2021) Raspberry Pi Zero. URL https://www .raspberrypi.org/products/raspberry-pi-zero/.

165 ARM (2021) ARM1176JZF-S Technical Reference Manual. URL https:// developer.arm.com/documentation/ddi0301/h/.

166 Zhong, G., Dubey, A., Tan, C., and Mitra, T. (2019) Synergy: An HW/SW Framework for High Throughput CNNs on Embedded Heterogeneous SoC. *ACM Transactions on Embedded Computing Systems*, 18 (2), 1–23.

167 Aimar, A., Mostafa, H., Calabrese, E., Rios-Navarro, A., Tapiador-Morales, R., Lungu, I., Milde, M.B., Corradi, F., Linares-Barranco, A., Liu, S., and Delbruck, T. (2019) NullHop: A Flexible Convolutional Neural Network Accelerator Based on Sparse Representations of Feature Maps. *IEEE Transactions on Neural Networks and Learning Systems*, 30 (3), 644–656.

168 Kala, S., Jose, B.R., Mathew, J., and Nalesh, S. (2019) High-Performance CNN Accelerator on FPGA Using Unified Winograd-GEMM Architecture. *IEEE Transactions on Very Large Scale Integration (VLSI) Systems*, 27 (12), 2816–2828.

169 Shen, J., Qiao, Y., Huang, Y., Wen, M., and Zhang, C. (2018) Towards a Multi-Array Architecture for Accelerating Large-Scale Matrix Multiplication on FPGAs, in *2018 IEEE International Symposium on Circuits and Systems (ISCAS)*, pp. 1–5.

170 Altera (2021) FPGA Architecture. URL https://www.intel.com/content/dam/www/programmable/us/en/pdfs/literature/wp/wp-01003.pdf.

171 Rabaey, J.M., Chandrakasan, A., and Nikolic, B. (2003) *Digital Integrated Circuits*, Prentice Hall Press, USA, 2nd edn.

172 Xilinx (2021) Xilinx Power Estimator. URL https://www.xilinx.com/products/technology/power/xpe.html.

173 Zhou, X., Du, Z., Guo, Q., Liu, S., Liu, C., Wang, C., Zhou, X., Li, L., Chen, T., and Chen, Y. (2018) Cambricon-S: Addressing Irregularity in Sparse Neural Networks through a Cooperative Software/Hardware Approach, in *Proceedings of the 51st Annual IEEE/ACM International Symposium on Microarchitecture*, IEEE Press, MICRO-51, pp. 15–28, doi:10.1109/MICRO.2018.00011.

174 Gupta, S., Agrawal, A., Gopalakrishnan, K., and Narayanan, P. (2015) Deep Learning with Limited Numerical Precision. *CoRR*, **abs/1502.02551**. URL http://arxiv.org/abs/1502.02551.

175 Srivastava, N., Jin, H., Smith, S., Rong, H., Albonesi, D., and Zhang, Z. (2020) Tensaurus: A Versatile Accelerator for Mixed Sparse-Dense Tensor Computations, in *2020 IEEE International Symposium on High Performance Computer Architecture (HPCA)*, pp. 689–702, doi:10.1109/HPCA47549.2020.00062.

176 Hegde, K., Asghari-Moghaddam, H., Pellauer, M., Crago, N., Jaleel, A., Solomonik, E., Emer, J., and Fletcher, C.W. (2019) ExTensor: An Accelerator for Sparse Tensor Algebra, in *Proceedings of the 52nd Annual IEEE/ACM International Symposium on Microarchitecture*, Association

for Computing Machinery, New York, NY, USA, MICRO '52, pp. 319–333, doi:10.1145/3352460.3358275.

177 Pal, S., Beaumont, J., Park, D.H., Amarnath, A., Feng, S., Chakrabarti, C., Kim, H.S., Blaauw, D., Mudge, T., and Dreslinski, R. (2018) OuterSPACE: An Outer Product Based Sparse Matrix Multiplication Accelerator, in *2018 IEEE International Symposium on High Performance Computer Architecture (HPCA)*, pp. 724–736, doi:10.1109/HPCA.2018.00067.

178 Szegedy, C., Vanhoucke, V., Ioffe, S., Shlens, J., and Wojna, Z. (2015) Rethinking the Inception Architecture for Computer Vision. *CoRR*, **abs/1512.00567**. URL http://arxiv.org/abs/1512.00567.

179 Ardakani, A., Condo, C., and Gross, W.J. (2020) Fast and Efficient Convolutional Accelerator for Edge Computing. *IEEE Transactions on Computers*, 69 (1), 138–152, doi:10.1109/TC.2019.2941875.

180 Zhu, C., Huang, K., Yang, S., Zhu, Z., Zhang, H., and Shen, H. (2020) An Efficient Hardware Accelerator for Structured Sparse Convolutional Neural Networks on FPGAs. *IEEE Transactions on Very Large Scale Integration (VLSI) Systems*, 28 (9), 1953–1965, doi:10.1109/TVLSI.2020. 3002779.

181 Xie, X., Lin, J., Wang, Z., and Wei, J. (2021) An Efficient and Flexible Accelerator Design for Sparse Convolutional Neural Networks. *IEEE Transactions on Circuits and Systems I: Regular Papers*, 68 (7), 2936–2949, doi:10.1109/TCSI.2021.3074300.

182 Lu, L., Xie, J., Huang, R., Zhang, J., Lin, W., and Liang, Y. (2019) An Efficient Hardware Accelerator for Sparse Convolutional Neural Networks on FPGAs, in *2019 IEEE 27th Annual International Symposium on Field-Programmable Custom Computing Machines (FCCM)*, pp. 17–25, doi:10.1109/FCCM.2019.00013.

183 Alwani, M., Chen, H., Ferdman, M., and Milder, P. (2016) Fused-Layer CNN Accelerators, in *2016 49th Annual IEEE/ACM International Symposium on Microarchitecture (MICRO)*, pp. 1–12, doi:10.1109/MICRO.2016. 7783725.

184 Cadence Design Systems, Inc. (2019) What is Hardware Software Co-Design and How Can it Benefit You or Your Business? URL https://resources.pcb.cadence.com/blog/2019-what-is-hardware-software-co-design-and-how-can-it-ben efit-you-or-your-business.

185 Darwish, T. and Bayoumi, M. (2005) Trends in Low-Power VLSI Design, in *The Electrical Engineering Handbook* (ed. W.K. Chen), Academic Press, pp. 263–280.

186 Wu, Q., Ding, G., Xu, Y., Feng, S., Du, Z., Wang, J., and Long, K. (2014) Cognitive Internet of Things: A New Paradigm Beyond Connection. *IEEE Internet of Things Journal*, 1 (2), 129–143.

187 Sugimoto, N., Mitsuishi, T., Kaneda, T., Tsuruta, C., Sakai, R., Shimura, H., and Amano, H. (2015) Trax Solver on Zynq with Deep Q-Network, in *2015 International Conference on Field Programmable Technology (FPT)*, pp. 272–275.

188 Lee, K., Kong, J., and Munir, A. (2020) HW/SW Co-Design of Cost-Efficient CNN Inference for Cognitive IoT, in *Proceedings of IEEE International Conference on Intelligent Computing in Data Sciences (ICDS)*.

189 Vanishree, K., George, A., Gunisetty, S., Subramanian, S., Kashyap R., S., and Purnaprajna, M. (2020) CoIn: Accelerated CNN Co-Inference Through Data Partitioning on Heterogeneous Devices, in *2020 6th International Conference on Advanced Computing and Communication Systems (ICACCS)*, pp. 90–95.

190 Zhu, J., Wang, L., Liu, H., Tian, S., Deng, Q., and Li, J. (2020) An Efficient Task Assignment Framework to Accelerate DPU-Based Convolutional Neural Network Inference on FPGAs. *IEEE Access*, 8, 83224–83237.

191 Kim, Y., Kim, J., Chae, D., Kim, D., and Kim, J. (2019) uLayer: Low Latency On-Device Inference Using Cooperative Single-Layer Acceleration and Processor-Friendly Quantization, in *Proceedings of the 14th EuroSys Conference 2019*, EuroSys '19, pp. 1–15.

192 McCalpin, J.D. (1995) Memory Bandwidth and Machine Balance in High Performance Computers, pp. 19–25.

193 Guo, K., Sui, L., Qiu, J., Yu, J., Wang, J., Yao, S., Han, S., Wang, Y., and Yang, H. (2018) Angel-Eye: A Complete Design Flow for Mapping CNN Onto Embedded FPGA. *IEEE Transactions on Computer-Aided Design of Integrated Circuits and Systems*, 37 (1), 35–47.

194 Li, Y., Ma, S., Guo, Y., Xu, R., and Chen, G. (2018) Configurable CNN Accelerator Based on Tiling Dataflow, in *2018 IEEE 9th International Conference on Software Engineering and Service Science (ICSESS)*, pp. 309–313.

195 Zhao, Y., Chen, X., Wang, Y., Li, C., You, H., Fu, Y., Xie, Y., Wang, Z., and Lin, Y. (2020) SmartExchange: Trading Higher-Cost Memory Storage/Access for Lower-Cost Computation, in *47th International Symposium on Computer Architecture*.

196 Xilinx (2022) Linaro Ultra96 Evaluation Board. URL https://www.96boards.org/product/ultra96/.

197 Xilinx (2022) ZCU104 Evaluation Board. URL https://www.xilinx.com/products/boards-and-kits/zcu104.html.

198 ADPower (2022) HPM-300A Digital Power Meter and Analyzer. URL http://adpower21.com/.

199 Qiao, X., Cao, X., Yang, H., Song, L., and Li, H. (2018) AtomLayer: A Universal ReRAM-Based CNN Accelerator with Atomic Layer Computation, in *2018 55th ACM/ESDA/IEEE Design Automation Conference (DAC)*, pp. 1–6, doi:10.1109/DAC.2018.8465832.

200 Ishida, K., Byun, I., Nagaoka, I., Fukumitsu, K., Tanaka, M., Kawakami, S., Tanimoto, T., Ono, T., Kim, J., and Inoue, K. (2020) SuperNPU: An Extremely Fast Neural Processing Unit Using Superconducting Logic Devices, in *2020 53rd Annual IEEE/ACM International Symposium on Microarchitecture (MICRO)*, pp. 58–72, doi:10.1109/MICRO50266.2020.00018.

Index

Accelerators for Convolutional Neural Networks, First Edition.
Arslan Munir, Joonho Kong, and Mahmood Azhar Qureshi.
© 2024 The Institute of Electrical and Electronics Engineers, Inc. Published 2024 by John Wiley & Sons, Inc.

Printed and bound by CPI Group (UK) Ltd, Croydon, CR0 4YY

27/10/2024

14580672-0002